The
BANGUDAE
PETROGLYPHS
in Ulsan

Authors

Jeon Hotae
Professor, University of Ulsan

Rhee Hawoo
Reserch Professor, Bangudae Petroglyphs Institute, University of Ulsan

Park Younghee
Researcher, Korea Prehistoric Art Institute

Translator

Jeon Hyejeon
Lecturer, Ohio State University

The
BANGUDAE
PETROGLYPHS
in Ulsan

Jeon Hotae, Rhee Hawoo, Park Younghee

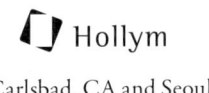 Hollym

Carlsbad, CA and Seoul

The Bangudae Petroglyphs in Ulsan

This book was funded by Jeon Hotae, Rhee Hawoo, Park Younghee and the Ulsan Institute of Cultural Properties.

First edition, 2019
by Hollym International Corp., Carlsbad, CA, USA
Phone 760 814 9880
http://www.hollym.com   **e−Mail** contact@hollym.com

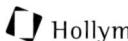 Hollym

Published simultaneously in Korea
by Hollym Corp., Publishers, Seoul, Korea
Phone +82 2 734 5087   **Fax** +82 2 730 5149
http://www.hollym.co.kr   **e−Mail** hollym@hollym.co.kr

ISBN: 978−1−56591−492−6
Library of Congress Control Number: 2019939014

Printed in Korea

Contents

Tables

Photos

Figures

Preface

Ulsan Daegok-ri Bangudae Petroglyphs (National Treasure No. 285) takes an important place in the prehistoric world art history as one of the often cited sites when discussing the prehistoric art trends. Bangudae Petroglyphs preserve the people's views on the world, nature and life in the prehistoric hunting and gathering society.

In 1971 when Bangudae Petroglyphs were found, the site had already been going through an annual cycle of being submerged then rising from water. Earlier, Sayeon Dam was constructed in the lower Daegok Stream behind which stands the cliff where the Bangudae Petroglyphs stand, causing the water levels to rise during the annual rainy seasons. When the Dongguk University Buddhist Site Research Team found the site, Bangudae Petroglyphs had already lost a portion of its natural environment.

The first academic report was made by the Dongguk University Museum in 1984. In the year 2000, the University of Ulsan Museum photographed and analyzed many different surfaces in addition to the main rock surface where most of the petroglyphs are concentrated and published a detailed report. Ulsan Petroglyph Museum which opened in 2008 reviewed the existing reports and published a new report with additional site examinations in 2013.

University of Ulsan Bangudae Petroglyph Institute since its founding in October 2011 continued to collaborate with domestic and international research institutions to study petroglyphs, prehistoric art sites and artifacts. The Institute released the results in the forms of research publication and research report for the academics and institutes domestic and abroad. National Treasure No. 285 Ulsan Bangudae Petroglyphs is the fourth volume published by the Institute which is part of the Korean petroglyph analysis report series.

Since its founding, the Institute had been asked by petroglyph researchers to publish a report on Bangudae Petroglyphs that can be used internationally. While the site had been examined three times, some petroglyphs needed re-categorization while some had been newly discovered. Many researchers suggested that the Institute publish a new official report and a book. When the researchers of the Institute conducted an additional examination of the Bangudae Petroglyphs, additional petroglyphs in addition to those suggested were found in the main and the peripheral surfaces.

Under the standards applied to all publications up to volume 3, the Institute provided numbers and measurements to each petroglyph, allowing researchers to objectively observe and utilize the information. In addition to a number of photographs, we included aerial shots that present the environmental changes to the Bangudae Petroglyphs and the surroundings since its founding. The detailed shots of the newly found rock surfaces near the main rock surface are also included.

Since the fall of 2011, the Institute conducted a detailed examination of the changes in the site for two years. The research team visited the site and worked in the blueprint room as often as possible since 2013. Even after the late 2015 when the comparative analysis of the petroglyphs for the publication began, the research team continued to visit the Bangudae Petroglyphs, also frequently observing any changes to the environment surrounding the site.

I express gratitude to Professor Rhee Hawoo and Dr. Park Yeonghee, Ulsan Cultural-heritage Institute in funding provided generous support for the publication of this volume. It is difficult to edit this report with numerous photographs, figures and tables. I thank the Hollym Publishers' editors who overtook such a task.

April, 2019

Dr. Jeon Hotae

Bangudae Petroglyph Institute Director, University of Ulsan

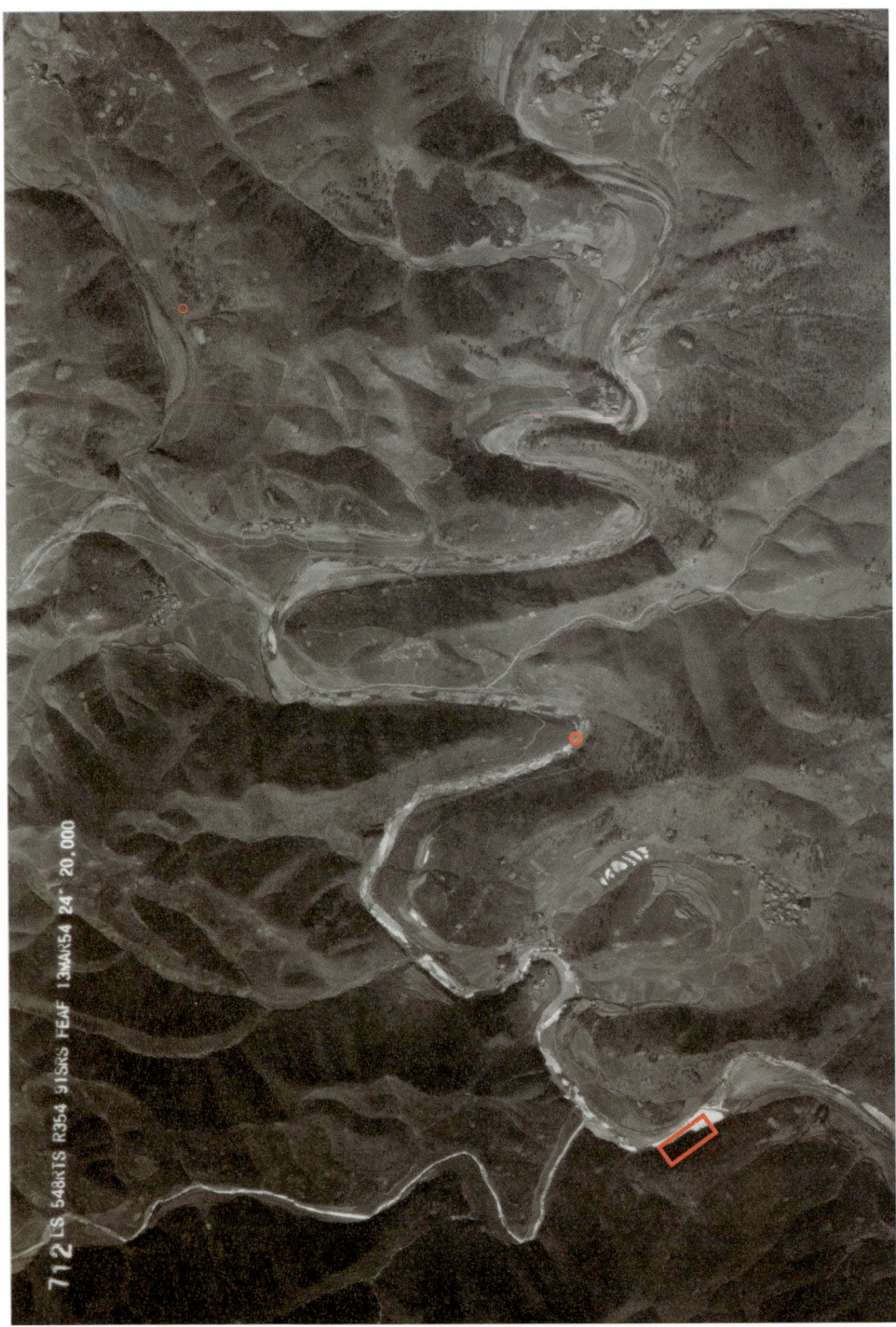

Photo 1. Aerial shots of the Bangudae Petroglyphs and surrounding in 1954 (http://www.ngii.go.kr)

The Bangudae Petroglyphs in Ulsan

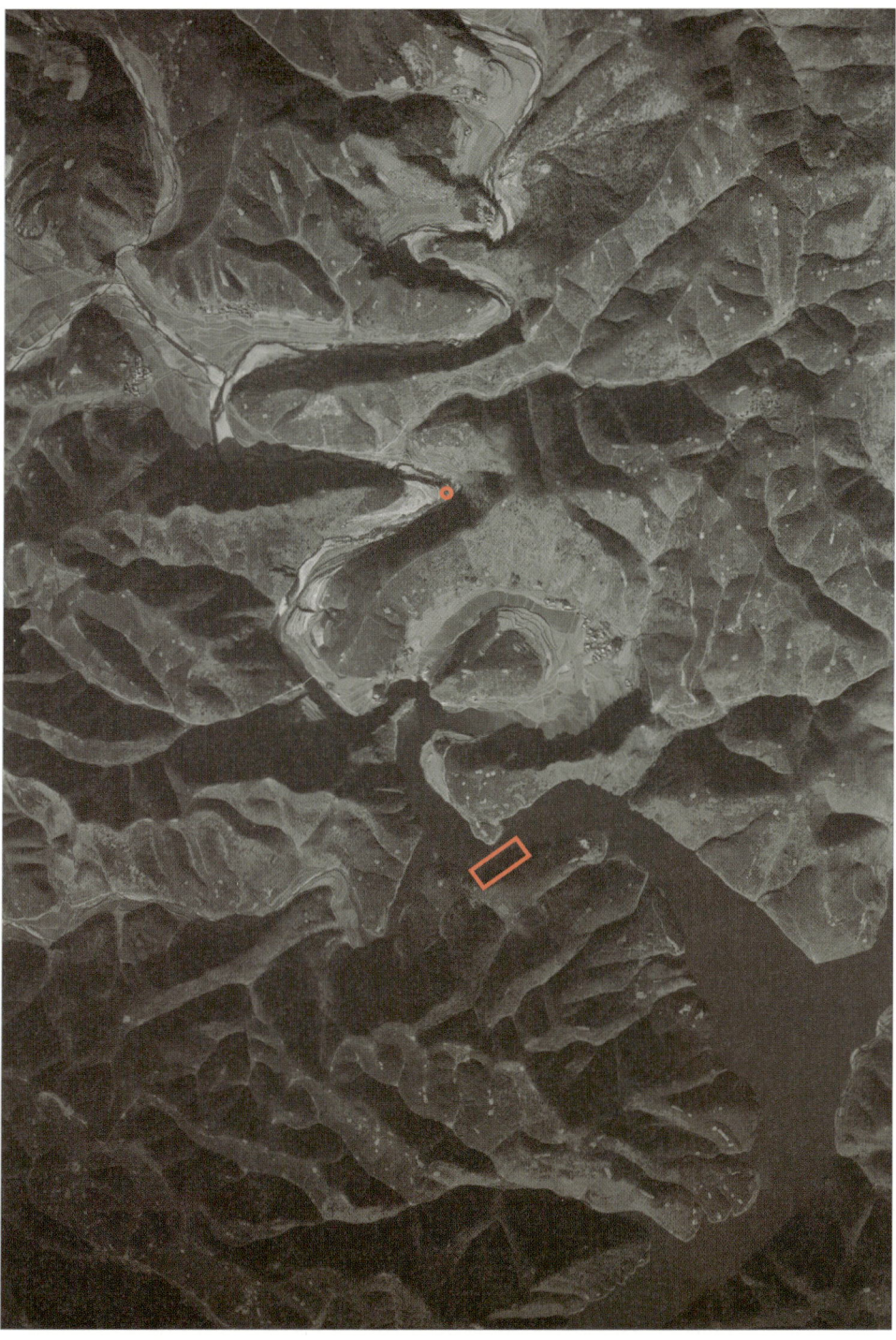

Photo 2. Aerial shots of the Bangudae Petroglyphs and surrounding in 1968 (http://www.ngii.go.kr)

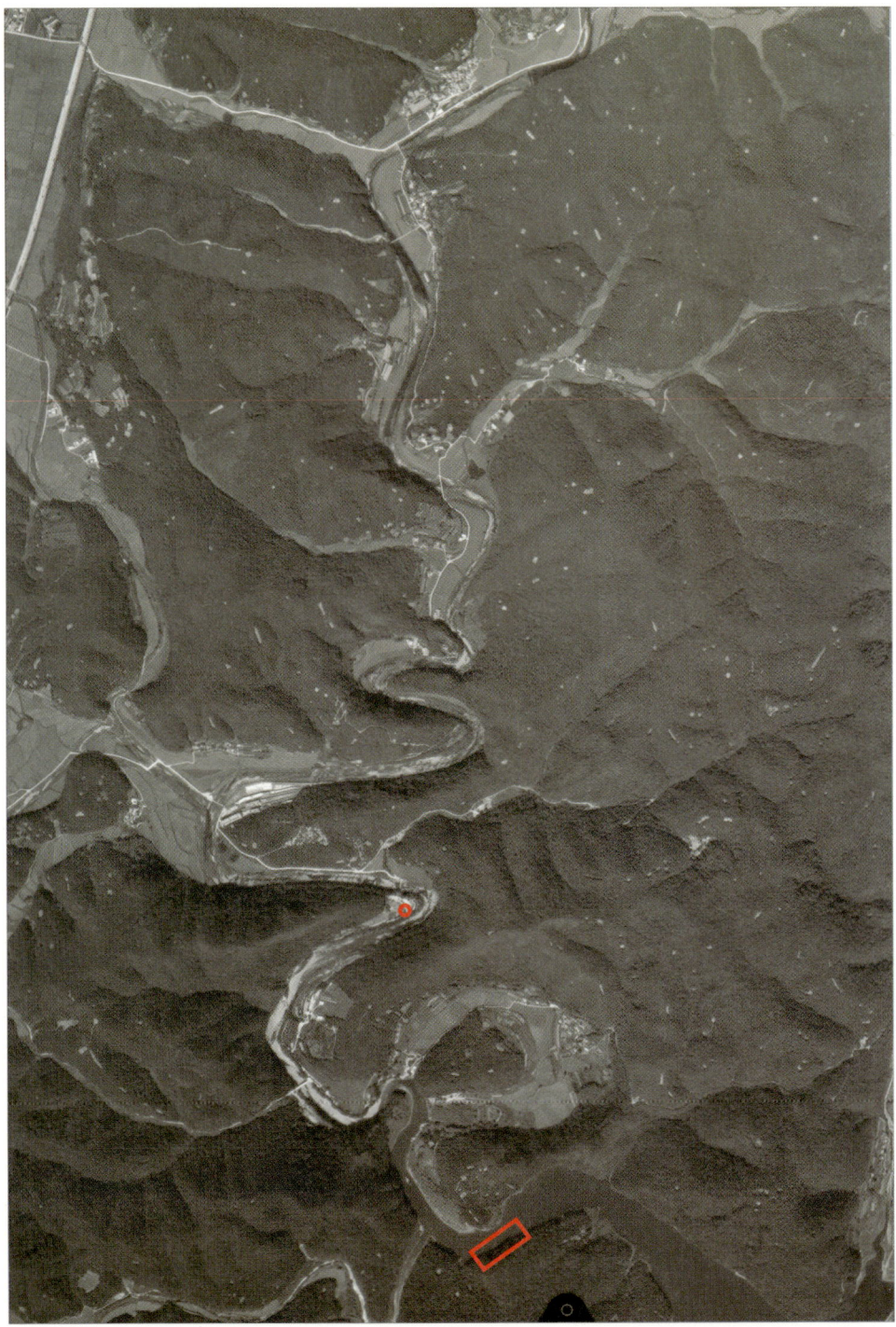

Photo 3. Aerial shots of the Bangudae Petroglyphs and surrounding in 1996 (http://www.ngii.go.kr)

The Bangudae Petroglyphs in Ulsan

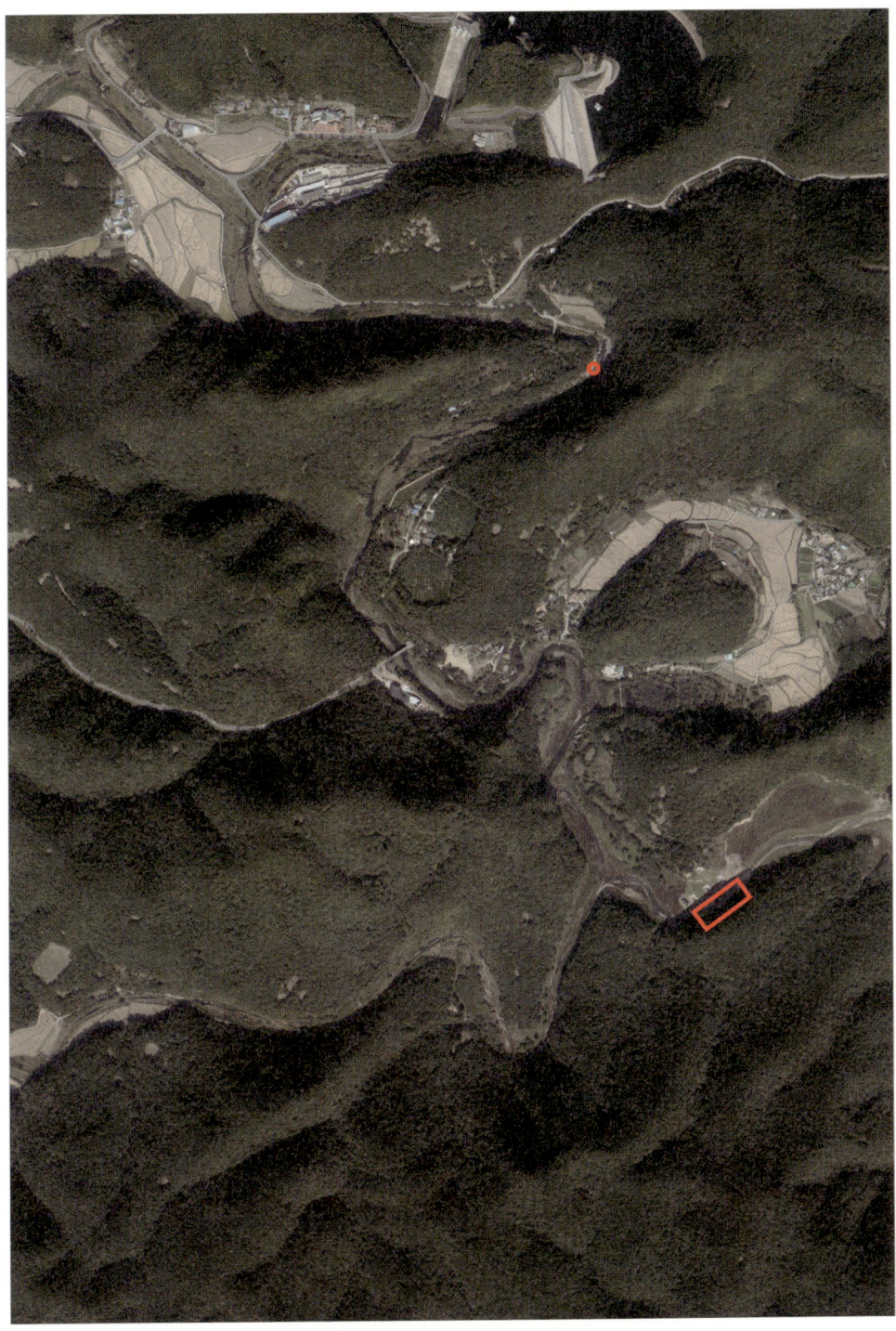

Photo 4. Aerial shots of the Bangudae Petroglyphs and surrounding in 2013 (http://www.ngii.go.kr)

Location and
Environment of the Archaeological Site

1. Environment and Geography

Ulju Daegok-ri Bangudae Petroglyphs is located in 285 Bangudaean-gil, Eonyang-eup, Ulju-gun of Ulsan Metropolitan city. Engraved on the cliffs surrounded by Daegok Stream, Bangudae Petroglyphs belong to the larger group of Daegok Stream Petroglyphs along with another petroglyph site nearby, Cheonjeon-ri Petroglyphs. Daegok Stream flows east from Mount Baekun (892.7m), Miho-ri, Duseo-myeon, Ulju-gun, Ulsan and turns south at Bokan Reserves. It joins the streams Yeonwha, Guryang, Bangu, and Daegok to form a deep valley which then winds toward Gokyeon Town, Sayeon-ri, Beomseo-eup, Ulju-gun, Ulsan to join Taewha River. Daegok Dam was constructed in June of 2005 in the upstream of Daegok Streams while Sayeon Dam was constructed in December of 1965. With the construction of Sayeon Dam, Bangudae Petroglyphs came to be submerged underwater during eight months annually. When the Dongguk University Museum found the site while examining Buddhist sites of Daegok Stream in 1971, the Petroglyphs were submerged underwater. Despite having been designated National Treasure No. 285 in June 23, 1995, the environment surrounding the site has not changed much.

The two petroglyphs in the Daegok Stream region lie where the Stream winds down south with Cheonjeon-ri Petroglyphs, National Treasure No. 146, located 1.2 km upstream of Bangudae Petroglyphs. Bangudae Petroglyphs are located on the rock cliffs south of Bangudae, named after its form resembling a turtle. Daegok Stream sometimes is called Bangu Stream after Bangudae and Mount Bangu. The winding Daegok Stream and the surrounding old forest create a unique atmosphere.

Around Daegok Stream are many wide river plateaus including the one across the Bangudae Petroglyphs. Bangudae Petroglyphs are placed on Geonneogakdan of Daegok Stream near what used to be Shinri Town. With the construction of Sayeon Dam, many towns around Bangudae Petroglyphs including Shinri Town were flooded. To the east of Bangudae Petroglyphs are Mount Yeonwha (532m) which borders Eunpyeon-ri and Daegok-ri in Dudong-myeon. To the west of the site are Mount Mabyeong (511m), Mount Ami (601m), and Mount Yongahm (589m).

The geology near Daegok Stream belong to Hayang Group of Gyeongsang Supergroup (Gyeongsang Basin) which is a Mesozoic sedimentary basin. The rocks around the Bangudae Petroglyphs belong to Mesozoic Cretaceous Gyeongsang Hayang Group Silla Series Daegu Formation's Sayeonri Formation's grey arenaceous mudstone. Many types of dinosaur footprints have been found around Daegok Stream area. Daegok-ri dinosaur print fossils (Ulsan Cultural Asset No. 13) which boast exceptional conditions out of all footprints found in the Daegok Stream area are located on the northeast side of the hills southeast of the Bangudae Petroglyphs.

2. Archaeology and History

Daegok Stream area presents awe-striking scenery with winding waters and curious rock formations. The name "Bangudae" can be confirmed in Yeojidoseo (Eonyang), written in 1757-1765, Haedongjido (Eonyang) published in late Joseon period, and Jibangjido 1872 (Eonyang). Yeojidoseo records that the area's resemblance to a turtle gave it a name "Bangudae." Due to the unique natural scape, various sites from prehistoric period when Bangudae Petroglyphs were created to Joseon period are found in the Daegok Stream Area.

The upper stream area now submerged due to Daegok Dam construction had low hills around the water, making it an ideal place for towns, houses, and tombs. Also part of the regions surrounding Daegok Dam are Ulju-gun Dudong-myeon Bang-ri and Cheonjeon-ri where a total of 1,000 archaeological remains emerged, including Bronze Age settlements, Samhan Period wooden tombs, the Three Kingdoms Period wooden tombs, clay sarcophagi, stone and wood tombs. Because of its location on the prime transport path from Gimhae, Yangsan, Eonyang and Gyeongju during the Silla Period, Bang-ri was home to the Three Kingdoms Period architecture including the site of Bango Temple.

Commemorating Poeun Mongju Jeong (1337-1392) of late Goryeo Period, Hoejae Eonjeok Lee (1491-1553) of early Joseon Period, and Hangang Gu Jeong (1543-1620) visiting and engraving poems in Bangudae, Yuheo and Yeongmo memorial stones were erected in Poeundae. Across Poeundae stands Bangu Seowon dedicated to Hangang Gu Jeong. On the rock surfaces of Bangudae are a number of texts and images including an image of a crane and the characters, 盤龜, all of which cannot be dated.

Eonyang-eup, Ulju-gun where Daegok-ri is part of used to be Geojihwa-hyeon during the Silla Period which name became Heonyang-hyeon in the year 757 (King Gyeongdeok 16) according to the restructuring of provinces. Later in 1143 (Goryeo, King Injong 21), it was renamed Eonyang-hyeon. In 1895 (Joseon, King Gojong 32), it was again, renamed Eonyang-gun and became Eonyang-myeon, which encompassed Sangbuk-myeon and Jungbuk-myeon, in Ulsan-gun in 1914. At this time, Daegok-ri became Daegok-ri, Eonyang-myeon, unifying Daegok-ri, Oenam-myeon of Gyeongju and Daegok-ri, Jungbuk-myeon of Eonyang-hyeon. As Eonyang-myeon became Eonyang-eup in 1996, the name became Daegok-ri, Eonyang-eup. With the construction of Sayeon Dam, Hanshil Town which was the central town of Daegok-ri became submerged underwater in 1965. Bangu-dong came to be the new center of Daegok-ri and Bangudae became the symbol of Daegok-ri.

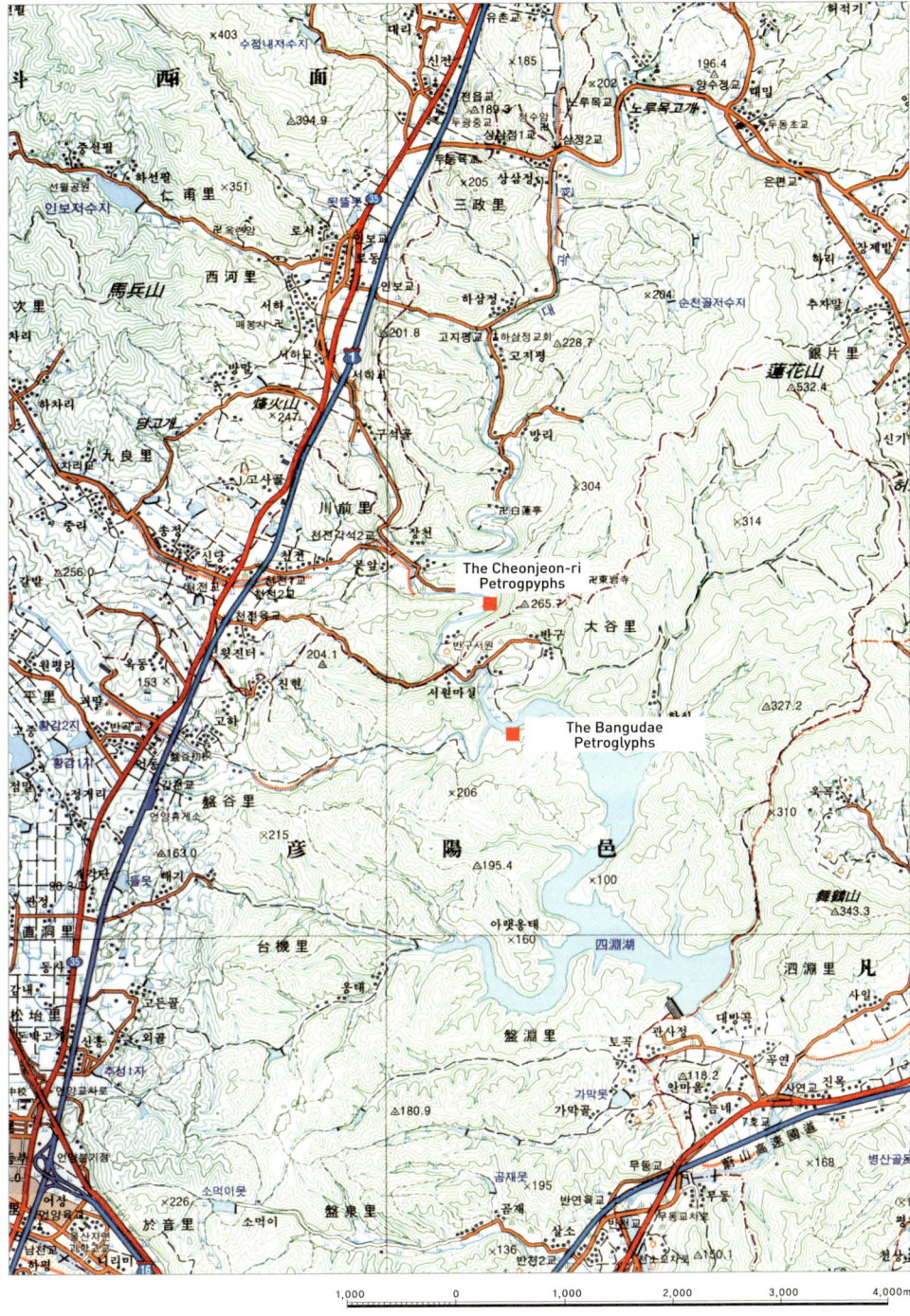

Fig. 1. Location of the Bangudae Petroglyphs and topography around the area

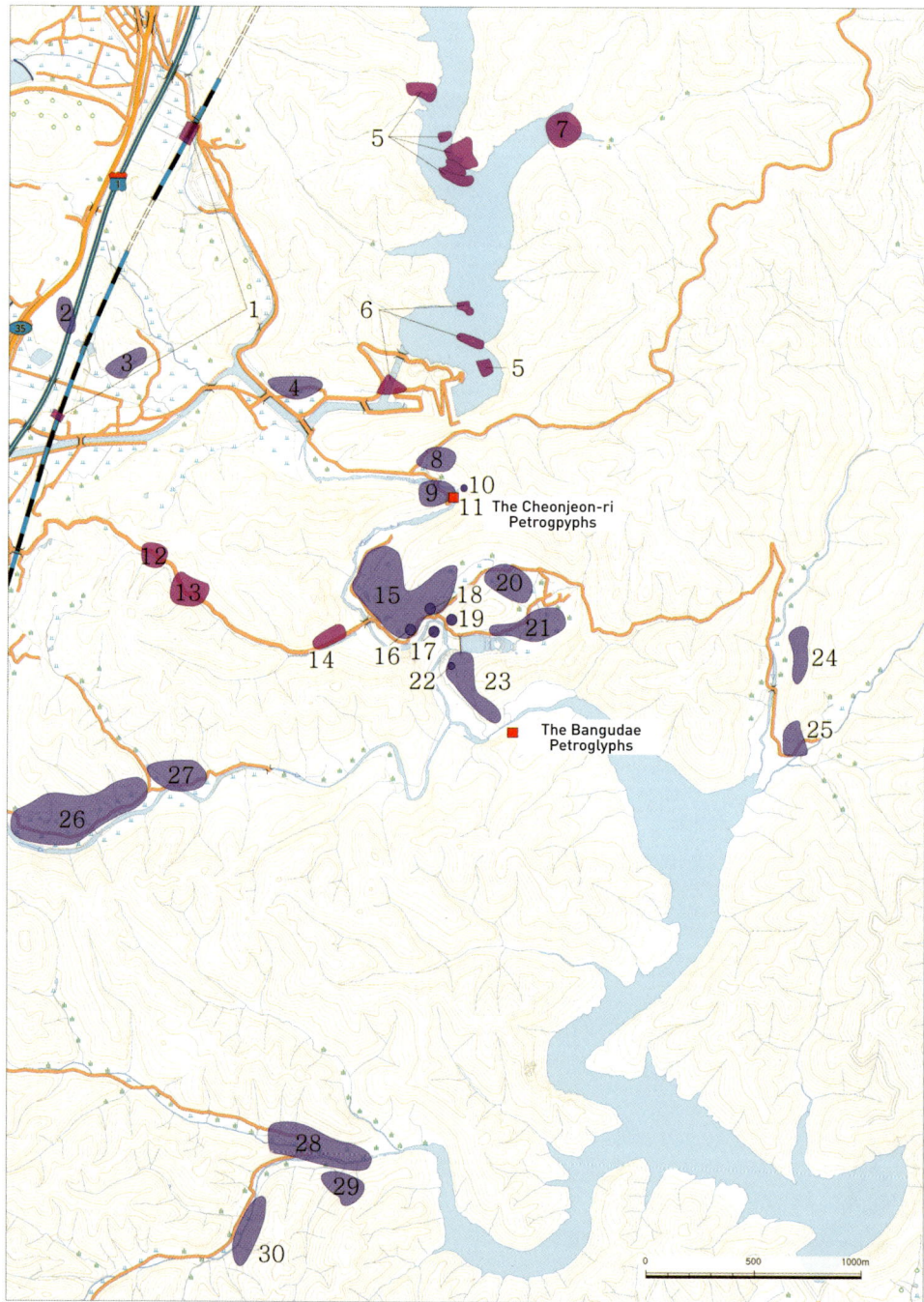

The Cheonjeon-ri
Petrogpyphs

The Bangudae
Petroglyphs

0   500   1000m

Fig. 2. Relic sites around the Bangudae Petroglyphs

Table 1. Distribution of relics around the Bangudae Petroglyphs

No.	Site	Period	Characteristics	Research Institute / Text Sources	Research
1	Archaeological Research Report on Sites within Gyeongbu Railway Construction Area (Ulsan)	Undated/ Bronze Age	The research area is Hwalcheon-ri site, Seoha-ri site and Cheonjeon-ri site. The investigation resulted in findings of 10 remains including a Bronze Age settlement in Hwalcheon-ri. *Gusungakmokgonyeolmun* clay ware and patternless clay ware bottom among others were excavated. In Seoha-ri, an undated stone group, a fine charcoal kiln for roof tiles, two pit sites, and two column pit sites were found. In Cheonjeon-ri, a Bronze Age settlement, round clay bowls and such were found.	Archaeological Research Report on Sites within Gyeongbu Railway Construction Area (Ulsan), Korea Cultural Heritage Foundation Cultural Property Investigation and Research Team, 2008.	Excavation
2	Ulju Cheonjeon-ri Tombs	Three Kingdoms Period	Located in the northwest hills of Daehyeon Town. About ten circular mounds with a diameters ranging from five to seven meters were found. Clay ware dated to the Three Kingdoms Period were found.	Cultural Site Map— Ulju-gun, Ulsan Metropolitan City, 2003.	Surface examination
3	Ulju Cheonjeon-ri Seodang Site	Joseon	Located on the hillside of hills north of Daehyeon Town. Pieces of *buncheong* ware, white porcelain, celadon, and kiln parts were found. The location is thought to be the site of Joseon Period kilns.	Cultural Site Map— Ulju-gun, Ulsan Metropolitan City, 2003.	Surface examination
4	Guksa Forest Archaeological Site, Ulju Cheonjeon-ri	Joseon	Located on the hillside of hills north of Jangcheon Town. Artifacts including *buncheong* ware, white porcelain, clay ware, onggi and others were collected. The location is thought to be the site of Joseon Period settlement and tombs.	Cultural Site Map— Ulju-gun, Ulsan Metropolitan City, 2003.	Surface examination
5	Archaeological Sites in Areas Submerged by Ulsan Daegok Dam (Second Investigation)	Three Kingdoms Period, Joseon	Three regions including Cheonjeon-ri, Bang-ri, and Gojipyeong within the areas surrounding Daegok Dam, constructed to secure metropolitan water sources for the city of Ulsan, were excavated and researched. In Cheonjeon-ri, closest to Daegok Dam, 34 remains including 10 roof tile kilns, one *onggi* kiln, and 3 *onggi* dumps were found. In Bang-ri, located 2.5km upstream of Daegok Dam, 44 remains including 4 architectural sites from the Unified Silla Period, one architectural site from Joseon Period, 3 wall sites, and 3 water drainage sites. In Gojipyeong, located on the hillside of hills 100-117m above water levels, 100m northwest of Bang-ri, 10 remains including 3 kilns (two charcoal kilns, a *buncheong* ware kiln) were found.	Second Excavation and Research of Ulsan Area Metropolitan Water System (Daegok Dam): Cheonjeon-ri, Bang-ri, Gojipyeong, Korea Cultural Heritage Foundation Cultural Property Investigation and Research Team, 2002.	Excavation

No.	Site	Period	Characteristics	Research Institute / Text Sources	Research
6	First Archaeological Excavation in Ulsan Daegok Dam Construction Site	Unified Silla-Joseon	Four regions including iron production sites, temple sites, and other archeological sites of Bang-ri were investigated. Roof tile kilns, porcelain kilns, and smelting hearths from the Unified Silla to Joseon Periods were found. Roof tiles, clay wares, and porcelain ware were collected.	Second Excavation and Research of Ulsan Area Metropolitan Water System (Daegok Dam), Korea Cultural Heritage Foundation Cultural Property Investigation and Research Team, 1999.	Excavation
7	Archaeological Sites in Areas Submerged by Ulju Daegok Dam (Third Investigation)	Bronze Age	Three archaeological remains in addition to 21 existing ones have been found. When additional excavation and research of the region is completed, a significant resource will be added to Ulsan region clay ware research.	Fourth Excavation and Research of Ulsan Area Metropolitan Water System (Daegok Dam), Korea Cultural Heritage Foundation	Excavation
8	Ulju Cheonjeon-ri Bango Temple Site	Unified Silla, Balhae	Located on the hillside of hills north of Cheonjeon-ri Rocks. Pagoda body and top parts were scattered around. The pagoda body has been moved to Pusan National University. The records and the style of the pagoda body suggest that the temple dates back to the Unified Silla Period.	Cultural Site Map— Ulju-gun, Ulsan Metropolitan City, 2003.	Surface examination
9	Archaeological site, Ulju Cheonjeon-ri	Three Kingdoms Period	Located on the hills of Cheonjeon-ri rocks. Clay ware parts from the Three Kingdoms Period and undated roof tile parts were collected. The location is thought to have had settlements and tombs from the Three Kingdoms Period.	Cultural Site Map— Ulju-gun, Ulsan Metropolitan City, 2003.	Surface examination
10	Cheonjeon-ri Dinosaur Footprint Fossils	Cretaceous	Located across the Cheonjeon-ri Rocks. About 200 footprints belonging to ten medium large dinosaurs including Ultrasaurus, and one Goseongosaurus belonging to Cretaceous Period.	Cultural Asset Vol. 6, Ulsan Metropolitan City	Surface examination
11	Ulju Cheonjeon-ri Rocks	Bronze Age	Designated National Treasure No. 147, it is located on the shores of midstream of Daegok. On the wide, rectangular rock surface, geometric patterns, Animals(zoomorphes), and stylized figures are engraved. A fine line engraving depicting a horseback procession, various species of beasts, dragons, and ships and Silla Period texts are found on the lower portions of the surface.	Cultural Site Map— Ulju-gun, Ulsan Metropolitan City, 2003.	Surface examination

No.	Site	Period	Characteristics	Research Institute / Text Sources	Research
12	Ulju Cheonjeon-ri Apgol Kiln Site I	Three Kingdoms Period	Located at the Apgol entry east of Jinhyeon Town. One remain of clay ware kiln that measure up to 375cm long, 114cm wide and 80cm deep from the Three Kingdoms Period was found. Inside the kiln were found short necked urns with cross-hatching patterns (*tanalmun*) among others.	Cultural Site Map– Ulju-gun, Ulsan Metropolitan City, 2003.	Excavation
13	Ulju Cheonjeon-ri Apgol Kiln Site II	Goryeo	Located at the center of Apgol. One celadon kiln remains with only lower portion measuring 140cm in diameter and 55cm in depth and the part of its front portion measuring 420cm wide and 30cm deep surviving. Large celadon plates, octagonal plates, patterned plates, pottery stands, clay stands and others were excavated.	Cultural Site Map– Ulju-gun, Ulsan Metropolitan City, 2003.	Excavation
14	Ulju Cheonjeon-ri Apgol Kiln Site III	Undated historic age	Located at the entrance of Apgol. Half of one semi underground charcoal kiln measuring 690cm long, 250cm wide and 72cm deep has been found.	Cultural Site Map– Ulju-gun, Ulsan Metropolitan City, 2003.	Excavation
15	Ulju Daegok-ri Seowon Archaeological Site	Goryeo -Joseon	Located on the west side of the hill where Bangu Seowon stands and the south side. Pieces of celadon, white porcelain, and clay ware were collected. It is likely that a Goryeo and Joseon Period architecture stood there.	Cultural Site Map– Ulju-gun, Ulsan Metropolitan City, 2003.	Surface examination
16	Ulju Daegok-ri Jipcheongjeong	Joseon	Located west of Bangu Seowon. A pavilion belonging to the House of Choi of Gyeongju, the current building was restored in 1932.	Cultural Site Map– Ulju-gun, Ulsan Metropolitan City, 2003.	Surface examination
17	Bango Seowon Yuheo Memorial Stone	Joseon	The regional scholars named Bangudae Poeundae to commemorate the late Goryeo Period Confucian scholar Poeun Mongju Jeong (圃隱 鄭夢周, 1337-1392) and erected Poeundae *Youngmo* Memorial Stone (1885), Poeundae *Sillok* Memorial Stone (1890) and Bango Seowon *Yuheo* Memorial Stone (1901). The Memorials were moved to the current location in 1965.	Cultural Site Map– Ulju-gun, Ulsan Metropolitan City, 2003.	Surface examination

No.	Site	Period	Characteristics	Research Institute / Text Sources	Research
18	Ulju Daegok-ri Bangu Seowon	Joseon	Bordering Established in 1712 (Joseon, King Sukjong Year 38) in honor of three eminent scholars including Mongju Jeong, it came to house ancestral tablets from 1713. The current building is a recent restoration.	Ulsan Metropolitan City, 2003, Cultural Site Map— Ulju-gun, 2003.	Surface examination
19	Ulju Daegok-ri Bangudae Texts	Undated historic age	Located on the northern surface of Bangudae. Characters "盤龜," crane motifs, and others were found. A number of texts remain on the rock surfaces leading to Bangudae.	Cultural Site Map— Ulju-gun, Ulsan Metropolitan City, 2003.	Surface examination
20	Ulju Daegok-ri Bangu Archaeological Site	Joseon	Located on the west hillside of hills north of Bangu Town. Pieces of white porcelain from Joseon Period as well as pieces of clay ware were collected. The location is thought to be the site of Joseon Period settlement and tombs.	Cultural Site Map— Ulju-gun, Ulsan Metropolitan City, 2003.	Surface examination
21	Ulju Daegok-ri Dongmaesil Archaeological Site	Joseon	Located in Dongmaesil south of Bangu Town. Pieces of clay ware with cross hatchings and porcelain were collected. The location is thought to be the site of Joseon Period settlement and tombs.	Cultural Site Map— Ulju-gun, Ulsan Metropolitan City, 2003.	Surface examination
22	Ulju Daegok-ri Dinosaur Footprints	Cretaceous	Located on the shores of Daegok Stream across Bangudae. 13 dinosaur footprints measuring 74-76cm in length and 7-10cm in width were found.	Cultural Asset Vol. 13, Ulsan Metropolitan City	Surface examination
23	Ulju Daegok-ri Bangudae Site	Joseon	Located on the west side of the hills north of Bangudae Petroglyphs. Roof tile kiln remains exposed on the surface and a large number of roof tiles and pieces of Joseon porcelain were collected. The location is thought to be the site of Joseon Period roof tile kilns, buildings, and settlements.	Ulsan Metropolitan City, 2003, Cultural Site Map- Ulju-gun, 2003.	Surface examination
24	Ulju Daegok-ri Amgol Archaeological Site	Unified Silla, Balhae	Located in Amgol, north of Hansil Town. Pieces of clay ware such as long-necked urn were collected. A group of tombs from the Unified Silla Period likely stood here.	Cultural Site Map— Ulju-gun, Ulsan Metropolitan City, 2003.	Surface examination

No.	Site	Period	Characteristics	Research Institute / Text Sources	Research
25	Ulju Daegok-ri Hansil Archaeological Site	Joseon	In the submerged Hansil Town, pieces of Joseon Period *buncheong* ware, white porcelain and *onggi* were collected. The location is thought to be the site of Joseon Period settlement.	Cultural Site Map— Ulju-gun, Ulsan Metropolitan City, 2003.	Surface examination
26	Ulju Bangok-ri Goha Tombs	Three Kingdoms Period	Located in Gohagol, east of Goha Town. A number of broken stone chamber tombs were found. A number of long-necked urns, short-necked urns, and goblets dating back to 5-6th century were found. The site is thought to be that of tombs from the Three Kingdoms Period.	Cultural Site Map— Ulju-gun, Ulsan Metropolitan City, 2003.	Surface examination
27	Ulju Bangok-ri Bangok Stream Archaeological Site	Three Kingdoms Period	Located on the hills facing the small valley east of Bangok-ri Goha Tombs. Pieces of clay ware, white porcelain, and *buncheong* ware were collected. The location is thought to be the site of the Three Kingdoms Period or Joseon Period settlement and tombs.	Cultural Site Map— Ulju-gun, Ulsan Metropolitan City, 2003.	Surface examination
28	Ulju Taegi-ri Archaeological Site	Joseon	Located on the hills east of Taegigol. Pieces of white porcelain and clay ware dated to Joseon Period were collected. A Joseon Period tombs or settlements likely stood on the place.	Cultural Site Map— Ulju-gun, Ulsan Metropolitan City, 2003.	Surface examination
29	Ulju Taegi-ri Porcelain Kiln Site	Joseon	Located in the valley west of Sayeon Dam. A significant number of damaged *buncheong* ware and porcelain as well as half-finished products, ceramic supports and furnace wall parts were collected. A kiln site of significant size from Joseon Period likely stood on the place.	Cultural Site Map— Ulju-gun, Ulsan Metropolitan City, 2003.	Surface examination
30	Ulju Taegi-ri Archaeological Site 2	Three Kingdoms Period-Joseon	In and around Taegiri Town, pieces of porcelain from the Three Kingdoms Period and Joseon Period were collected. It is highly likely that tombs or settlements from the Three Kingdoms to Joseon Period stood on the location.	Cultural Site Map— Ulju-gun, Ulsan Metropolitan City, 2003.	Surface examination

Categories of Motifs in Bangudae Petroglyphs

Bangudae Petroglyphs (National Treasure No. 285), Daegok-ri, Ulju-gun, Ulsan Metropolitan City is an archaeological remains located on the perpendicular rock surfaces at N35°35′56″, E129°11′07″. From the top, the rock faces curve at the angle resembling Hangeul "ㄱ" with the top of the cliff jutting forward like Hanok roofs, protecting the petroglyphs from rain and wind. The bottom part of the rock shows a developed joint. The petroglyphs are distributed within 25.5m to the east and the west of the natural rock. The location also provides natural sound resonance.

With the main rock surface at the center, various motifs decorate the walls to the

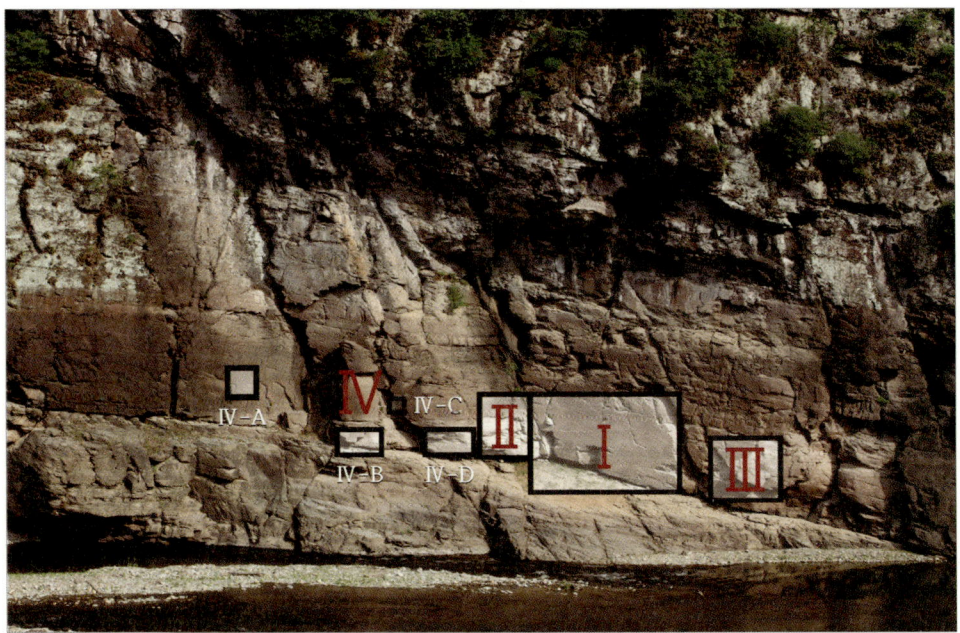

Photo 5. Location of rock surface, the Bangudae Petroglyphs (surface I–IV)

The Bangudae Petroglyphs in Ulsan

east and the west. Considering the chronology of the petroglyphs, we will designate the main rock surface as surface I, surfaces to the east and the west as surfaces II and III and the small separate surface to the west of surface II as surface IV.

The current research, the latest conducted by the Institute, began in October of 2015. With the support of the Cultural Heritage Administration, we conducted multiple site examinations and found a number of petroglyphs. From March 2, 2016, additional research was conducted for ten days, measuring and tracing each new petroglyph motifs. Afterward, the research results were substantiated and verified. We verified the precursory and the actual research results from May 15 to 17 in 2017.

Based on the results of detailed measurements and examination of Ulju Daegok-ri Bangudae Petroglyphs, we organized the petroglyphs in the following Table 2 and Figures 1, 2. Total of 353 individual petroglyphs were examined. We found 16 (4.5%) human figures, 202 animal figures (57.2%), 21 tool images (5.9%) and 114 unidentified motifs (32.2%). The detailed categorizations of motifs are as following in Tables 4 to 20. The measurements for each petroglyph found in surfaces I to IV are given in ㎜. The number is S=1:1 for measurements in the drawings.

The research results for Ulju Daegok-ri Bangudae Petroglyphs were given in a report or a book form in three separate occasions. Dongguk University Museum in 1984 (191 petroglyphs), University of Ulsan Museum in 2000 (296 petroglyphs), and Ulsan Petroglyph Museum of Bangudae in 2013 (231 petroglyphs) each published a research report.

We made tracings of motifs using waterproof pens on non-adhesive OPP films to enhance the accuracy of the traced image. What the researchers focused on during the process was determining whether or not the artificial marks form a uniform pattern. By examining pattern-forming marks, we could find multiple new petroglyphs previously unidentified.

Table 2. Classification of individual figures of the Bangudae Petroglyphs

	Humans (anthromorphes)		Animals (zoomorphes)								Tools (tool figures)						Unidentified		Total
	Full Body	Face	Even-toed ungulates (artiodactyla)	Carnivora-terrestial (carnivora-earth)	Carnivora-marine (pinnipedia)	Cetacean (cetacea)	Birds (aves)	Testudine (chelonia)	Fish (piscis)	Unidentified species	Ships (boats)	Nets (net)	Weir (fish trap)	Floats (float)	Harpoons (fish spear)	Unidentified figures	Unidentified forms	Unrecognizable forms	Total
I — A	1																		1
I — B	2		3	6		22	1	3	1	3	2	1	1	4	1		12	9	71
I — C	1		4	6		3	2		2	1							2	12	33
I — D	5	2	29	7	2	17	1	2	3	9	1			1		5	26	7	117
I — E	3		21	7	2	4				3	2						12	7	61
I — F			1			1				1							2		5
I Sub Total	12	2	58	26	4	47	4	5	6	17	5	1	1	5	1	5	54	35	288
II — A	1		4	1		1											1		8
II — B						3			3			2					3		11
II — C																		1	1
II — D																		1	1
II Sub Total	1		4	1		4			3			2					4	2	21
III — A			4	1		4			1	1	1						3		15
III — B				1						1							1		3
III — C	1									1							1		3
III Sub Total	1		4	2		4			1	3	1						5		21
IV — A				1		2											2		5
IV — B			1	1						1							7	3	13
IV — C			1														1	1	3
IV — D			1	1															2
IV Sub Total			3	3		2				1							10	4	23
Total	14	2	69	32	4	57	4	5	10	21	6	3	1	5	1	5	73	41	353

Category totals — Humans: 16; Animals: 202; Tools: 21; Unidentified: 114; Total: 353.

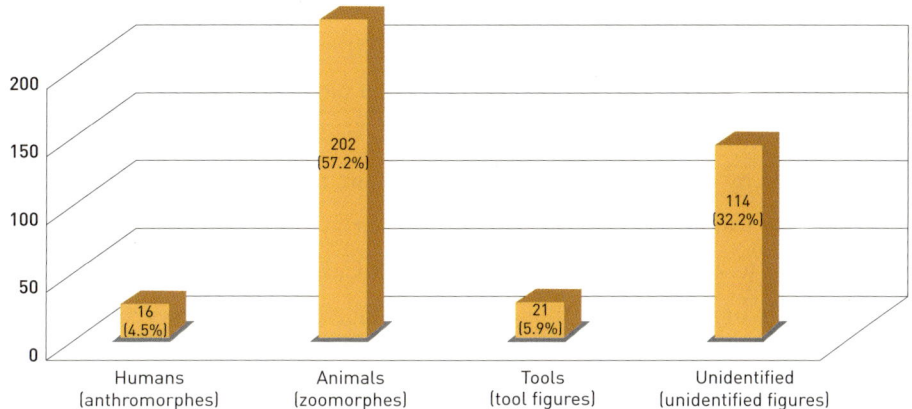

Fig. 3. Distribution of figure types (surface I–IV) 1

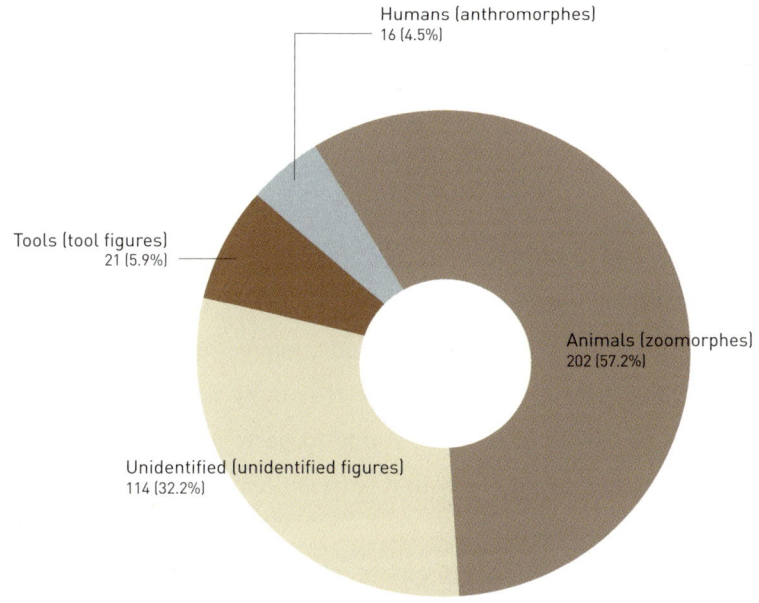

Fig. 4. Distribution of figure types (surface I–IV) 2

1. Surface I - Main Rock Surface

Surface I has the highest concentration of petroglyphs and is referred to as the main rock surface. The main rock surface resembles an elongated rhombus leaning west, but a large part of the lower surface in the middle has broken off. The whole surface leans eastward by about 13°. From the shape of the rock and the natural fissures as the border, we can observe that the main rock surface flows from east to west and can be divided to six separate surfaces I-A, I-B, I-C, I-D, I-E, and I-F.

The number of petroglyphs found in the Surface I is 288, comprising 81.6% of the total. Engraved on the small Surface I-A in the east end is one human figure. On the Surface I-B, we can find 71 various motifs centered on cetacean (cetacea). The number of petroglyphs found on Surface I-B comprises 24.6% of the total. On the upper part of the surface are three turtles and one human figure. Below those are different species of cetacean (cetacea) swimming upward. We can find profiles of cetaceans (cetacea) and sharks as well as one very large cetacean (cetacea) posing as if to dive downward. A number of terrestrial animals (zoomorphes) are also found in the same scene. On the lower eastern part of the scene, one human figure stands with the limbs spread apart. Aside from these figures, we can find two ships related to whaling, four floats, one harpoon, one net, and weirs. The group of motifs may be telling one story.

Surface I-C is located on the center of the main rock surface. 33 petroglyphs, which is 11.4% of the total number found, are on this surface. With tigers (panthera tigris), deer (cervus nippon), cetaceans (cetacea) and whaling ships often intersecting with one another, the scene shows a complicated composition. Much of the bottom part of the surface has broken off. Part of the remaining surface shows a number of petroglyphs that are difficult to discern due to parts having been ground off. We could identify one human figure with a harpoon and two carnivorous animals (zoomorphes) of ambiguous species.

Surface I-D has 117 petroglyphs, comprising 40.6% of the total number. Half of the petroglyph motifs of Bangudae Petroglyphs are found on this surface. On the surface are a number of cetaceans (cetacea) and two human faces of different sizes and locations. Of the human figures, we can find one seemingly waving both arms, one hunter-like figure with a bow, and one figure with an arm raised. At the middle of the top part of the surface, we can also find three animals (zoomorphes) with crosshatching patterns on their bodies. The cetacean (cetacea) and the two birds (aves) each to left and right also draw attention among the motifs of this surface. The scene shows various unidentified tools in addition to floats. Deer (cervus nippon) and tigers (panthera tigris) of different sizes and shapes also adorn the surface. Of the animal motifs of the Surface I-D, the even-toed ungulates (artiodactyla) species comprise the majority with total of 29 found.

The number of petroglyphs found in the Surface I-E is 61, comprising 21.2% of the total number. Multiple deer (cervus nippon) have been found below one ship on the top of the scene. What catches eye on the Surface I-E is the number of animals (zoomorphes) in pairs, seemingly mates. One deer (cervus nippon) with the same crosshatched pattern from that of I-D on the body is also found on I-E. The representative carnivore of I-E is the tiger (panthera tigris). From the Surface I-F, measuring 26×45cm and on the eastern edge of the surface I-E, we found one cetacean (cetacea), one even-toed ungulate animal, one unidentified species, and two petroglyphs of unidentifiable shape.

Bangudae Petroglyphs were mostly engraved using the pecking method. All petroglyphs were first engraved with thin lines or series of dots to distinguish the silhouette, and then the surfaces were brought into more detail using the pecking method. However, some petroglyphs also show grinding method.

Although this is limited to a specific few, it is likely that people added grinding on existing petroglyphs made with line engraving or pecking after a certain period of time passed. Most of the petroglyphs with visible grinding are found around at the height of an average person's eye level.

Considering the overlapping and the repetition of petroglyph motifs, line engraving the earliest dating method found in Bangudae Petroglyphs. On top of the initial line engraving, newer line engravings or surface peckings were layered on. The overlapping petroglyph on the main rock surface confirms that Bangudae Petroglyphs accumulated over different periods of time. The number of petroglyphs found on the main rock surface, Surface I, comprises 81.6% of the total. The human figures, animal figures, tools, and unidentified petroglyphs of the Surface I can be summarized as following.

1) Humans (anthromorphes)

The number of human figures found was 14 (4.9% of the petroglyphs in Surface I). Of the human figures, the full body figures were engraved using pecking on the surface method while the human faces were made with line engraving. Such human figures were found in five rock surfaces from I-A to I-E.

The figure on I-A (I-A-1) raises a harpoon above the head as if about to make a throw. The figure on the top part of I-B is a man, standing with knees bent, both hands on his brow surveying afar (I-B-6). On the lower part of the surface is a woman with her limbs spread wide. Generally, figures with such posture are understood to be representing shamans. One human figure was also found on I-C (I-C-22). Although the details remain unclear due to grinding on top, the figure stands with one hand on the waste and one holding a harpoon.

From I-D, seven human figures were found. Five figures each show different poses while the remaining two are human faces. The figure on the upper part of the surface seems as though waving both arms up and down in front of an animal while the middle figure aims a bow at the beast. Another figure poses to throw a harpoon while two have their hands raised. The two human faces resemble masks (I-D-12, 83). From I-E, two human figures aiming arrows at animals (zoomorphes) (I-E-36, 47) and one standing facing forward have been found (I-E-58).

2) Animals (zoomorphes)

Total of 167 animal figures were found on the Surface I, comprising 58% of all petroglyphs on the surface. More than half of the petroglyphs are even-toed ungulates (artiodactyla) and cetaceans (cetacea). Others are carnivorous mammals (mammalia), testudines (chelonia), reptiles (reptilia), birds (aves) and fish (piscis). 17 animal figures of unidentifiable species also have been found.

The number of even-toed ungulates (artiodactyla) including deer (cervus nippon) is 58, comprising as much as 34.7% of all animal figures on the Surface I. Most of the animals (zoomorphes) are in pairs, seemingly mates. Most are described with surface engravings but some such as small-sized deer (cervus nippon) are drawn with line engraving. Many of the line-engraved animals (zoomorphes) are found on the lower layers of overlapped petroglyphs.

The number of carnivora including deer (cervus nippon) is 26, comprising 15.6% of all animal figures of the Surface I. The majority are felines. Canines such as foxes or what seem to be wolves also show up. A few seem to be mustelids.

Four even-toed ungulates (artiodactyla) and two carnivora from the Surface I have cross hatchings on the bodies. The bulging bellies of these animals (zoomorphes) suggest that they are pregnant. It is possible that the patterns on the bodies mark the pregnant animals (zoomorphes) (I-B-40, I-D-8, 9, 13, I-E-21, 23).

Following the even-toed ungulates (artiodactyla), the cetaceans (cetacea) are the second highest in number. 47 cetaceans (cetacea) are found, comprising 28.1% of all animals (zoomorphes) on the Surface I. On I-B, multiple cetaceans (cetacea) were engraved using line engraving and surface engraving technique. The cetaceans (cetacea) representative of the Bangudae Petroglyphs are mostly found on I-B, surface engraved.

The line-engraved cetaceans (cetacea) on the bottom layer which date the earliest seem to be connected to the whaling ships and the floats. The cetacean (cetacea) carrying her calf (I-B-7, 8) and the cetacean (cetacea) with a harpoon on its body (I-B-26, 27) is among the most remarkable works in the Bangudae Petroglyphs. Some cetaceans (cetacea) overlap with one another.

While most of the cetaceans (cetacea) head upward, some turn their heads sideways or towards the bottom. One cetacean (cetacea) has lines dividing its body. This one, connected to the floats, is thought to be already caught with lines representing the cuts (I-D-111). To both sides of the cetacean (cetacea) I-D-19 on the surface I-D, two birds (aves), which seem to be cormorants, one on each side, fly alongside. The motif of a bird and a whale heading toward same direction requires more insight. Most of the cetaceans (cetacea) are described in the bird's eye view, but some are shown in profile. At times, we see an example of cetacean (cetacea) representing observations from two different angles.

We find five sea turtle motifs: three on the upper portion of I-B and two on I-D. I-D-38, 39, I-E-25, 26 are thought to be marine carnivores. These four shows forms distinct from fish (piscis) or cetaceans (cetacea) and seem to come in pairs. On the main rock surface, Surface I, we find four birds (aves) and six fish (piscis). Two of the fish (piscis) seem to be sharks.

3) Tools

Total of 18 tools, including ships (boat), nets (net), weirs (fish trap), floats (float) and harpoons (fish spear) have been confirmed, comprising 6.2% of all petroglyphs on the main rock surface. Most have unidentified category or purpose, we can find five ships total. Other than one ship on the upper portion of I-E, other four are connected to the cetacean (cetacea) on the side with a thin line, confirming that they are whaling ships. These ships have characteristic front and rear which point upward.

The net on the surface I-B has a U curve. The tigers (panthera tigris) and cetaceans (cetacea) inside the net suggest that this is the case of overlapping petroglyphs. Below the net is what seems to be a weir, but it is difficult to confirm with certainty. The five floats relate to ships or cetaceans (cetacea). The harpoon on the body of the cetacean (cetacea) has been described first with pecking method and then sharpened with grinding.

4) Unidentified

The unidentified petroglyphs can be categorized to those with unidentified shape and those with unidentifiable shape. The unidentified shape refers to cases in which the petroglyph shows a distinct form but the reference is unclear. The unidentifiable shape refers to cases in which the artificial marks make it clear the intention to describe something but erosion and other damage renders the remaining shape unidentifiable. We can find 55 unidentified shapes on the main rock surface and 34 unidentifiable shapes, adding up to 89 in total.

Table 3. Classification of individual figures (surface I–A)

No.			Type	Shape	Length (cm)	Height (cm)	Method
I	A	1	Human	Full Body	24.5	19.1	Pecking

Table 4. Classification of individual figures (surface I–B)

No.			Type	Shape	Length (cm)	Height (cm)	Method
I	B	1	Animal	Testudine (chelonia)	14.7	16.5	Pecking then grinding
		2	Animal	Testudine (chelonia)	15.3	23.7	Pecking then grinding
		3	Animal	Testudine (chelonia)	11.5	14.3	Pecking then grinding
		4	Unidentified	Unidentifiable Shape	7	16.3	Pecking
		5	Unidentified	Unidentifiable Shape	2.2	16.9	Pecking
		6	Human	Full Body	10.2	20.1	Pecking
		7	Animal	Cetacean (cetacea)	42.4	61.4	Pecking then grinding
		8	Animal	Cetacean (cetacea)	10.9	17.5	Pecking
		9	Animal	Birds (aves)	15	13.4	Pecking
		10	Animal	Even-toed ungulates (artiodactyla)	18.5	12.3	Pecking
		11	Unidentified	Unidentifiable Shape	5.7	6.6	Pecking
		12	Animal	Even-toed ungulates (artiodactyla)	14	10.4	Pecking
		13	Tools	Nets (net)	29.4	38.6	Pecking
		14	Unidentified	Unidentifiable Shape	1.5	9	Pecking
		15	Animal	Carnivora	11.7	17	Pecking
		16	Animal	Cetacean (cetacea)	21.8	30.7	Pecking
		17	Animal	Cetacean (cetacea)	18	14.4	Pecking
		18	Unidentified	Unidentifiable Shape	8.8	5.8	Pecking
		19	Tools	Weir (fish trap)	41	15.7	Pecking
		20	Animal	Cetacean (cetacea)	13.3	33	Pecking
		21	Animal	Cetacean (cetacea)	10	22.8	Pecking
		22	Tools	Whaling ship	11.7	9.4	Pecking
		23	Tools	Floats (float)	6.7	11.8	Pecking
		24	Animal	Cetacean (cetacea)	27	40.3	Pecking then grinding
		25	Animal	Cetacean (cetacea)	16	16.8	Pecking
		26	Animal	Cetacean (cetacea)	33.7	63.8	Pecking
		27	Tools	Harpoons (fish spear)	7.2	30.7	Pecking then grinding
		28	Unidentified	Unidentified Shape	5.9	18	Pecking
		29	Animal	Unidentified Species	10.2	8.1	Pecking
		30	Unidentified	Unidentifiable Shape	12.4	19.8	Pecking

No.			Type	Shape	Length (cm)	Height (cm)	Method
		31	Tools	Whaling ship	24	6.9	Pecking
		32	Tools	Floats (float)	4	10.3	Pecking
		33	Animal	Cetacean (cetacea)	9.8	20.2	Pecking
		34	Animal	Unidentified Species	9.5	6	Pecking
		35	Animal	Cetacean (cetacea)	15.8	45.3	Pecking then grinding
		36	Animal	Cetacean (cetacea)	22	7.7	Pecking
		37	Animal	Cetacean (cetacea)	29	54	Pecking then grinding
		38	Unidentified	Unidentified Shape	10	9.5	Pecking
		39	Tools	Floats (float)	9.3	12.1	Pecking
		40	Animal	Carnivora	44.5	22.1	Pecking then grinding
		41	Animal	Even-toed ungulates (artiodactyla)	16.5	9.8	Pecking
		42	Unidentified	Unidentified Shape	5.4	25.6	Pecking
		43	Animal	Carnivora	13.2	5.7	Pecking
		44	Unidentified	Unidentified Shape	20.7	9.4	Pecking
		45	Animal	Cetacean (cetacea)	26	43	Pecking
		46	Tools	Floats	10	12	Pecking
		47	Animal	Cetacean (cetacea)	14.7	34	Pecking
I	B	48	Animal	Cetacean (cetacea)	20	41.5	Pecking
		49	Unidentified	Unidentified Shape	6	5	Pecking
		50	Animal	Cetacean (cetacea)	18.3	40	Pecking then grinding
		51	Unidentified	Unidentified Shape	8.8	5.6	Pecking
		52	Unidentified	Unidentified Shape	6.6	6.5	
		53	Unidentified	Unidentified Shape	5.2	7.4	Pecking
		54	Animal	Carnivora	11.2	5	Pecking
		55	Animal	Carnivora	18.7	7.4	Pecking
		56	Animal	Fish (piscis)	16.5	43	Pecking then grinding
		57	Unidentified	Unidentifiable Shape	7	6.5	Pecking
		58	Animal	Cetacean (cetacea)	18	41	Pecking then grinding
		59	Unidentified	Unidentifiable Shape	5.7	11.6	Pecking
		60	Unidentified	Unidentified Shape	22	25	Pecking then grinding
		61	Animal	Cetacean (cetacea)	13	27.2	Pecking
		62	Unidentified	Unidentified Shape	13	4.8	Pecking
		63	Animal	Carnivora	26	11	Pecking
		64	Animal	Cetacean (cetacea)	48	80	Pecking then grinding
		65	Unidentified	Unidentifiable Shape	11.5	12.5	Pecking

No.			Type	Shape	Length (cm)	Height (cm)	Method
I	B	66	Animal	Unidentified Species	24	17.8	Pecking
		67	Animal	Cetacean (cetacea)	12	27.8	Pecking
		68	Animal	Cetacean (cetacea)	23	42.2	Pecking
		69	Unidentified	Unidentified Shape	3.4	27.7	Pecking
		70	Unidentified	Unidentified Shape	11.5	23.6	Pecking
		71	Human	Full Body	24.6	19.8	Pecking

Table 5. Classification of individual figures (surface I–C)

No.			Type	Shape	Length (cm)	Height (cm)	Method
I	C	1	Animal	Cetacean (cetacea)	14.5	24.5	Pecking
		2	Unidentified	Unidentified Shape	15.5	19.3	Pecking
		3	Animal	Carnivora	42	16.8	Pecking
		4	Tools	Whaling ship	52.4	27	Pecking
		5	Animal	Cetacean (cetacea)	20.2	64.5	Pecking
		6	Unidentified	Unidentifiable Shape	14	6.4	Pecking
		7	Animal	Carnivora	29	14.2	Pecking then grinding
		8	Animal	Even-toed ungulates (artiodactyla)	21.1	20	Pecking
		9	Tools	Whaling ship	40.4	13.9	Pecking
		10	Unidentified	Unidentified Shape	7	11	Pecking
		11	Animal	Cetacean (cetacea)	16.5	39.3	Pecking
		12	Animal	Unidentified Species	8.5	19.8	Pecking
		13	Animal	Even-toed ungulates (artiodactyla)	9.8	7.3	Pecking
		14	Animal	Even-toed ungulates (artiodactyla)	27.5	33.9	Pecking then grinding
		15	Animal	Carnivora	14.2	8.5	Pecking
		16	Unidentified	Unidentifiable Shape	16.1	14.3	Pecking
		17	Animal	Carnivora	28.3	11	Pecking then grinding
		18	Animal	Even-toed ungulates (artiodactyla)	18	8	Pecking
		19	Animal	Fish (piscis)	11	29.3	Pecking
		20	Animal	Fish (piscis)	12	14	Pecking
		21	Animal	Carnivora	29	16	Pecking
		22	Human	Full Body	29.5	16.7	Pecking
		23	Unidentified	Unidentifiable Shape	8	15.5	Pecking
		24	Unidentified	Unidentifiable Shape	14.8	20.5	Pecking
		25	Unidentified	Unidentifiable Shape	7.6	8.9	Pecking
		26	Unidentified	Unidentifiable Shape	11.5	14	Pecking

No.			Type	Shape	Length (cm)	Height (cm)	Method
I	C	27	Unidentified	Unidentifiable Shape	12	20.3	Pecking
		28	Unidentified	Unidentifiable Shape	5.4	6.3	Pecking
		29	Unidentified	Unidentifiable Shape	15	8.8	Pecking
		30	Unidentified	Unidentifiable Shape	2.5	7	Pecking
		31	Unidentified	Unidentifiable Shape	4.5	10.9	Pecking
		32	Animal	Carnivora	15.4	7.1	Pecking
		33	Unidentified	Unidentifiable Shape	8.5	9	Pecking

Table 6. Classification of individual figures (surface I–D)

No.			Type	Shape	Length (cm)	Height (cm)	Method
I	D	1	Unidentified	Unidentified Shape	4	20	Pecking
		2	Animal	Even-toed ungulates (artiodactyla)	43	13.8	Pecking
		3	Human	Full Body	6.6	13	Pecking
		4	Unidentified	Unidentifiable Shape	10.5	9	Pecking
		5	Unidentified	Unidentified Shape	9.3	18.5	Pecking
		6	Animal	Even-toed ungulates (artiodactyla)	40.5	13	Pecking
		7	Animal	Unidentified Species	14	7.8	Pecking
		8	Animal	Even-toed ungulates (artiodactyla)	52.3	21	Pecking
		9	Animal	Even-toed ungulates (artiodactyla)	57	21	Pecking
		10	Animal	Unidentified Species	33.5	16.5	Pecking
		11	Unidentified	Unidentified Shape	12.8	3.3	Pecking
		12	Human	Face	5.2	5.2	Pecking
		13	Animal	Even-toed ungulates (artiodactyla)	31.8	18.6	Pecking
		14	Unidentified	Unidentified Shape	9.7	8.8	Pecking
		15	Unidentified	Unidentified Shape	12.9	16.5	Pecking
		16	Animal	Carnivora	24	36.3	Pecking then grinding
		17	Animal	Birds (aves)	15.2	20.3	Pecking
		18	Unidentified	Unidentified Shape	5.4	8	Pecking
		19	Animal	Cetacean (cetacea)	33.2	52	Pecking
		20	Animal	Birds (aves)	21.8	22.8	Pecking
		21	Animal	Even-toed ungulates (artiodactyla)	14.4	7.9	Pecking
		22	Unidentified	Unidentifiable Shape	5.5	2	Pecking
		23	Unidentified	Unidentifiable Shape	14.3	5.5	Pecking
		24	Animal	Cetacean (cetacea)	29	23.1	Pecking

	No.	Type	Shape	Length (cm)	Height (cm)	Method
I D	25	Animal	Cetacean (cetacea)	8.5	17.6	Pecking
	26	Animal	Even-toed ungulates (artiodactyla)	33.8	18.5	Pecking
	27	Animal	Even-toed ungulates (artiodactyla)	8.4	7.3	Pecking
	28	Animal	Even-toed ungulates (artiodactyla)	14.2	8.4	Pecking
	29	Animal	Even-toed ungulates (artiodactyla)	9.3	5.7	Pecking
	30	Unidentified	Unidentified Shape	10.2	2.2	Pecking
	31	Animal	Carnivora	22.3	15.4	Pecking
	32	Animal	Cetacean (cetacea)	21.2	35	Pecking then grinding
	33	Unidentified	Unidentified Shape	20.3	10.3	Pecking
	34	Animal	Carnivora	20.5	14.5	Pecking
	35	Animal	Unidentified Species	16	17	Pecking
	36	Unidentified	Unidentifiable Shape	6.2	7.8	Pecking
	37	Animal	Carnivora	45.3	21	Pecking
	38	Animal	Carnivora-marine (pinnipedia)	6	10.6	Pecking
	39	Animal	Carnivora-marine (pinnipedia)	4.9	11	Pecking
	40	Animal	Even-toed ungulates (artiodactyla)	28	19.5	Pecking
	41	Human	Full Body	10.4	15.7	Pecking
	42	Animal	Even-toed ungulates (artiodactyla)	8	5.1	Pecking
	43	Animal	Even-toed ungulates (artiodactyla)	9	7.3	Pecking
	44	Animal	Fish (piscis)	4	5.1	Pecking
	45	Unidentified	Unidentified Shape	12.2	8.8	Pecking
	46	Animal	Unidentified Species	18.2	18.5	Pecking
	47	Unidentified	Unidentifiable Shape	17.4	4.7	Pecking
	48	Animal	Even-toed ungulates (artiodactyla)	48.2	25	Pecking then grinding
	49	Human	Full Body	31.7	34.7	Pecking
	50	Unidentified	Unidentified Shape	20	13.8	Pecking
	51	Unidentified	Unidentified Shape	16	9.1	Pecking
	52	Unidentified	Unidentified Shape	31	40.7	Pecking
	53	Unidentified	Unidentified Shape	12.7	1.5	Pecking
	54	Animal	Even-toed ungulates (artiodactyla)	12.8	9.3	Pecking
	55	Animal	Even-toed ungulates (artiodactyla)	16.5	12.9	Pecking
	56	Animal	Unidentified Species	11.5	15.8	Pecking
	57	Animal	Cetacean (cetacea)	21	22.5	Pecking
	58	Animal	Fish (piscis)	9.7	12.5	Pecking

Categories of Motifs in Bangudae Petroglyphs

No.		Type	Shape	Length (cm)	Height (cm)	Method
		59	Unidentified	Unidentifiable Shape	6.8	10.2	Pecking
		60	Unidentified	Unidentified Shape	12.3	16.2	Pecking
		61	Animal	Even-toed ungulates (artiodactyla)	9.2	8.4	Pecking
		62	Animal	Cetacean (cetacea)	22	28.1	Pecking
		63	Animal	Unidentified Species	16	14	Pecking
		64	Animal	Testudine (chelonia)	14.8	15	Pecking
		65	Animal	Cetacean (cetacea)	27.1	13	Pecking
		66	Tools	Unidentified Species	16.8	9.6	Pecking
		67	Animal	Testudine (chelonia)	6.3	6.8	Pecking
		68	Unidentified	Unidentified Shape	6.6	14.2	Pecking
		69	Unidentified	Unidentified Shape	10.5	16.2	Pecking
		70	Animal	Cetacean (cetacea)	43.4	23.7	Pecking
		71	Animal	Even-toed ungulates (artiodactyla)	21.8	21.2	Pecking then grinding
		72	Animal	Unidentified Species	8.8	17.8	Pecking then grinding
		73	Animal	Cetacean (cetacea)	24.4	35.8	Pecking
		74	Human	Full Body	11.2	16.3	Pecking then grinding
		75	Unidentified	Unidentified Shape	14.5	15.3	Pecking
I	D	76	Animal	Carnivora	26	15	Pecking
		77	Animal	Even-toed ungulates (artiodactyla)	12.5	11.2	Pecking
		78	Animal	Even-toed ungulates (artiodactyla)	23.3	23.6	Pecking
		79	Tools	Unidentified Species	13.8	14.3	Pecking
		80	Animal	Fish (piscis)	2.7	3.4	Pecking
		81	Animal	Cetacean (cetacea)	6.5	14	Pecking
		82	Unidentified	Unidentified Shape	8	8.3	Pecking
		83	Human	Face	13.3	20.4	Pecking
		84	Unidentified	Unidentified Shape	10	9.9	Pecking
		85	Animal	Carnivora	43.8	30	Pecking
		86	Human	Full Body	9.8	15.8	Pecking then grinding
		87	Unidentified	Unidentified Shape	10	12.5	Pecking
		88	Animal	Even-toed ungulates (artiodactyla)	18.7	11.8	Pecking
		89	Animal	Unidentified Species	21.5	18.3	Pecking
		90	Animal	Cetacean (cetacea)	37.9	13.3	Pecking
		91	Animal	Unidentified Species	7.3	4.3	Pecking
		92	Animal	Even-toed ungulates (artiodactyla)	8.5	9.8	Pecking
		93	Animal	Even-toed ungulates (artiodactyla)	27	21.7	Pecking

No.			Type	Shape	Length (cm)	Height (cm)	Method
		94	Animal	Cetacean (cetacea)	9.4	12.8	Pecking
		95	Animal	Cetacean (cetacea)	16.5	23.4	Pecking
		96	Unidentified	Unidentified Shape	6.2	8.2	Pecking
		97	Animal	Even-toed ungulates (artiodactyla)	23	38.8	Pecking
		98	Animal	Even-toed ungulates (artiodactyla)	10.3	12.4	Pecking
		99	Unidentified	Unidentified Shape	7	11.3	Pecking
		100	Unidentified	Unidentified Shape	10	8.2	Pecking
		101	Animal	Cetacean (cetacea)	7.3	13.2	Pecking
		102	Animal	Cetacean (cetacea)	11.7	16.5	Pecking
		103	Unidentified	Unidentified Shape	1.3	23.2	Pecking
		104	Tools	Unidentified Species	5.5	13.9	Pecking
I	D	105	Unidentified	Unidentified Shape	11.5	5.2	Pecking
		106	Unidentified	Unidentified Shape	27	9.5	Pecking
		107	Animal	Even-toed ungulates (artiodactyla)	14.5	8.2	Pecking
		108	Unidentified	Unidentifiable Shape	31	7.5	Pecking
		109	Animal	Cetacean (cetacea)	25.6	11.7	Pecking
		110	Tools	Floats	13	11.2	Pecking
		111	Animal	Cetacean (cetacea)	46.5	16.8	Pecking
		112	Animal	Even-toed ungulates (artiodactyla)	16.8	12	Pecking
		113	Tools	Unidentified Species	14	9.5	Pecking
		114	Animal	Carnivora	16.2	9.1	Pecking
		115	Tools	Unidentified Species	16	16.6	Pecking
		116	Animal	Even-toed ungulates (artiodactyla)	18.8	9.5	Pecking
		117	Animal	Even-toed ungulates (artiodactyla)	21.1	15	Pecking

Table 7. Classification of individual figures (surface I–E)

No.			Type	Shape	Length (cm)	Height (cm)	Method
		1	Unidentified	Unidentified Shape	13.6	7.3	Pecking
		2	Tools	Ships	28.3	12.2	Pecking
		3	Unidentified	Unidentified Shape	11.7	10.5	Pecking
I	E	4	Unidentified	Unidentifiable Shape	2.5	10.8	Pecking
		5	Animal	Cetacean (cetacea)	8	13.8	Pecking
		6	Animal	Even-toed ungulates (artiodactyla)	9.4	11.5	Pecking
		7	Animal	Even-toed ungulates (artiodactyla)	13.7	8.4	Pecking

No.			Type	Shape	Length (cm)	Height (cm)	Method
		8	Animal	Even-toed ungulates (artiodactyla)	8.8	6.7	Pecking
		9	Animal	Cetacean (cetacea)	9	19	Pecking
		10	Animal	Cetacean (cetacea)	6.8	12	Pecking
		11	Unidentified	Unidentifiable Shape	3.5	4	Pecking
		12	Animal	Unidentified Species	12	3	Pecking
		13	Unidentified	Unidentified Shape	7.3	5.5	Pecking
		14	Unidentified	Unidentified Shape	8.5	3	Pecking
		15	Animal	Unidentified Species	18.3	9.2	Pecking
		16	Animal	Even-toed ungulates (artiodactyla)	15.9	11.6	Pecking
		17	Unidentified	Unidentifiable Shape	18	13	Pecking
		18	Unidentified	Unidentified Shape	10.4	13	Pecking
		19	Animal	Even-toed ungulates (artiodactyla)	13.5	15.6	Pecking
		20	Animal	Even-toed ungulates (artiodactyla)	17.2	11.4	Pecking
		21	Animal	Carnivora	42.5	16.6	Pecking
		22	Unidentified	Unidentified Shape	12	12.8	Pecking
		23	Animal	Even-toed ungulates (artiodactyla)	42	23.5	Pecking
		24	Animal	Even-toed ungulates (artiodactyla)	10.9	10.3	Pecking
I	E	25	Animal	Carnivora-marine (pinnipedia)	4.8	11.6	Pecking
		26	Animal	Carnivora-marine (pinnipedia)	5.3	12	Pecking
		27	Animal	Unidentified Species	24.3	18.7	Pecking
		28	Unidentified	Unidentified Shape	22.5	2.6	Pecking
		29	Animal	Carnivora	29.7	17.7	Pecking
		30	Unidentified	Unidentifiable Shape	8.8	14.4	Pecking
		31	Animal	Carnivora	27	28	Pecking
		32	Animal	Even-toed ungulates (artiodactyla)	11	8.8	Pecking
		33	Animal	Even-toed ungulates (artiodactyla)	9.5	17.3	Pecking
		34	Animal	Even-toed ungulates (artiodactyla)	23.1	19.9	Pecking
		35	Animal	Even-toed ungulates (artiodactyla)	25.7	24.5	Pecking
		36	Human	Full Body	9.8	14.1	Pecking
		37	Animal	Even-toed ungulates (artiodactyla)	12.5	9.4	Pecking
		38	Animal	Even-toed ungulates (artiodactyla)	9.8	7.4	Pecking
		39	Unidentified	Unidentifiable Shape	21.5	6.2	Pecking
		40	Animal	Even-toed ungulates (artiodactyla)	11.1	11.3	Pecking
		41	Animal	Even-toed ungulates (artiodactyla)	21.2	15.4	Pecking

No.			Type	Shape	Length (cm)	Height (cm)	Method
		42	Animal	Carnivora	6.5	7.6	Pecking
		43	Animal	Carnivora	9.8	7.9	Pecking
		44	Animal	Even-toed ungulates (artiodactyla)	31.5	33.6	Pecking
		45	Animal	Carnivora	32.9	17.9	Pecking then grinding
		46	Animal	Even-toed ungulates (artiodactyla)	38	34.3	Pecking
		47	Human	Full Body	15.1	17.2	Pecking then grinding
		48	Animal	Even-toed ungulates (artiodactyla)	28.2	17.4	Pecking
		49	Animal	Even-toed ungulates (artiodactyla)	10.4	5	Pecking
		50	Animal	Even-toed ungulates (artiodactyla)	15.3	12.4	Pecking
I	E	51	Unidentified	Unidentifiable Shape	9.5	9.8	Pecking
		52	Animal	Birds (aves)	27.5	24.2	Pecking
		53	Animal	Cetacean (cetacea)	16.5	42.5	Pecking
		54	Unidentified	Unidentified Shape	10	12.2	Pecking
		55	Unidentified	Unidentifiable Shape	8.7	8	Pecking
		56	Animal	Carnivora	38.7	21.3	Pecking
		57	Unidentified	Unidentified Shape	12.8	10.2	Pecking
		58	Human	Full Body	17	21.1	Pecking
		59	Unidentified	Unidentified Shape	8.9	19.8	Pecking
		60	Unidentified	Unidentified Shape	15	9.1	Pecking
		61	Unidentified	Unidentified Shape	7.4	5.2	Pecking

Table 8. Classification of individual figures (surface I–F)

No.			Type	Shape	Length (cm)	Height (cm)	Method
		1	Unidentified	Unidentified Shape	7.8	9.8	Pecking
		2	Animal	Cetacean (cetacea)	11.4	13.5	Pecking
I	F	3	Animal	Even-toed ungulates (artiodactyla)	17.3	6	Pecking
		4	Animal	Unidentified Species	10.8	5.3	Pecking
		5	Unidentified	Unidentified Shape	8	3	Pecking

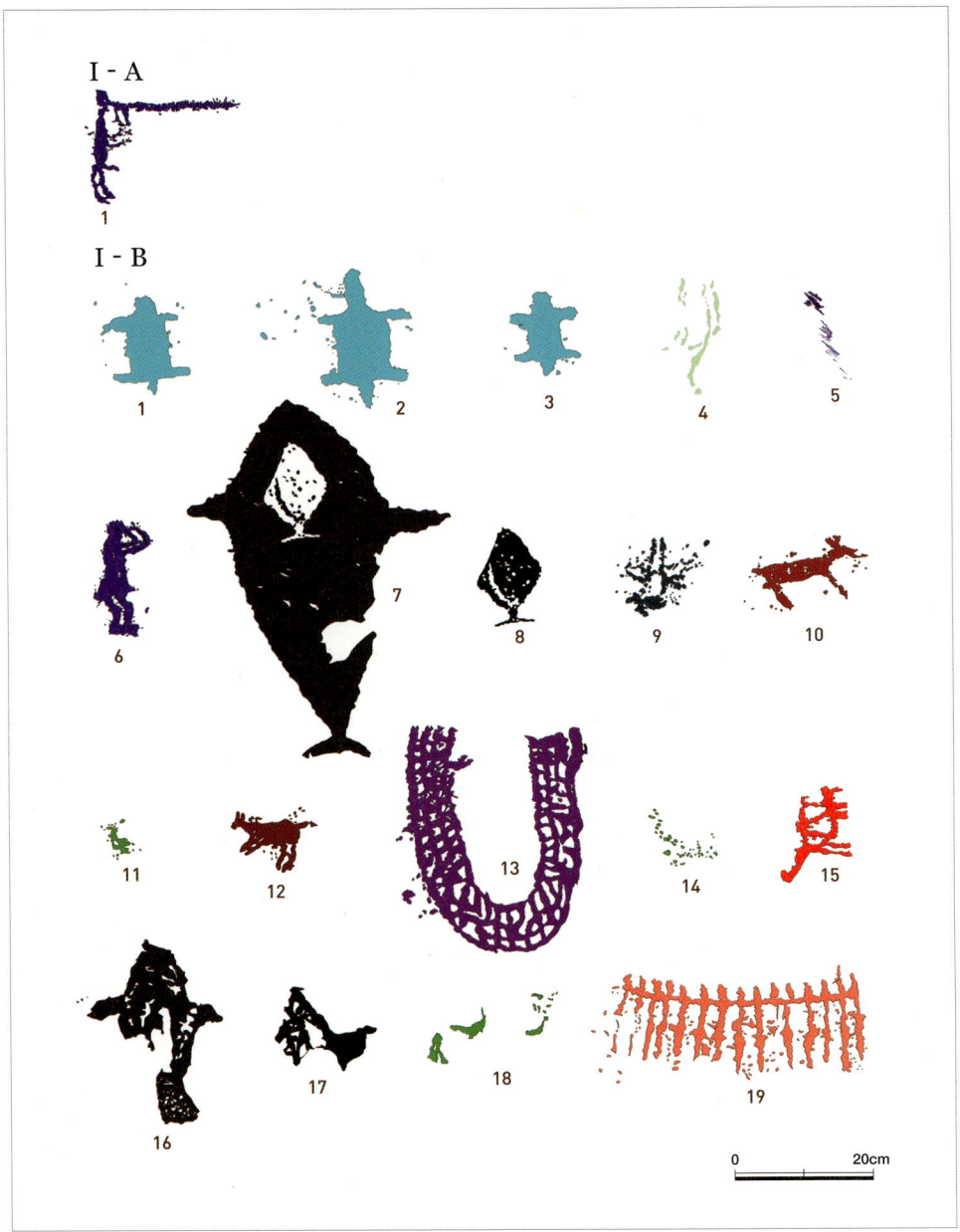

Fig. 5. Surface I–A, individual figures (1); surface I–B, individual figures (1–19)

The Bangudae Petroglyphs in Ulsan

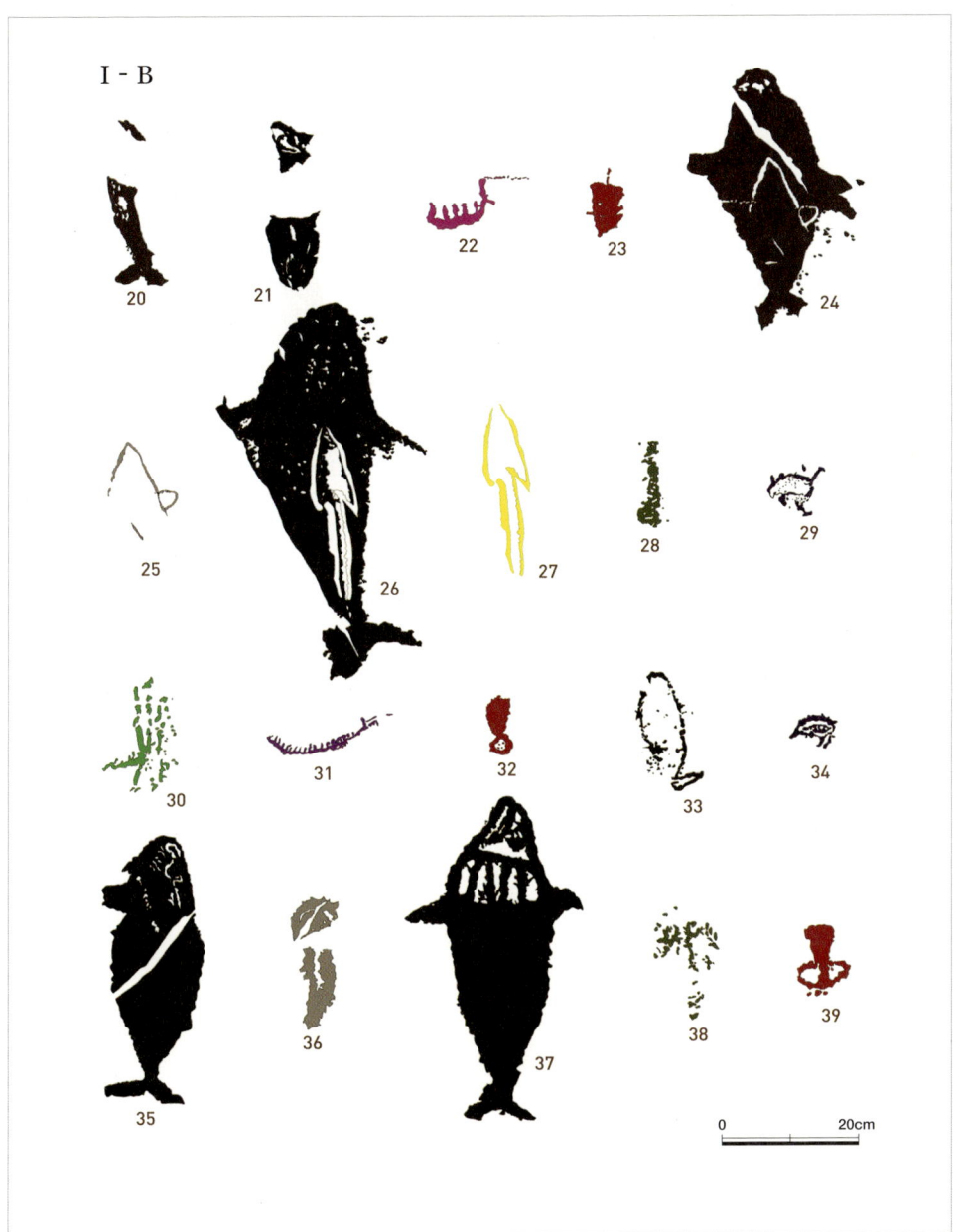

I - B

Fig. 6. Surface I–B, individual figures (20–39)

I - B

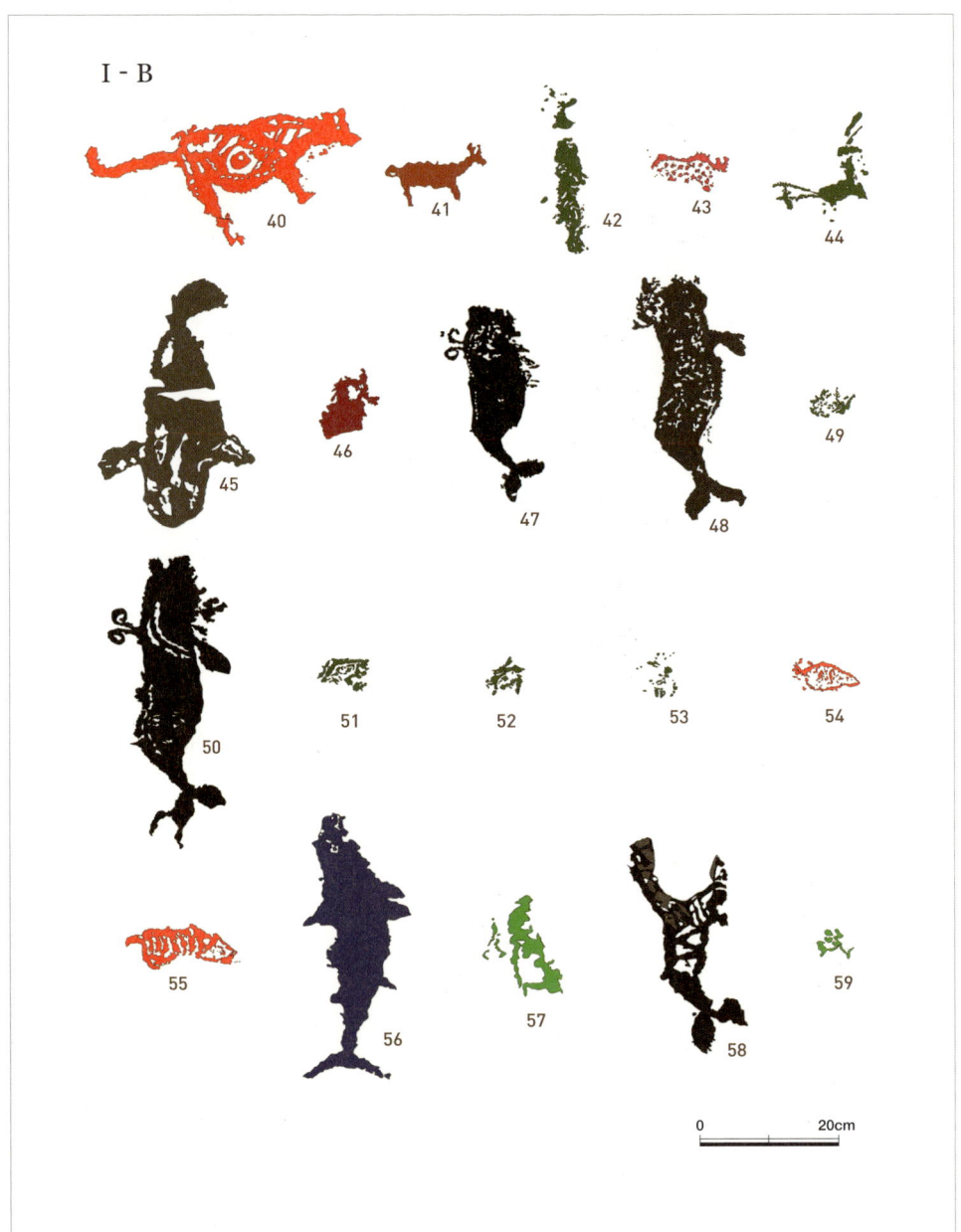

Fig. 7. Surface I–B, individual figures (40–59)

The Bangudae Petroglyphs in Ulsan

I - B

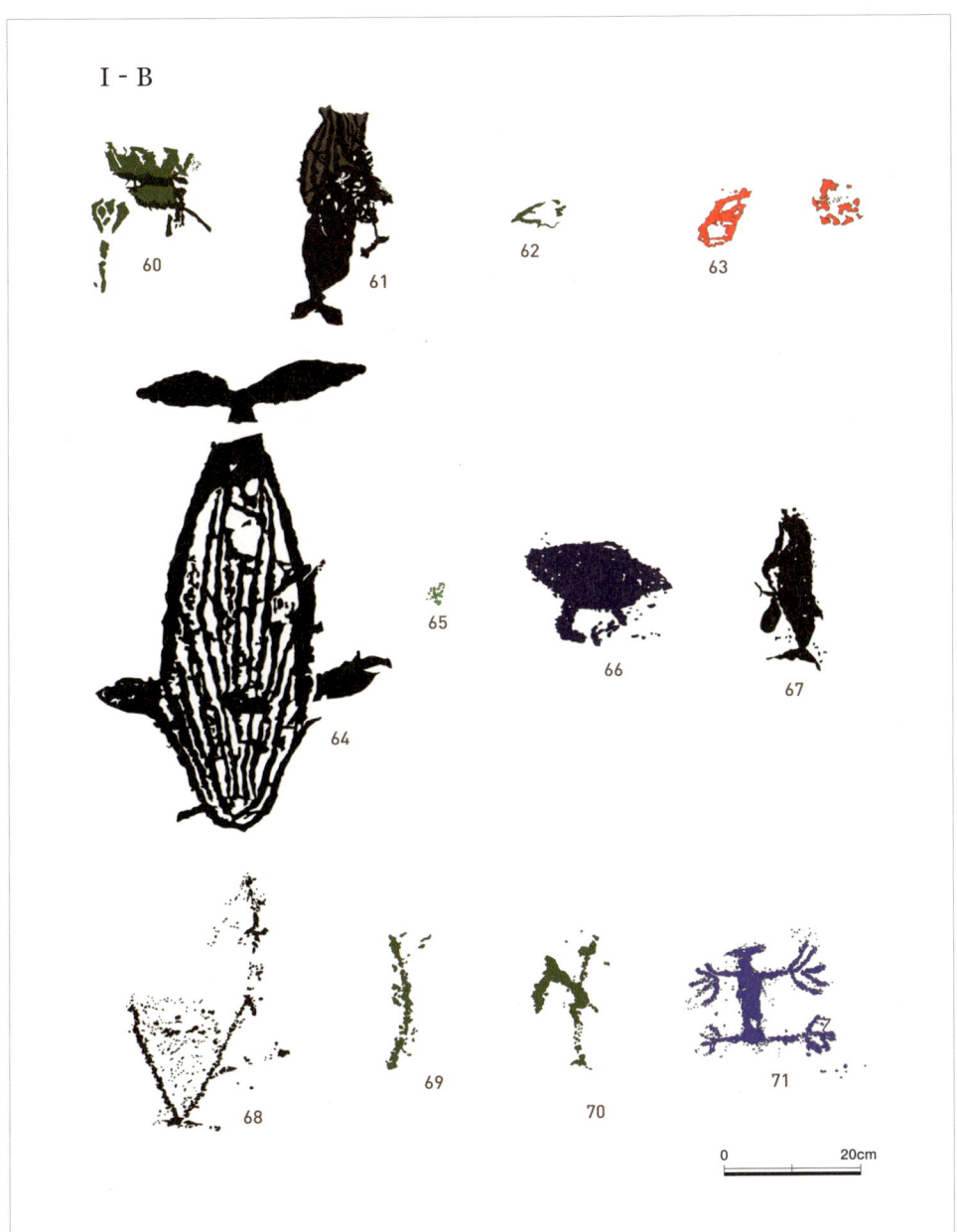

Fig. 8. Surface I–B, individual figures (60–71)

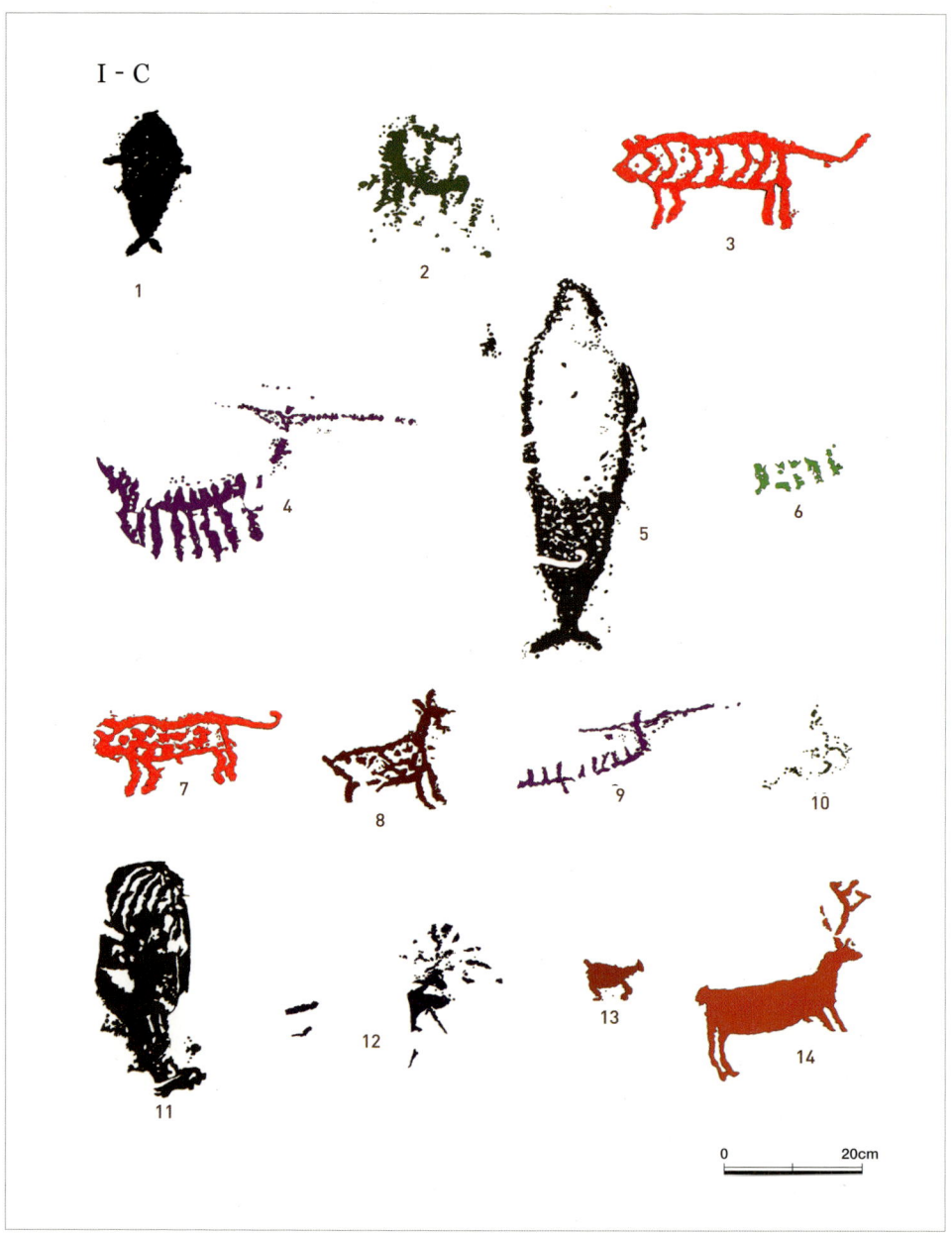

Fig. 9. Surface I–C, individual figures (1–14)

The Bangudae Petroglyphs in Ulsan

I - C

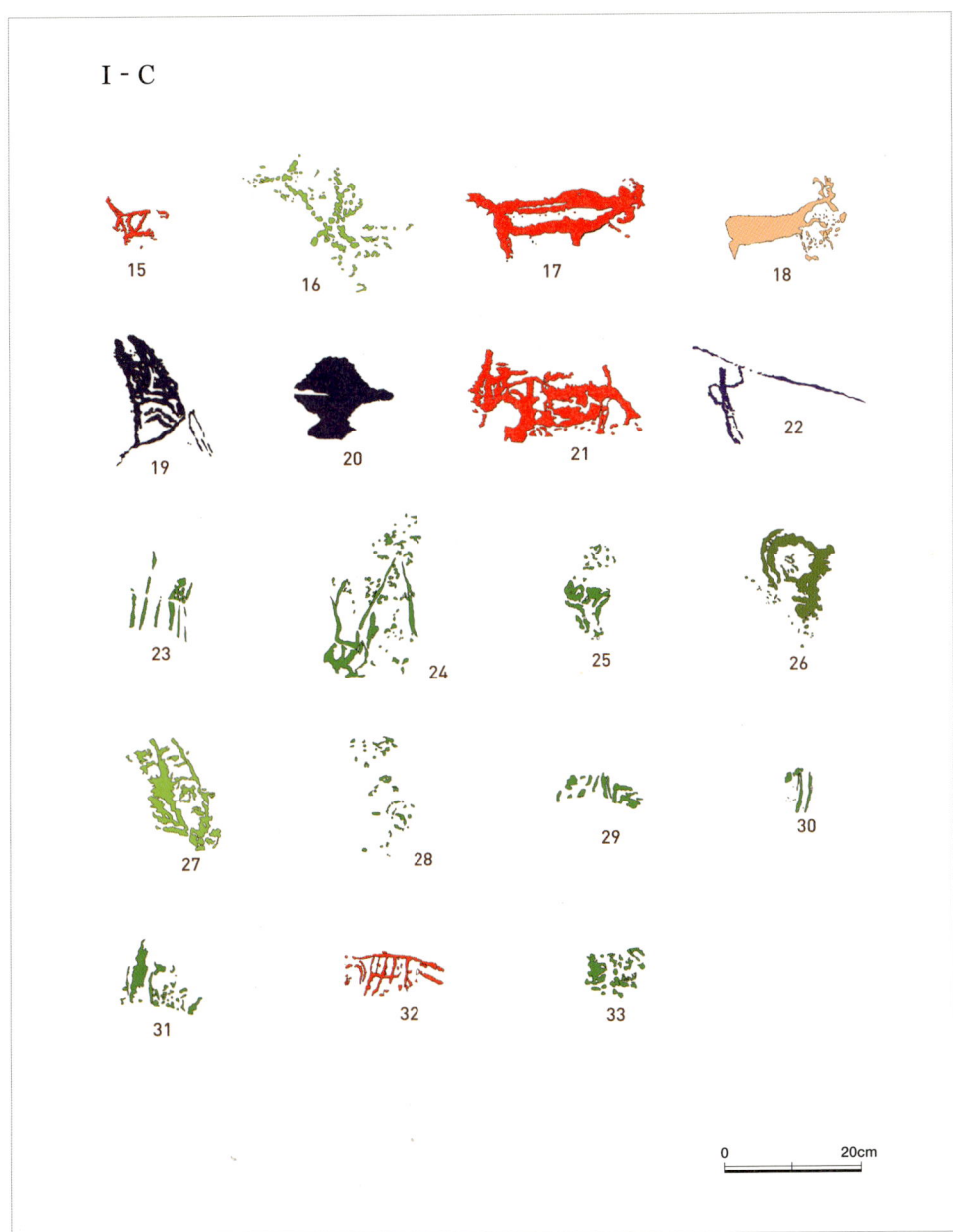

Fig. 10. Surface I–C, individual figures (15–33)

I - D

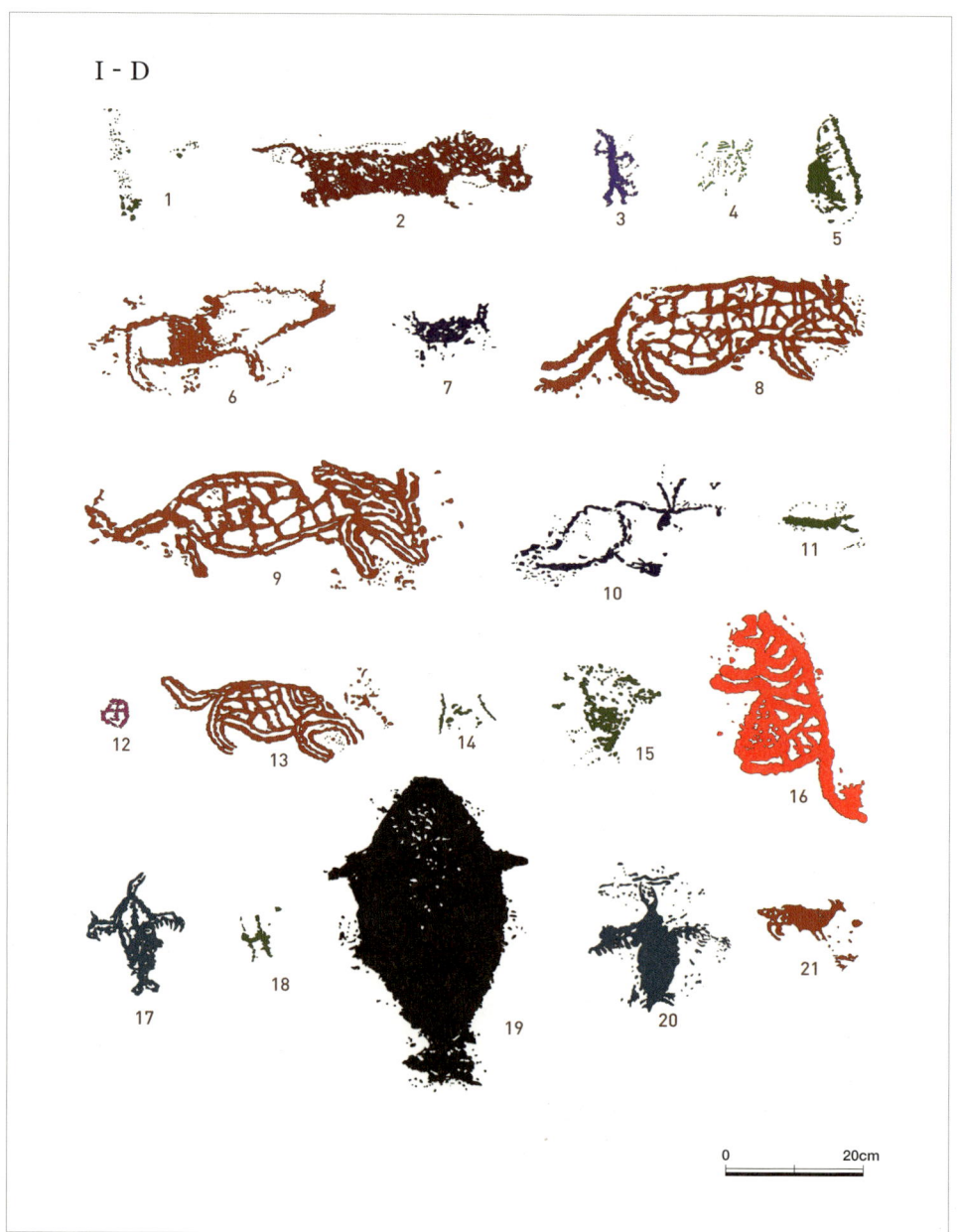

Fig. 11. Surface I–D, individual figures (1–21)

I - D

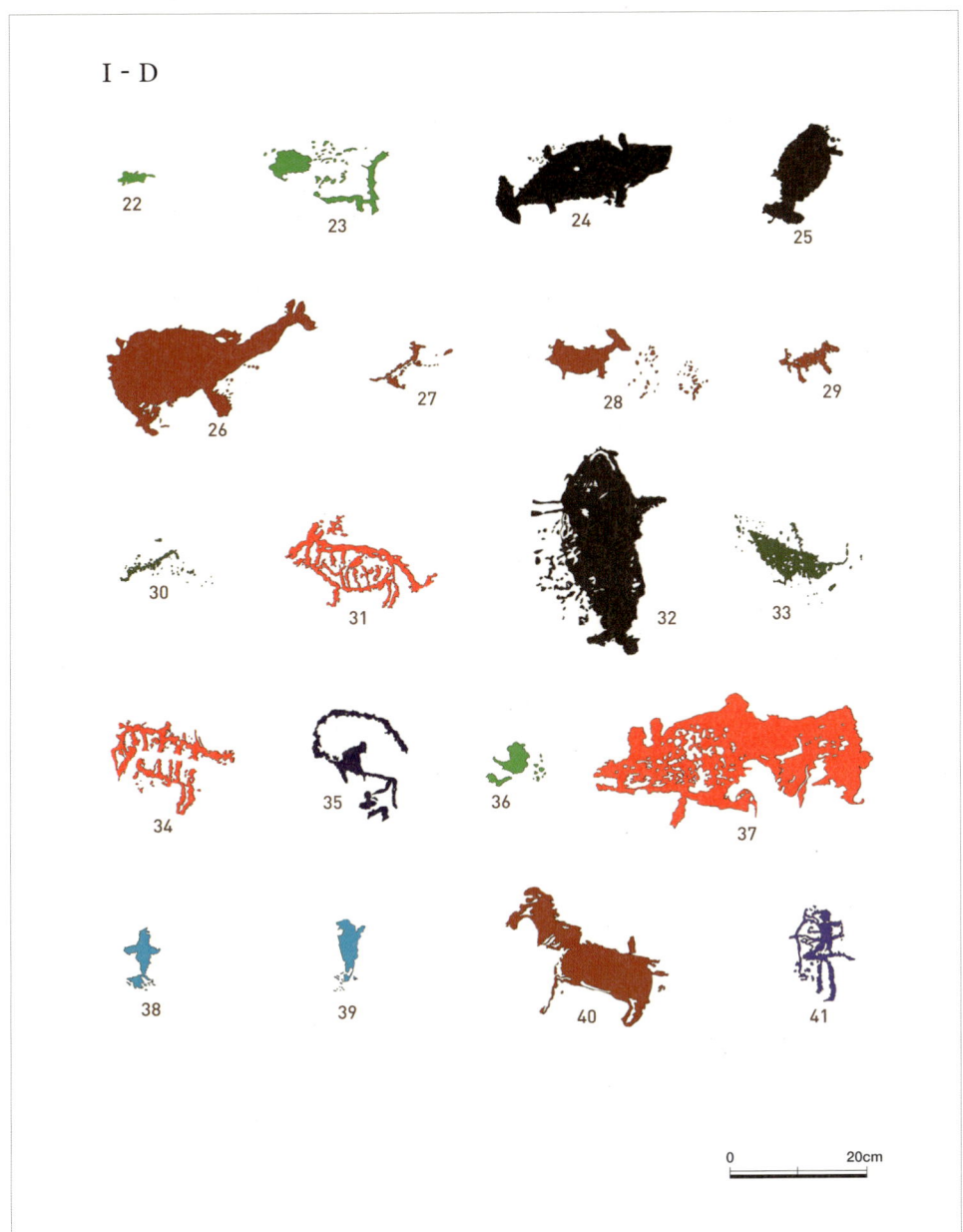

Fig. 12. Surface I–D, individual figures (22–41)

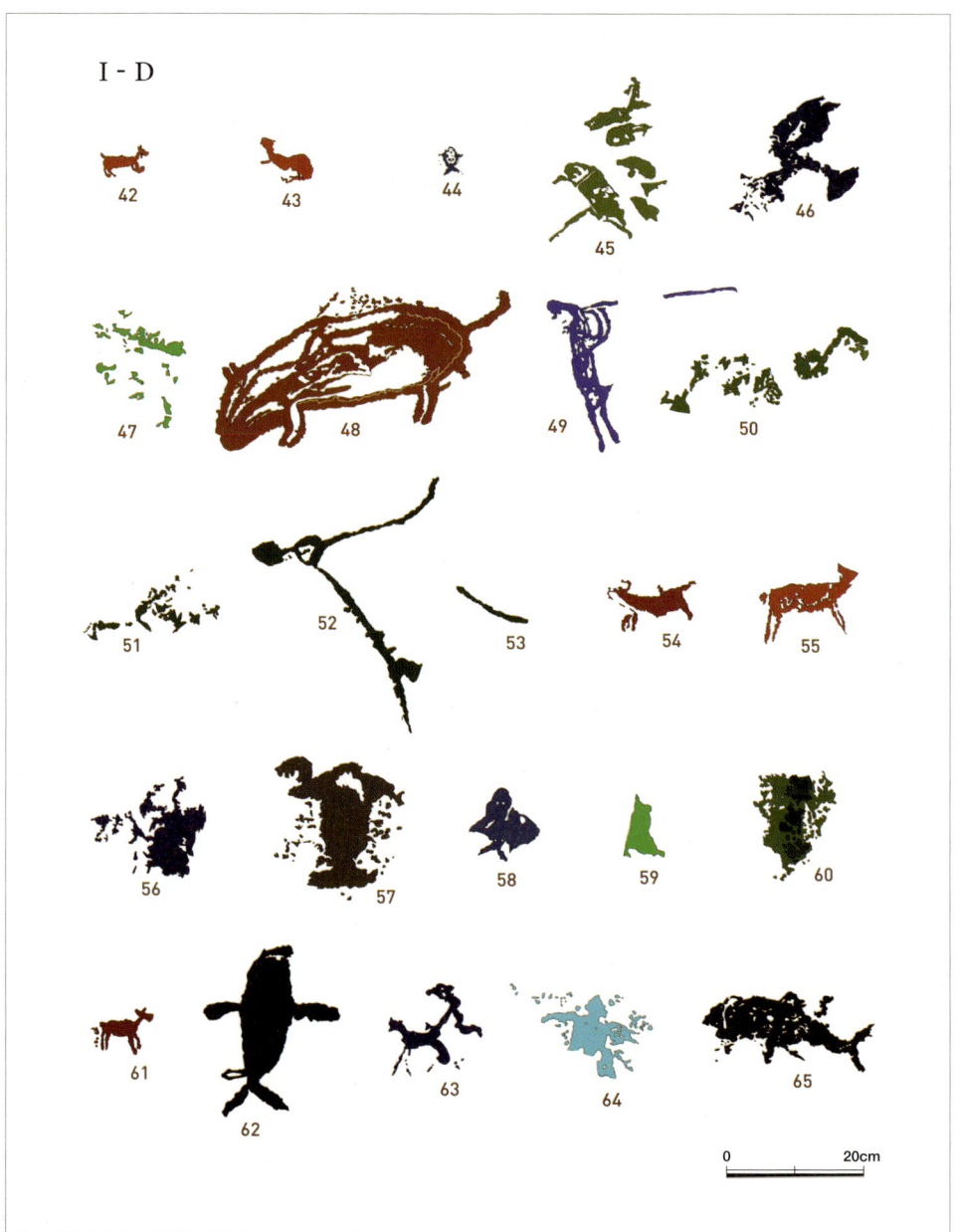

I - D

Fig. 13. Surface I–D, individual figures (42–65)

The Bangudae Petroglyphs in Ulsan

I - D

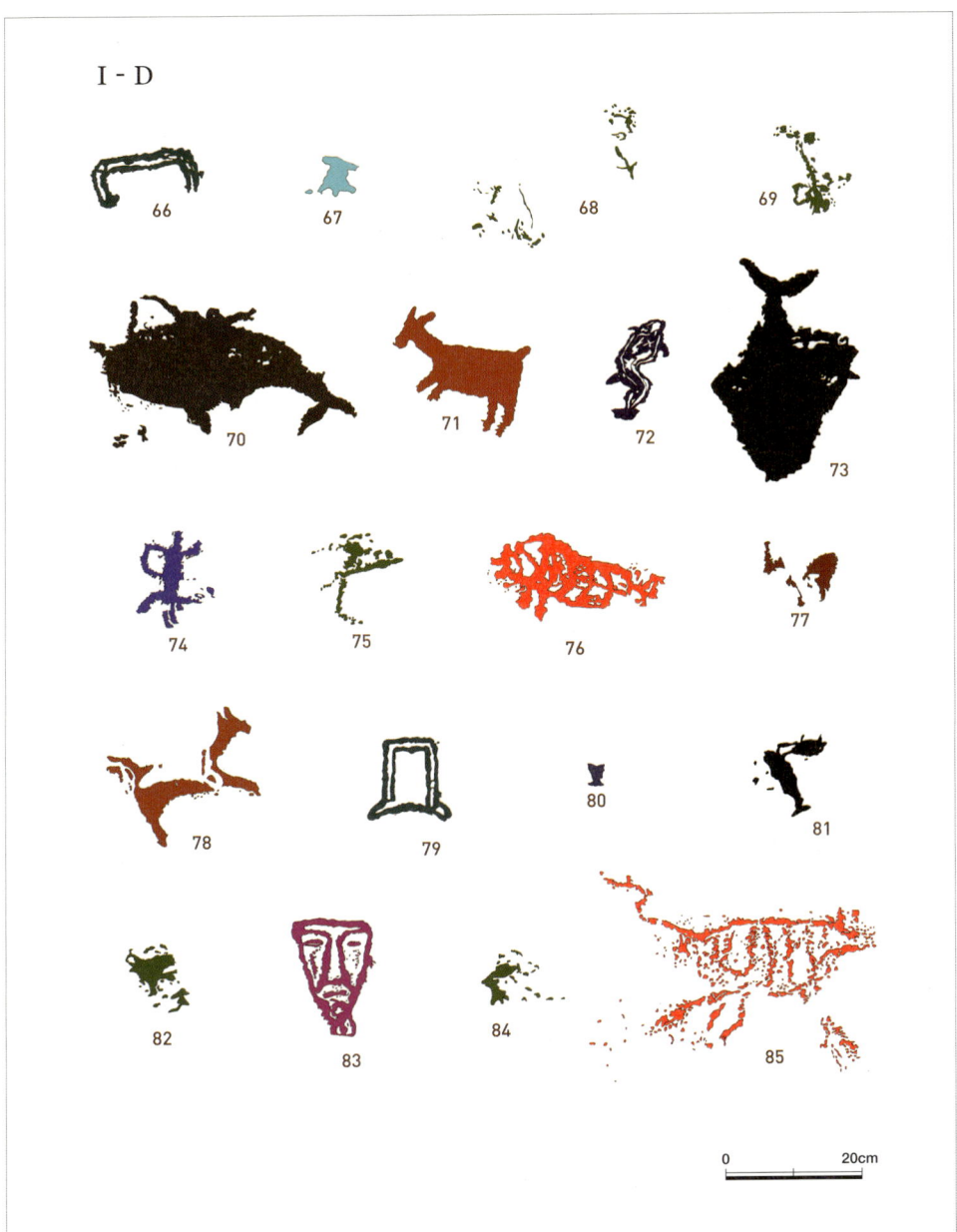

Fig. 14. Surface I–D, individual figures (66–85)

I - D

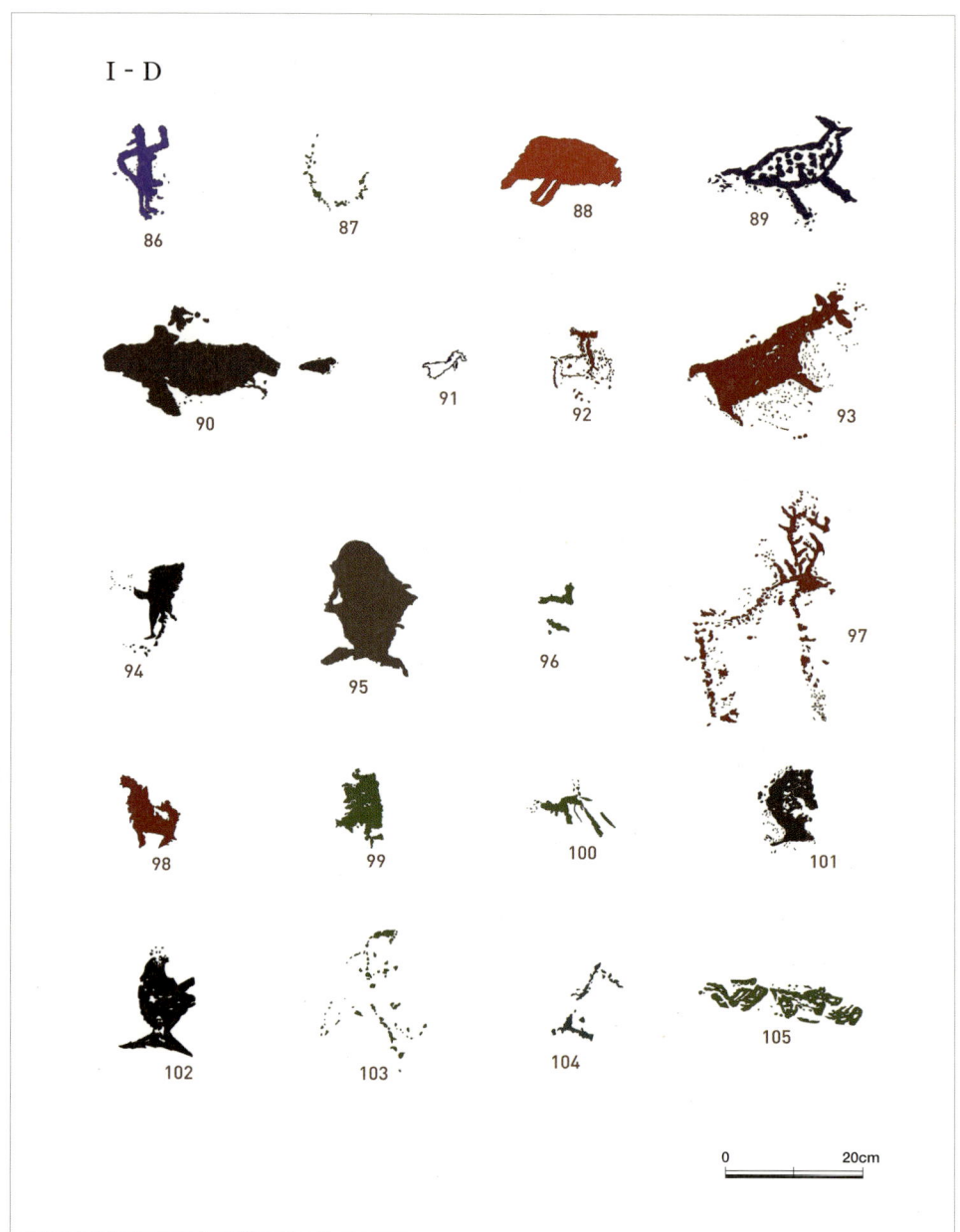

Fig. 15. Surface I–D, individual figures (86–105)

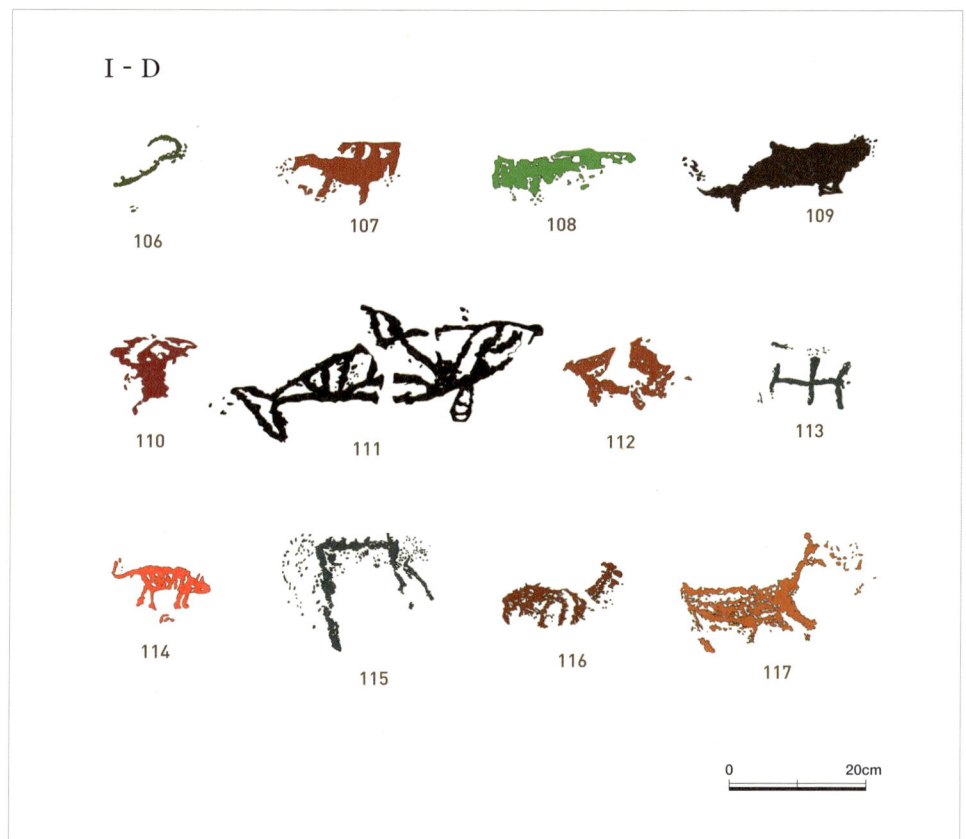

I - D

106
107
108
109
110
111
112
113
114
115
116
117

0   20cm

Fig. 16. Surface I–D, individual figures (106–117)

I - E

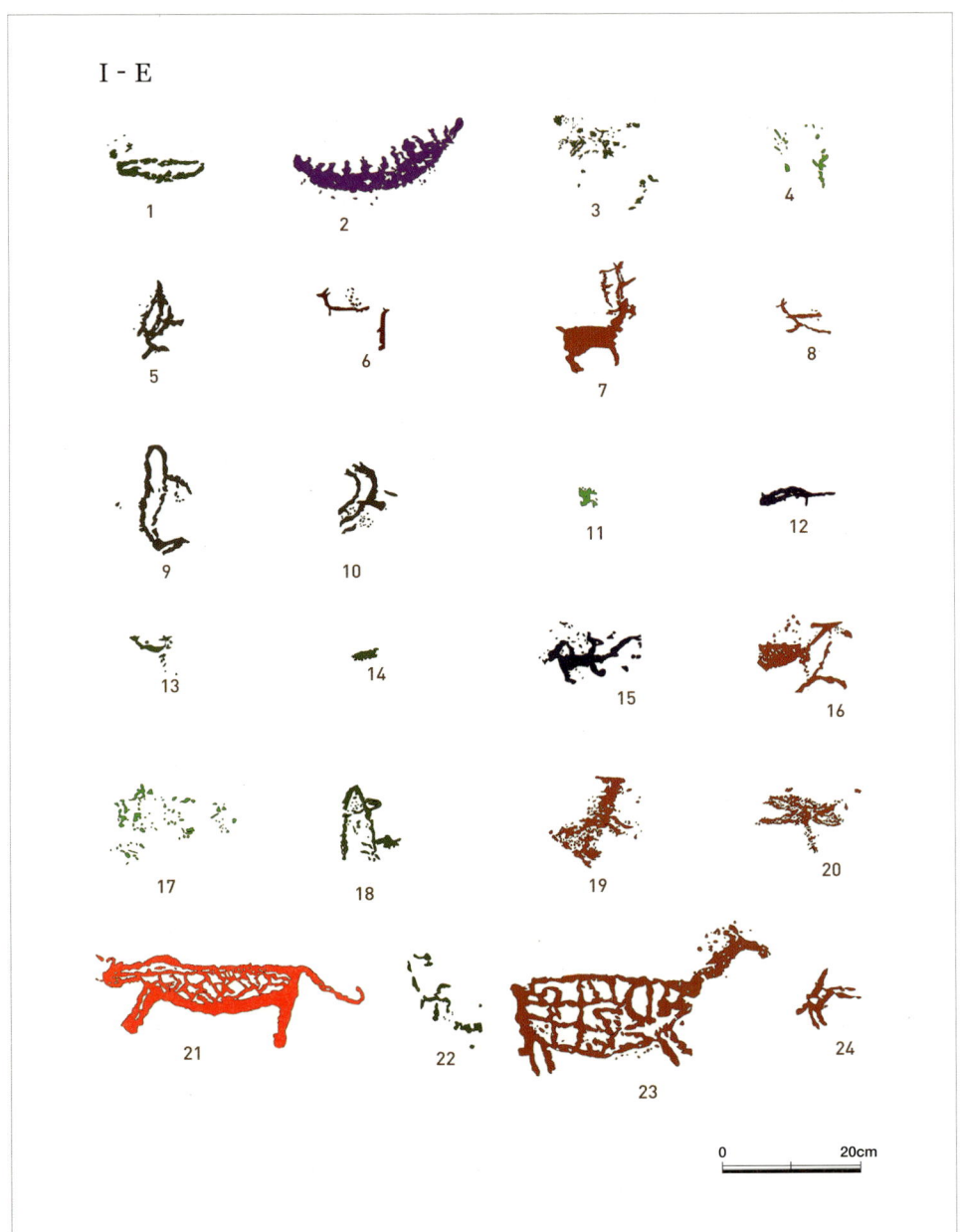

Fig. 17. Surface I–E, individual figures (1–24)

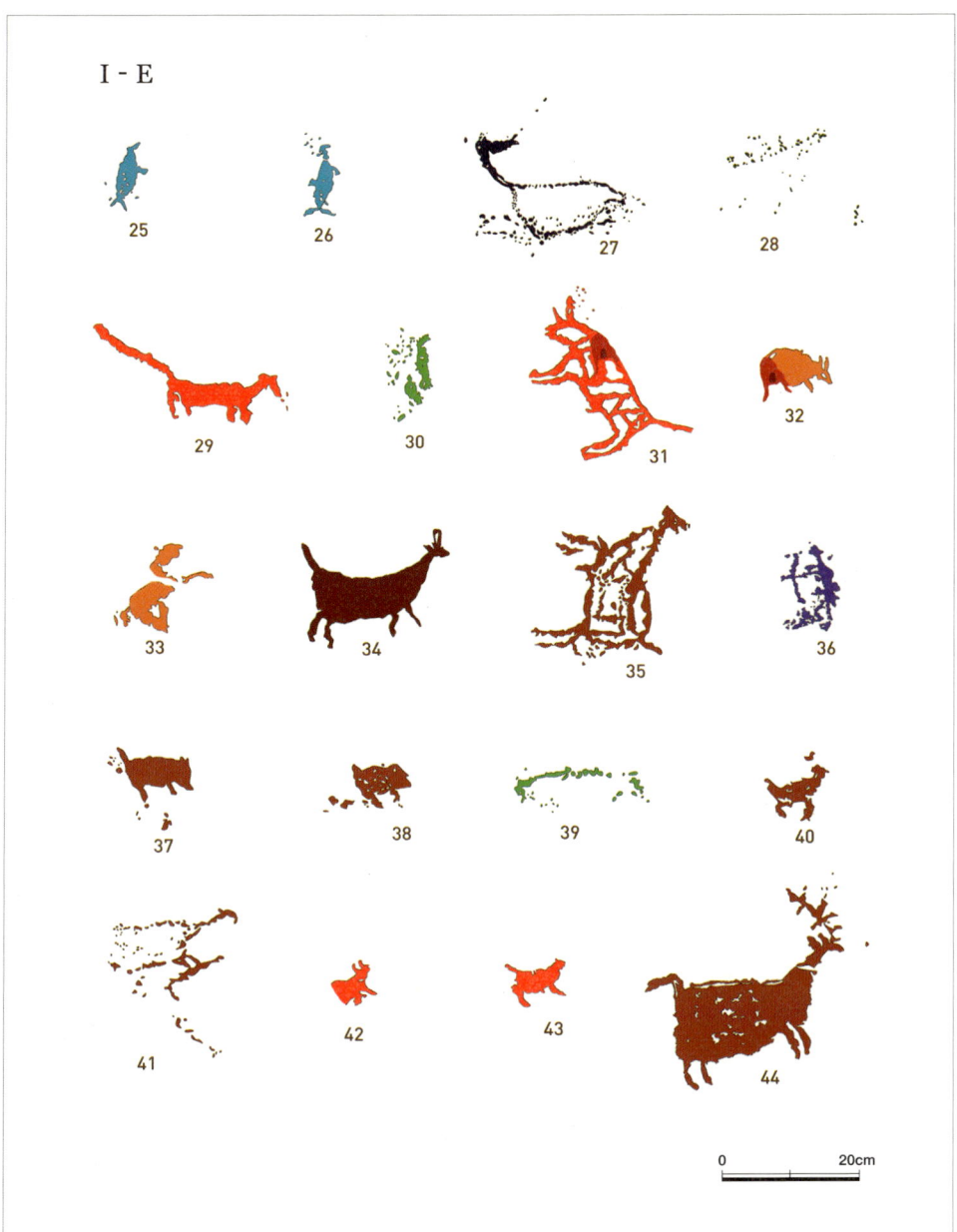

I - E

25 26 27 28
29 30 31 32
33 34 35 36
37 38 39 40
41 42 43 44

0   20cm

Fig. 18. Surface I–E, individual figures (25–44)

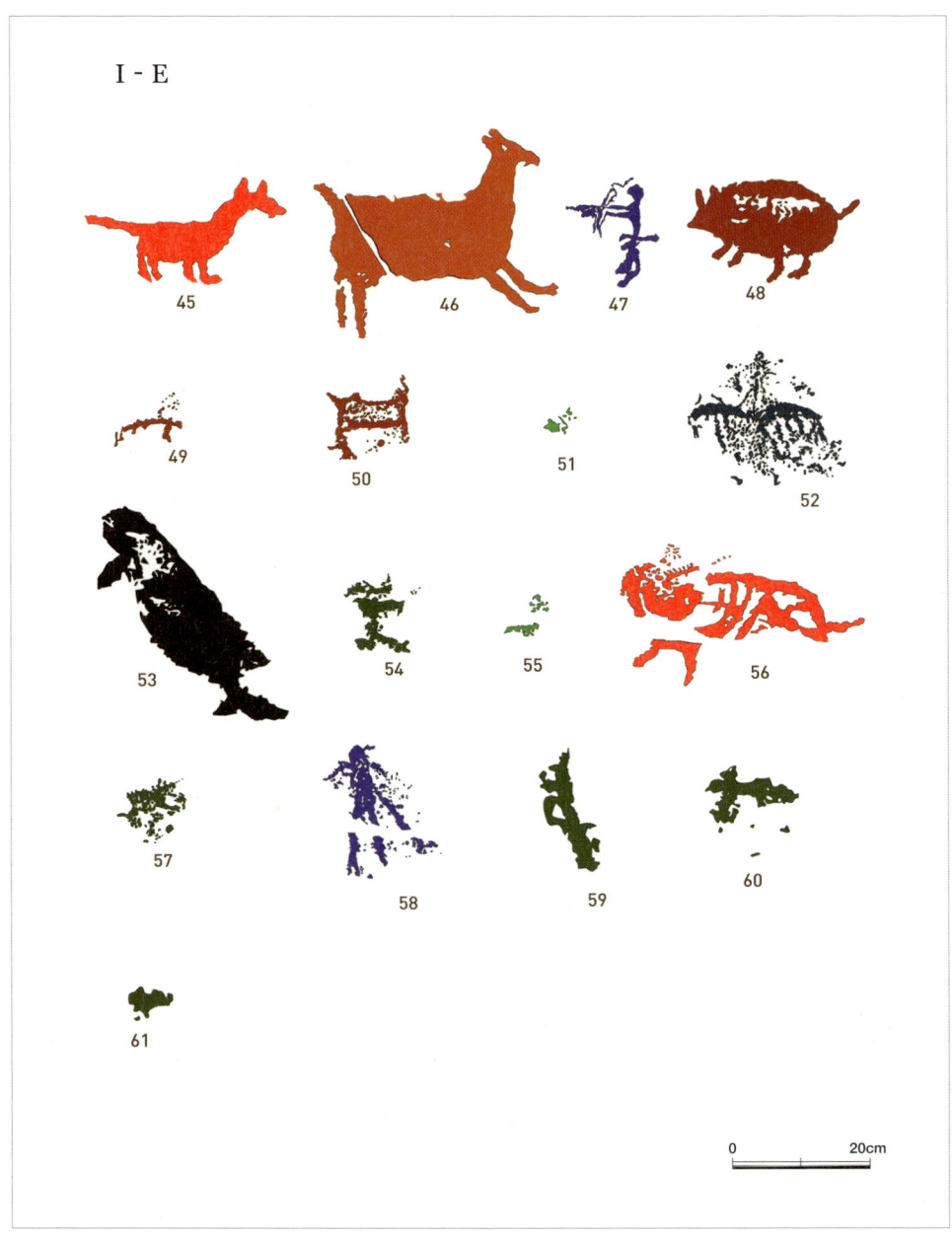

I - E

45 46 47 48 49 50 51 52 53 54 55 56 57 58 59 60 61

0 20cm

Fig. 19. Surface I–E, individual figures (45–61)

The Bangudae Petroglyphs in Ulsan

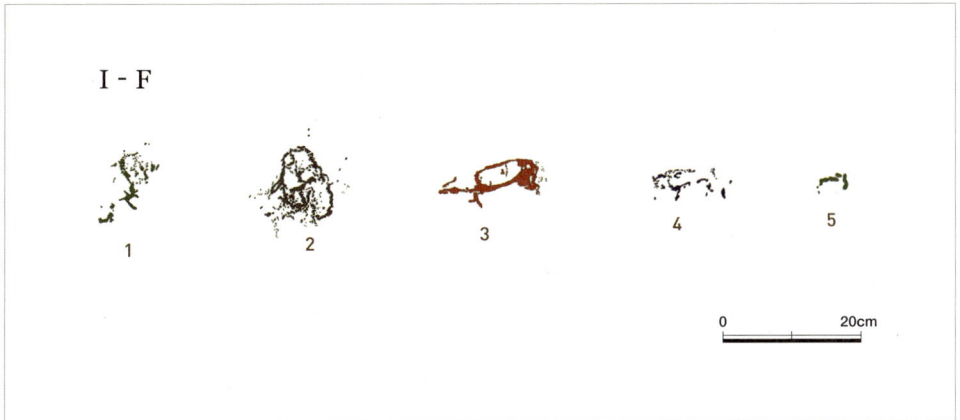

Fig. 20. Surface I–F, individual figures (1–5)

2. Surface II

Surface II lies east of the main rock surface where the cliff turns at the angle, facing the Surface I. When floods cause sediments from the upper stream of Daegok Stream to flow downward, the Surface II faces the first hit. Perhaps due to such environmental disadvantage, the surface has suffered from chipping, etc. losing much of its rock body. This surface may have had as many petroglyphs as the main rock surface, but only 21 survives to this day.

Surface II consists of fourrock surfaces within a frame with the width of 4.2m. From the top, the surface can be divided into II-A, II-B, II-C and II-D. On II-A, we found one human figure, four even-toed ungulates (artiodactyla), one carnivorous animal, and one whale. Including unidentified shapes, the total number rises to 11 (52.4% of surface II). On II-B, we found total of four petroglyphs: two resembling nets, one surface engraved cetacean (cetocea), and one unidentifiable shape.

On the small surface of II-C below II-B, we found three shapes which are thought to be fish (piscis). Two of the fish (piscis) face upward while the other faces down. On the lower area, one surface engraved cetacean (cetocea) and one line engraved cetacean (cetocea) were confirmed. In addition, we found a line engraved petroglyph with unclear shape on the surface leading northward.

Table 9. Classification of individual figures (surface II–A)

No.			Type	Shape	Length (cm)	Height (cm)	Method
II	A	1	Animal	Even-toed ungulates (artiodactyla)	14	8.5	Pecking
		2	Animal	Even-toed ungulates (artiodactyla)	5	5	Pecking
		3	Animal	Carnivora	25	12.5	Pecking
		4	Human	Full Body	9.5	16	Pecking
		5	Unidentified	Unidentifiable Shape	5	6	Pecking
		6	Animal	Even-toed ungulates (artiodactyla)	23	14	Pecking
		7	Animal	Even-toed ungulates (artiodactyla)	6.8	6	Pecking
		8	Unidentified	Unidentified Shape	15	17	Pecking
		9	Animal	Cetacean (cetacea)	14	28.5	Pecking
		10	Unidentified	Unidentified Shape	3.5	5	Pecking
		11	Unidentified	Unidentified Shape	16.5	6.5	Pecking

Table 10. Classification of individual figures (surface II–B)

No.			Type	Shape	Length (cm)	Height (cm)	Method
II	B	1	Tools	Nets (net)	21	14	Pecking
		2	Tools	Nets (net)	30	26	Pecking
		3	Animal	Cetacean (cetacea)	58	33.5	Pecking
		4	Unidentified	Unidentifiable Shape	18.5	13	Pecking

Table 11. Classification of individual figures (surface II–C)

No.			Type	Shape	Length (cm)	Height (cm)	Method
II	C	1	Animal	Fish (piscis)	9	12	Pecking
		2	Animal	Fish (piscis)	6.8	12	Pecking
		3	Animal	Fish (piscis)	3.5	6.3	Pecking

Table 12. Classification of individual figures (surface II–D)

No.			Type	Shape	Length (cm)	Height (cm)	Method
II	D	1	Animal	Cetacean (cetacea)	15	31	Pecking then grinding
		2	Animal	Cetacean (cetacea)	9.5	23.5	Pecking
		3	Unidentified	Unidentified Shape	30	14.5	Pecking

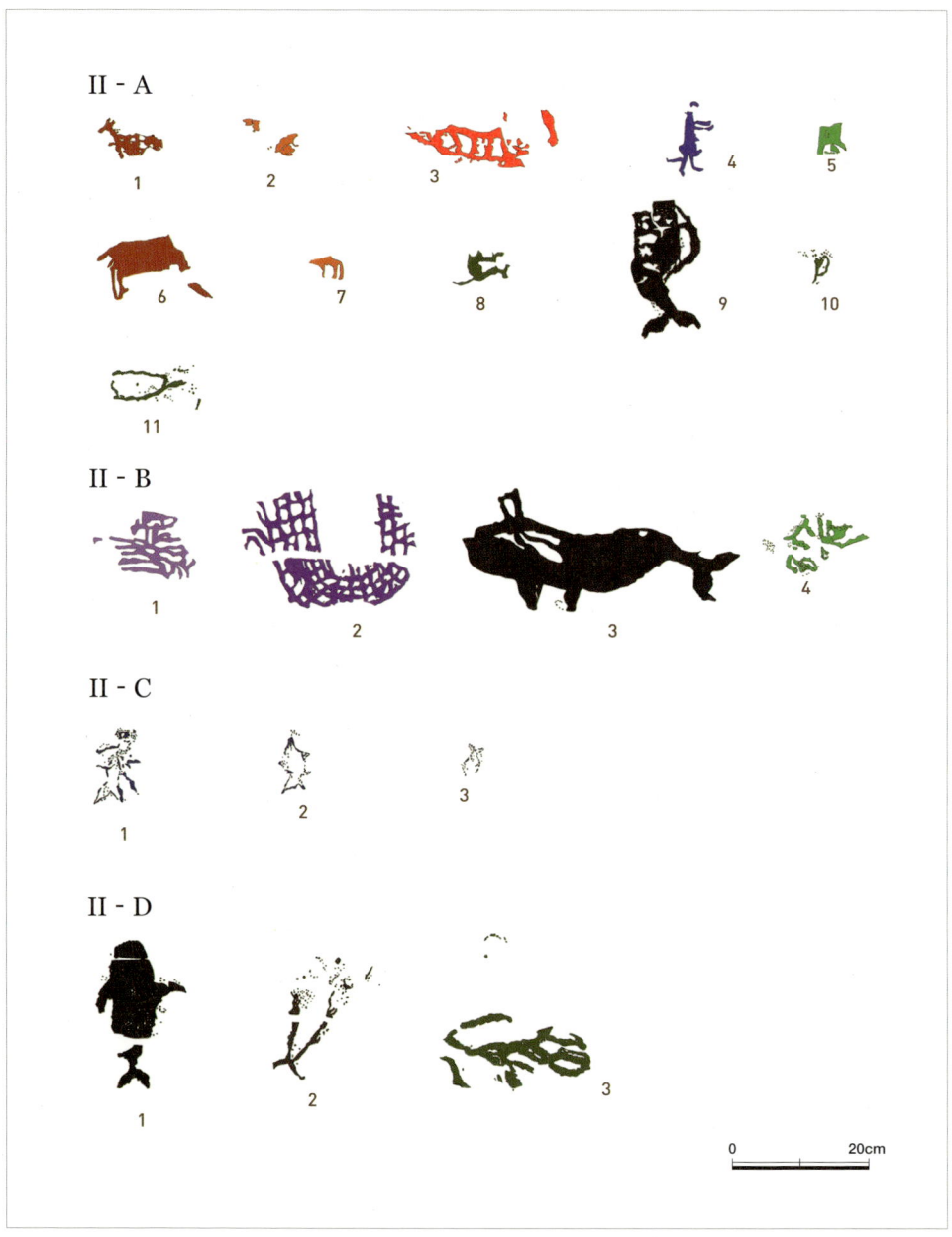

Fig. 21. Surface II–A, individual figures (1–11); surface II–B, individual figures (1–4); surface II–C, individual figures (1–3); surface II–D, individual figures (1–3)

The Bangudae Petroglyphs in Ulsan

3. Surface Ⅲ

Surface III, a 3.9m wide rock surface west of the main rock surface, can be subdivided into III-A, III-B, and III-C. From here, 21 petroglyphs, comprising 5.9% of the total number of petroglyphs found were confirmed. On III-A, the highest section of the surface, seven petroglyphs were found. On the western side, we found one line engraved tiger (panthera tigris) and one whale below with its belly upward. Below the cetacean (cetacea) is a ship and a tail of the whale. The flipped body of the line engraved whale suggests that it has been hunted by humans (anthromorphes). The line on the body of the cetacean (cetacea) seems to describe the cutting of the meat. On the eastern edge of the surface, we also find one tail of the cetacean (cetacea), one animal of unidentified species and one unidentifiable shape.

III-B is the surface that just forward from the whole cliff area. We found total of nine petroglyphs on the surface including one full bodied human and one cetacean (cetacea) which head fell off with the breaking of the rock. On the east, we find three line engraved deer (cervus nippon). These deer (cervus nippon) are the largest among the motifs of Bangudae Petroglyphs. The attention to detail in the animal form makes these deer (cervus nippon) distinct from other beasts. In addition, we can find even-toed ungulates (artiodactyla) and animals (zoomorphes) of unidentified species on the small surface leading to the east.

III-C is the lowest part of the rock surface. Four animal motifs and one unidentifiable shape were found. An animal of unidentified species, one fish (piscis), and one canine attacking an even-toed ungulate adorn the surface. The fish (piscis) motif shows a distinct shape and engraving methods that set it apart from other petroglyphs.

Table 13. Classification of individual figures (surface III–A)

No.			Type	Shape	Length (cm)	Height (cm)	Method
III	A	1	Animal	Cetacean (cetacea)	20.2	20.7	Pecking
		2	Unidentified	Unidentified Shape	16.7	3.5	Pecking
		3	Animal	Unidentified Shape	8.5	2.9	Pecking
		4	Animal	Carnivora	32.7	30	Pecking then grinding
		5	Animal	Cetacean (cetacea)	37.8	17.3	Pecking then grinding
		6	Tools	Whaling ship	15.2	5.8	Pecking
		7	Animal	Cetacean (cetacea)	8.5	11.7	Pecking

Table 14. Classification of individual figures (surface III–B)

No.			Type	Shape	Length (cm)	Height (cm)	Method
III	B	1	Human	Full Body	7	11.7	Pecking
		2	Animal	Cetacean (cetacea)	14.4	18.4	Pecking then grinding
		3	Unidentified	Unidentified Shape	5.7	6.5	Pecking
		4	Animal	Even-toed ungulates (artiodactyla)	53.6	40.8	Pecking
		5	Animal	Even-toed ungulates (artiodactyla)	52.9	44.3	Pecking
		6	Unidentified	Unidentified Shape	14.6	17.4	Pecking
		7	Animal	Even-toed ungulates (artiodactyla)	35	34.5	Pecking
		8	Unidentified	Unidentified Shape	20	6	Pecking
		9	Animal	Unidentified Species	13.5	17.5	Pecking

Table 15. Classification of individual figures (surface III–C)

No.			Type	Shape	Length (cm)	Height (cm)	Method
III	C	1	Animal	Unidentified Species	19	11	Pecking
		2	Animal	Fish (piscis)	19	8.8	Pecking
		3	Animal	Carnivora	18.7	11.2	Pecking
		4	Animal	Even-toed ungulates (artiodactyla)	37.5	33.7	Pecking
		5	Unidentified	Unidentified Shape	10.5	20.2	Pecking

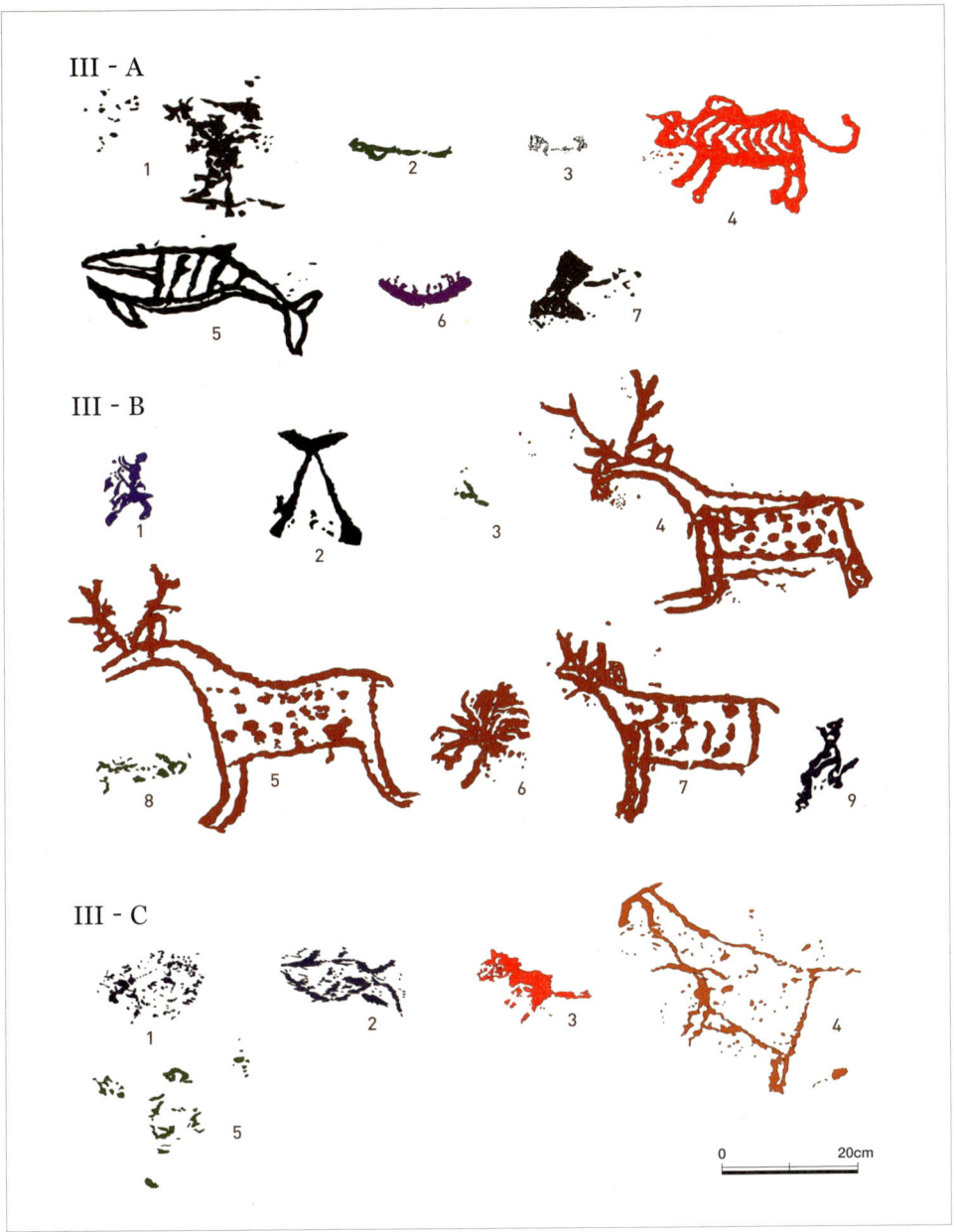

III - A

III - B

III - C

Fig. 22. Surface Ⅲ–A, individual figures (1–7); surface Ⅲ–B, individual figures (1–9); surface Ⅲ–C, individual figures (1–5)

Categories of Motifs in Bangudae Petroglyphs

4. Surface IV

Surface II curves again parallel to the Daegok Stream. Surface IV, where the rock cliff stretches across, consists of various smaller rock surfaces scattered throughout the area. Petroglyphs were found in a total of four locations. On IV-A, IV-B, IV-C, and IV-D which exist sporadically from east to west, we found 23 petroglyphs, comprising 6.5% of the total number of petroglyphs found.

On the far east surface of IV-A, two animals (zoomorphes) are engraved top and bottom. The animal engraved with pecking method located beneath the line engraved tiger (panthera tigris) is of unidentifiable species. This beast, seemingly half-finished, is likely a carnivore.

IV-B is below where the middle of the surface IV juts forward. We found total of seven petroglyphs on the surface. On the strip of three connected rock surfaces, all the petroglyphs found other than one even-toed ungulate found on the eastern end are unidentifiable or unidentified.

To the west of IV-B, a piece of rock has fallen off, creating a deep indent. The rock surface inside this area is IV-C. We found one even-toed ungulate, likely a mountain goat.

IV-D is located at the western end. It is the flat oval of a rock below the area between Surface II and IV where the rock turns at the angle. Total of 13 petroglyphs were found on this surface. Due to a serious erosion, the shapes are unclear. Other than two that seems to be cetaceans (cetacea), two that resembles carnivorous beasts, and one even-toed ungulate, the remaining eight are unidentified or unidentifiable. Of the images of carnivora, one seems to be a canine.

Table 16. Classification of individual figures (surface IV–A)

No.			Type	Shape	Length (cm)	Height (cm)	Method
IV	A	1	Animal	Carnivora	27.5	11	Pecking
		2	Animal	Unidentified species	21	13	Pecking

Table 17. Classification of individual figures (surface IV–B)

No.			Type	Shape	Length (cm)	Height (cm)	Method
IV	B	1	Unidentified	Unidentifiable Shape	9	7.3	Pecking
		2	Unidentified	Unidentified Shape	7.8	3.5	Pecking
		3	Unidentified	Unidentified Shape	7.7	10.2	Pecking
		4	Animal	Even-toed ungulates (artiodactyla)	14.7	6.4	Pecking
		5	Unidentified	Unidentifiable Shape	13.3	3.4	Pecking
		6	Unidentified	Unidentifiable Shape	6.4	4.2	Pecking
		7	Unidentified	Unidentifiable Shape	7.2	4.5	Pecking

Table 18. Classification of individual figures (surface IV–C)

No.			Type	Shape	Length (cm)	Height (cm)	Method
IV	C	1	Animal	Even-toed ungulates (artiodactyla)	11	8.5	Pecking

Table 19. Classification of individual figures (surface IV–D)

No.			Type	Shape	Length (cm)	Height (cm)	Method
IV	D	1	Unidentified	Unidentified Shape	7	10	Pecking
		2	Unidentified	Unidentified Shape	4.5	6.5	Pecking
		3	Animal	Cetacean (cetacea)	36.5	11.5	Pecking
		4	Animal	Cetacean (cetacea)	9	8	Pecking
		5	Unidentified	Unidentified Shape	5	8.9	Pecking
		6	Animal	Even-toed ungulates (artiodactyla)	25.5	14.5	Pecking
		7	Unidentified	Unidentified Shape	12.5	14.5	Pecking
		8	Animal	Carnivora	32	14	Pecking then grinding
		9	Unidentified	Unidentified Shape	8	4	Pecking
		10	Unidentified	Unidentified Shape	6.5	8	Pecking then grinding
		11	Animal	Carnivora	17.5	9	Pecking then grinding
		12	Unidentified	Unidentified Shape	7.2	3.4	Pecking
		13	Unidentified	Unidentifiable Shape	3.2	2.3	Pecking

Categories of Motifs in Bangudae Petroglyphs

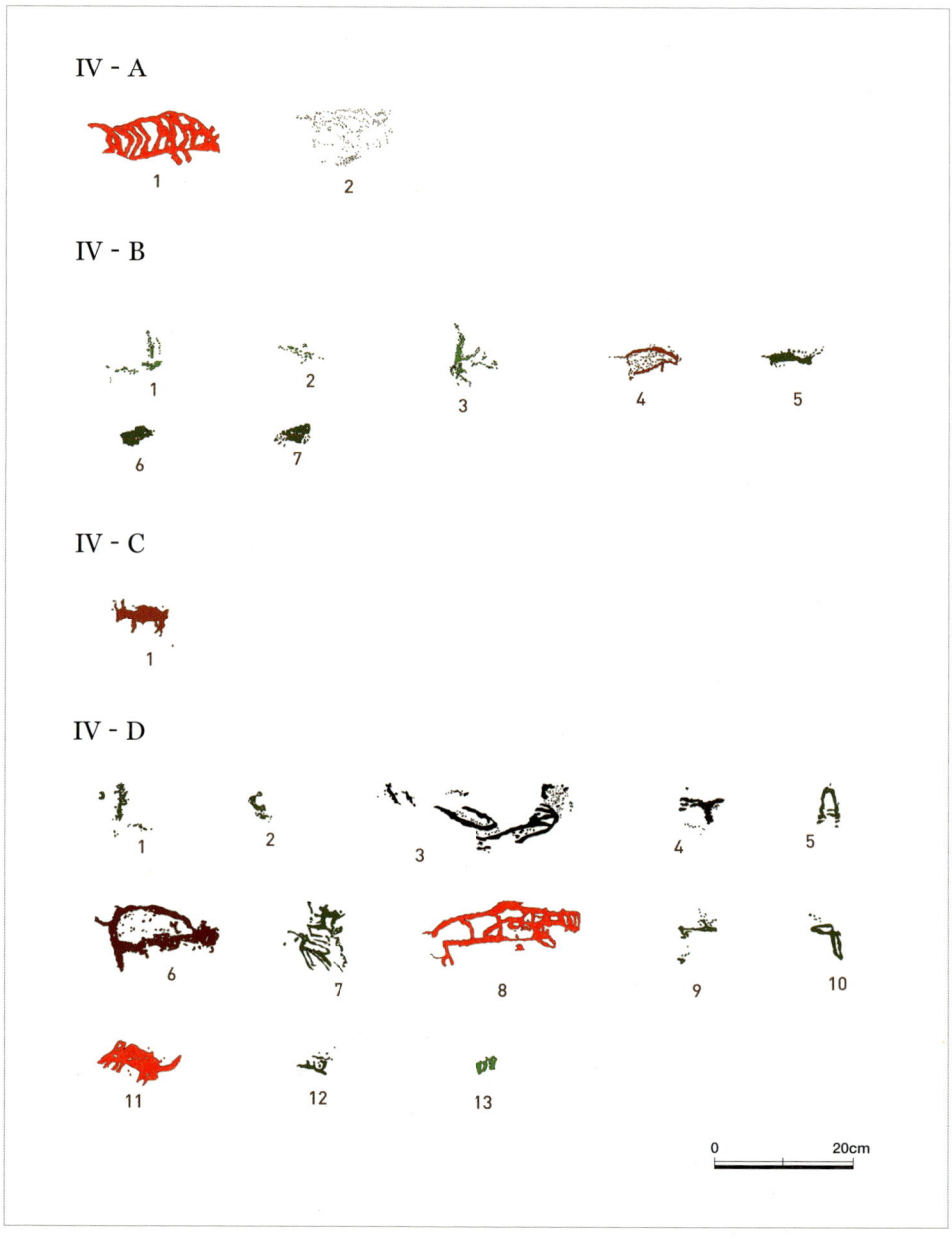

Fig. 23. Surface IV–A, individual figures (1–2); surface IV–B individual figures (1–7); surface IV–C individual figures (1); surface IV–D individual figures (1–13)

The Bangudae Petroglyphs in Ulsan

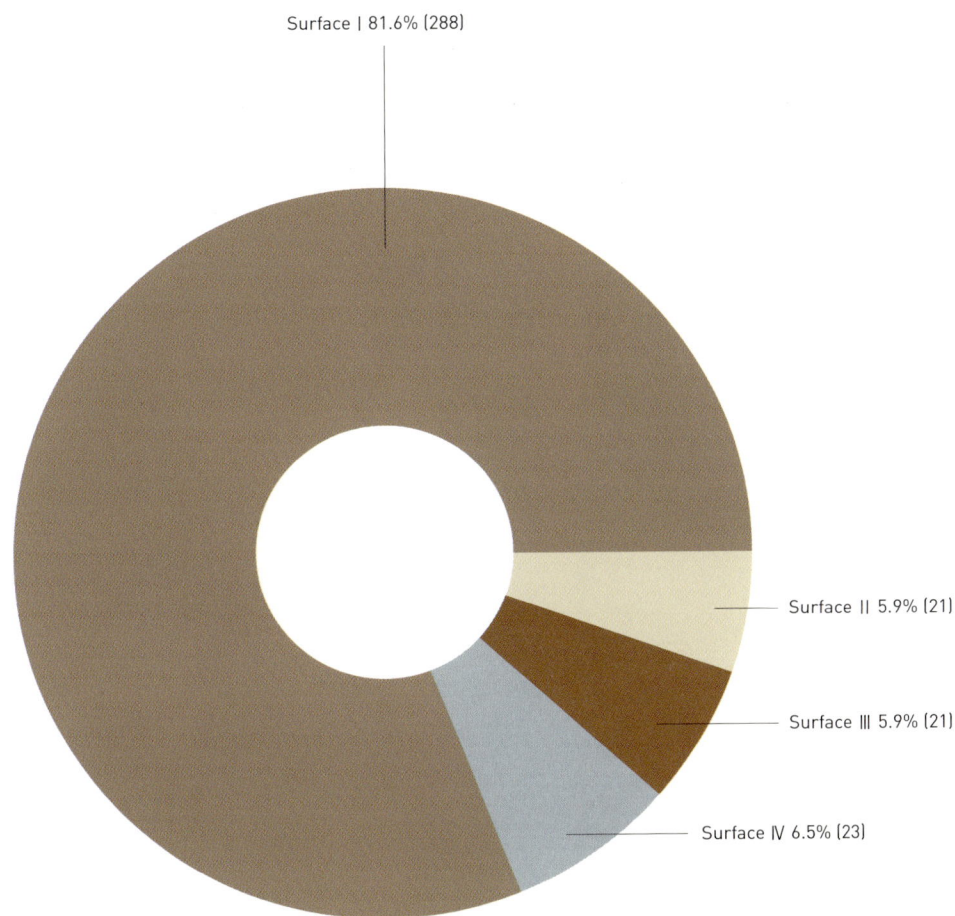

Surface I 81.6% (288)

Surface II 5.9% (21)

Surface III 5.9% (21)

Surface IV 6.5% (23)

Fig. 24. Distribution of surface I–IV

5. Classification of Images

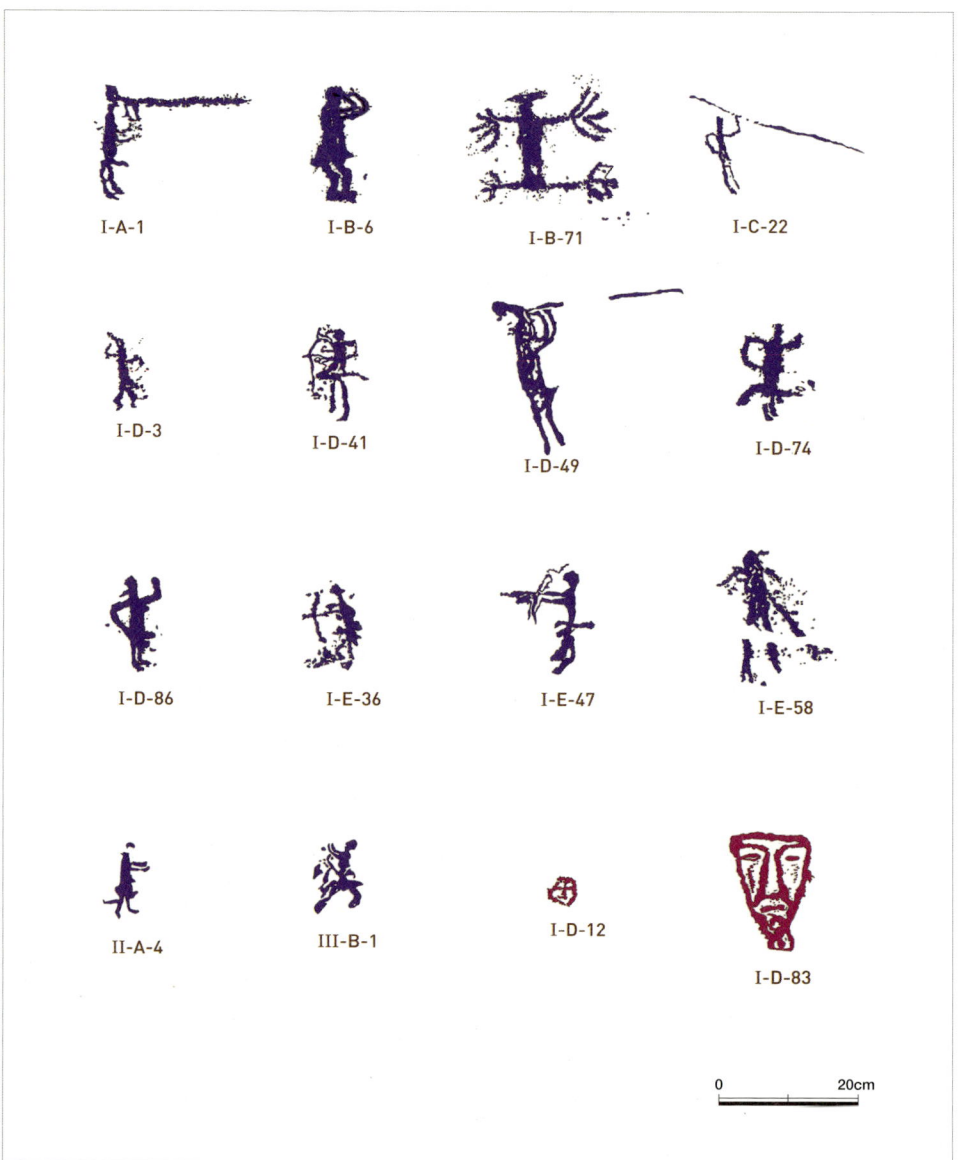

I-A-1

I-B-6

I-B-71

I-C-22

I-D-3

I-D-41

I-D-49

I-D-74

I-D-86

I-E-36

I-E-47

I-E-58

II-A-4

III-B-1

I-D-12

I-D-83

0   20cm

Fig. 25. Humans (anthromorphes)

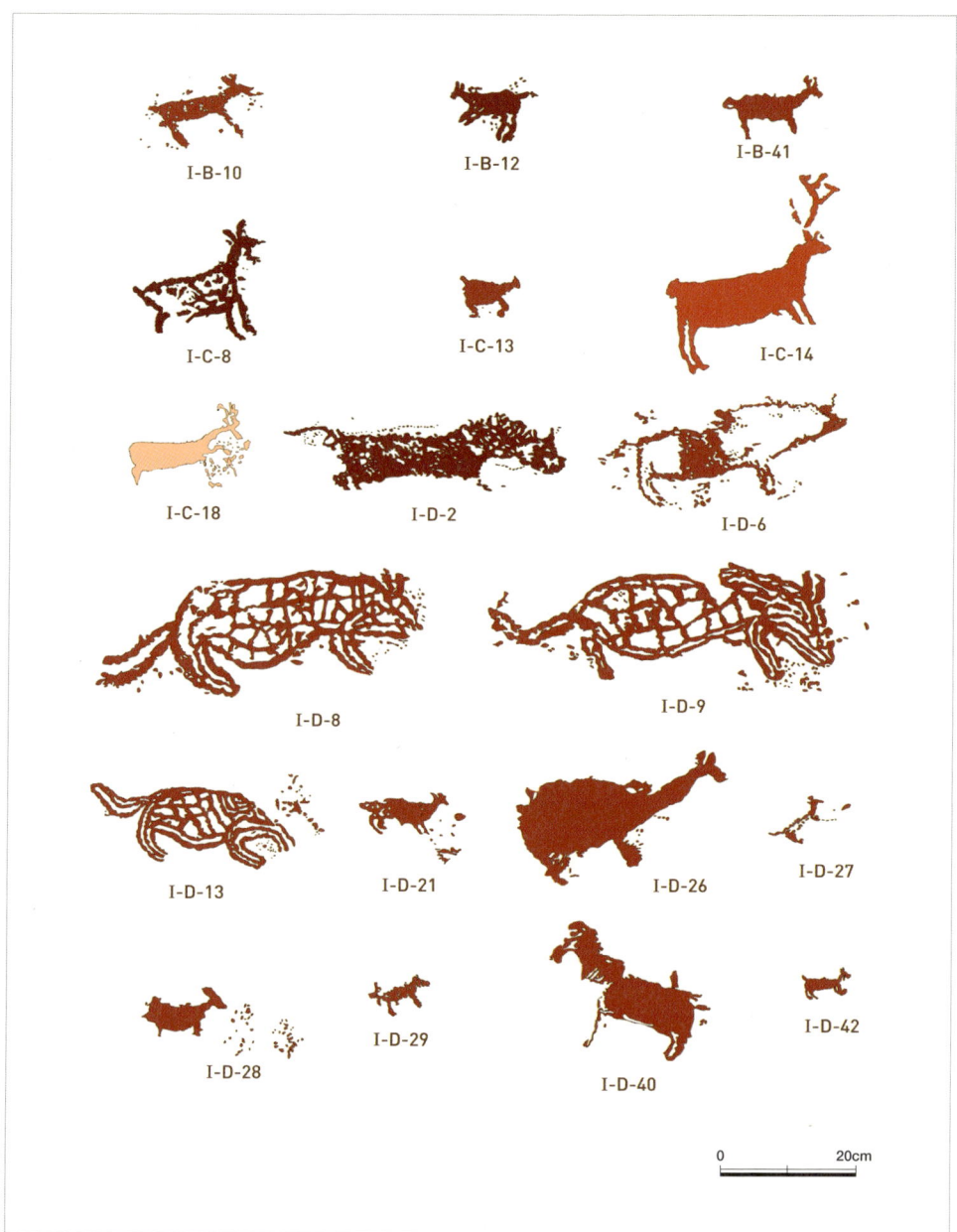

I-B-10

I-B-12

I-B-41

I-C-8

I-C-13

I-C-14

I-C-18

I-D-2

I-D-6

I-D-8

I-D-9

I-D-13

I-D-21

I-D-26

I-D-27

I-D-28

I-D-29

I-D-40

I-D-42

0   20cm

Fig. 26. Even–toed ungulates (artiodactyla) 1

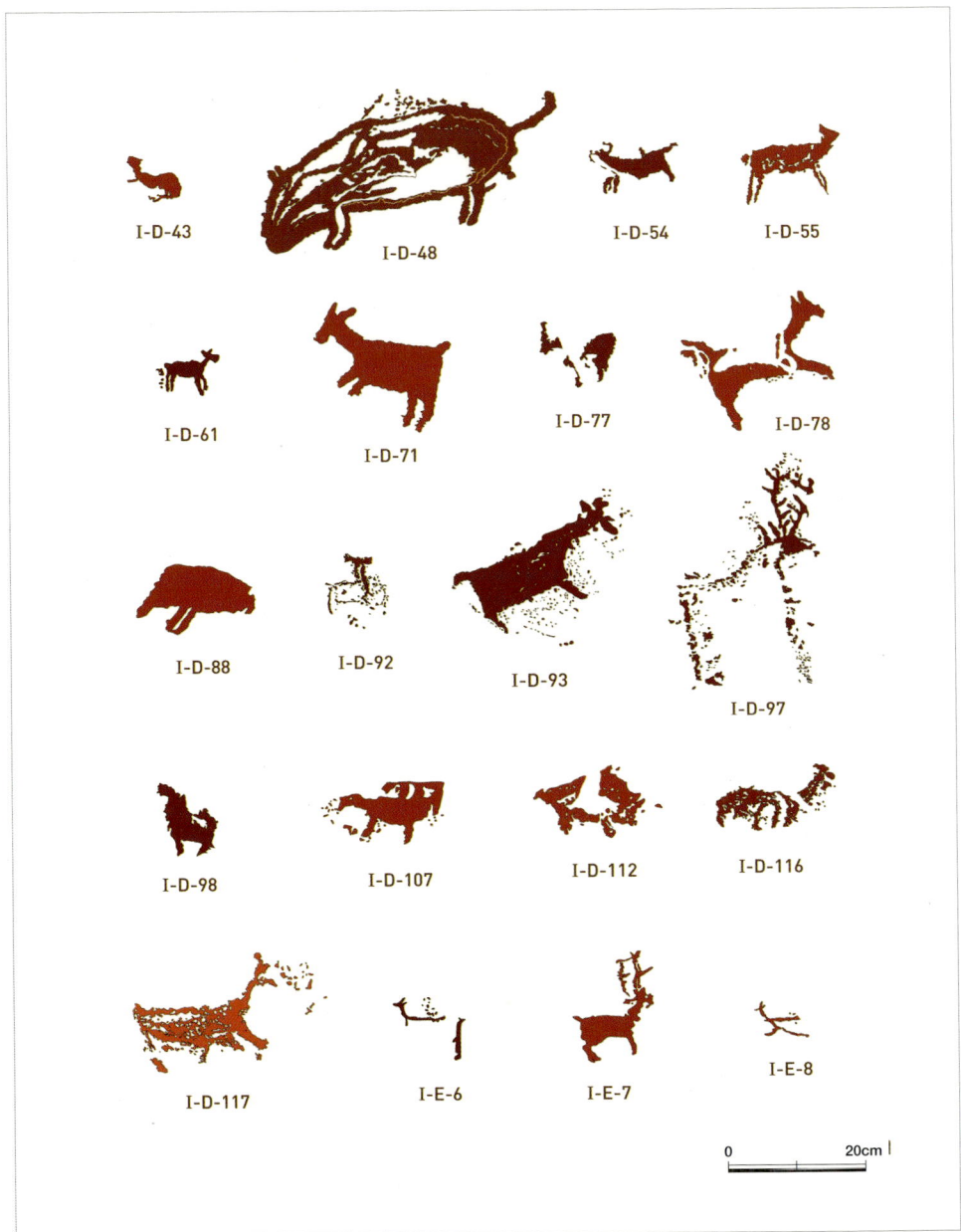

Fig. 27. Even–toed ungulates (artiodactyla) 2

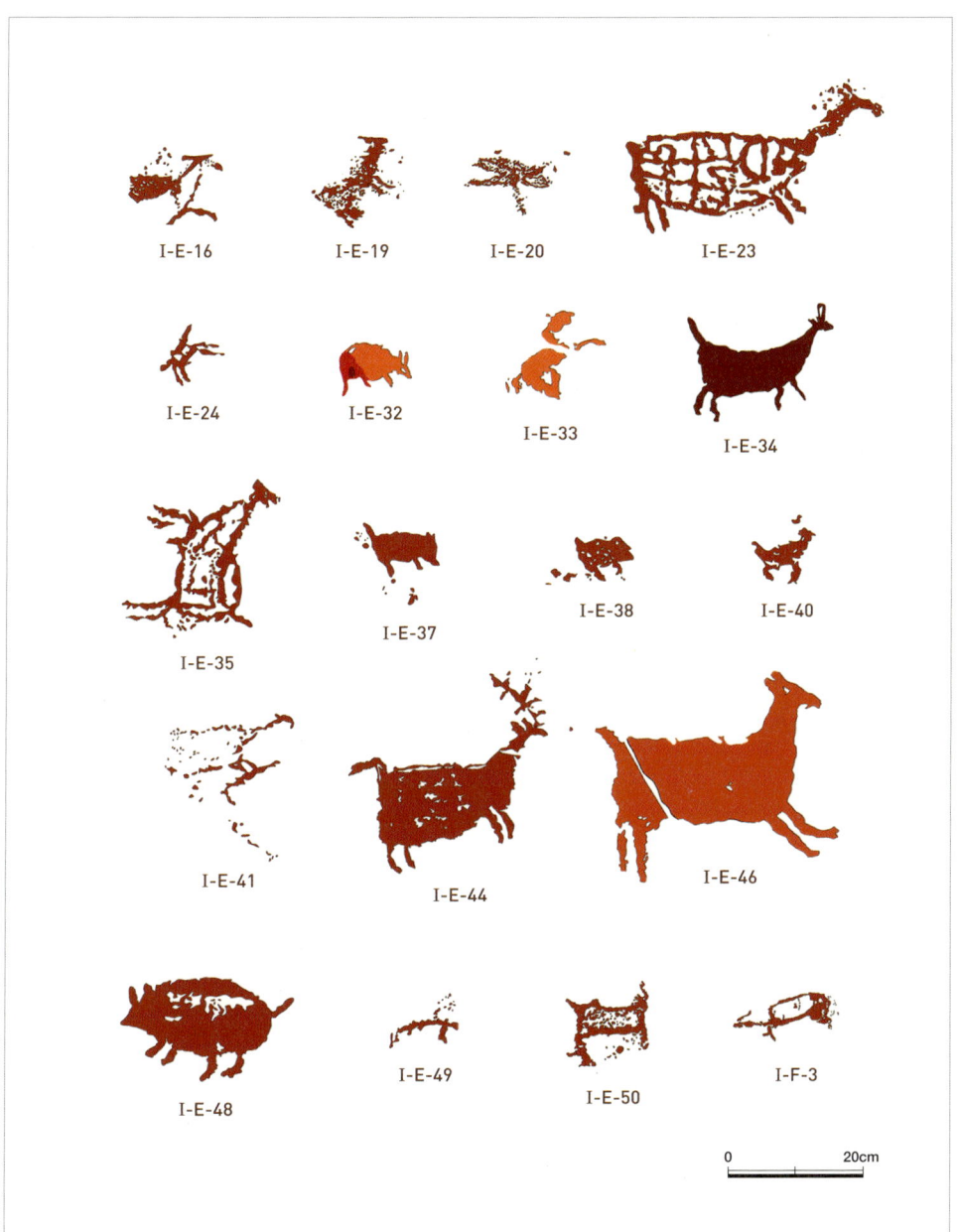

Fig. 28. Even–toed ungulates (artiodactyla) 3

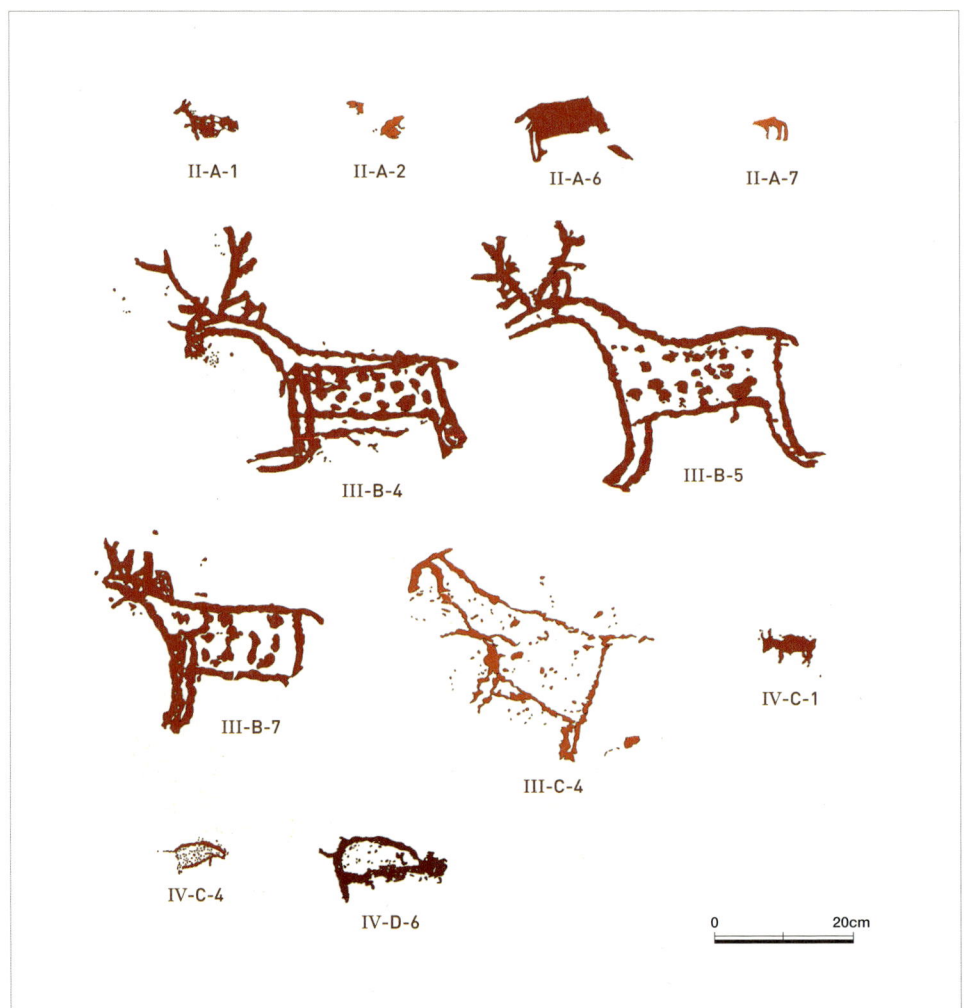

II-A-1 II-A-2 II-A-6 II-A-7

III-B-4 III-B-5

III-B-7 III-C-4 IV-C-1

IV-C-4 IV-D-6

0 20cm

Fig. 29. Even–toed ungulates (artiodactyla) 4

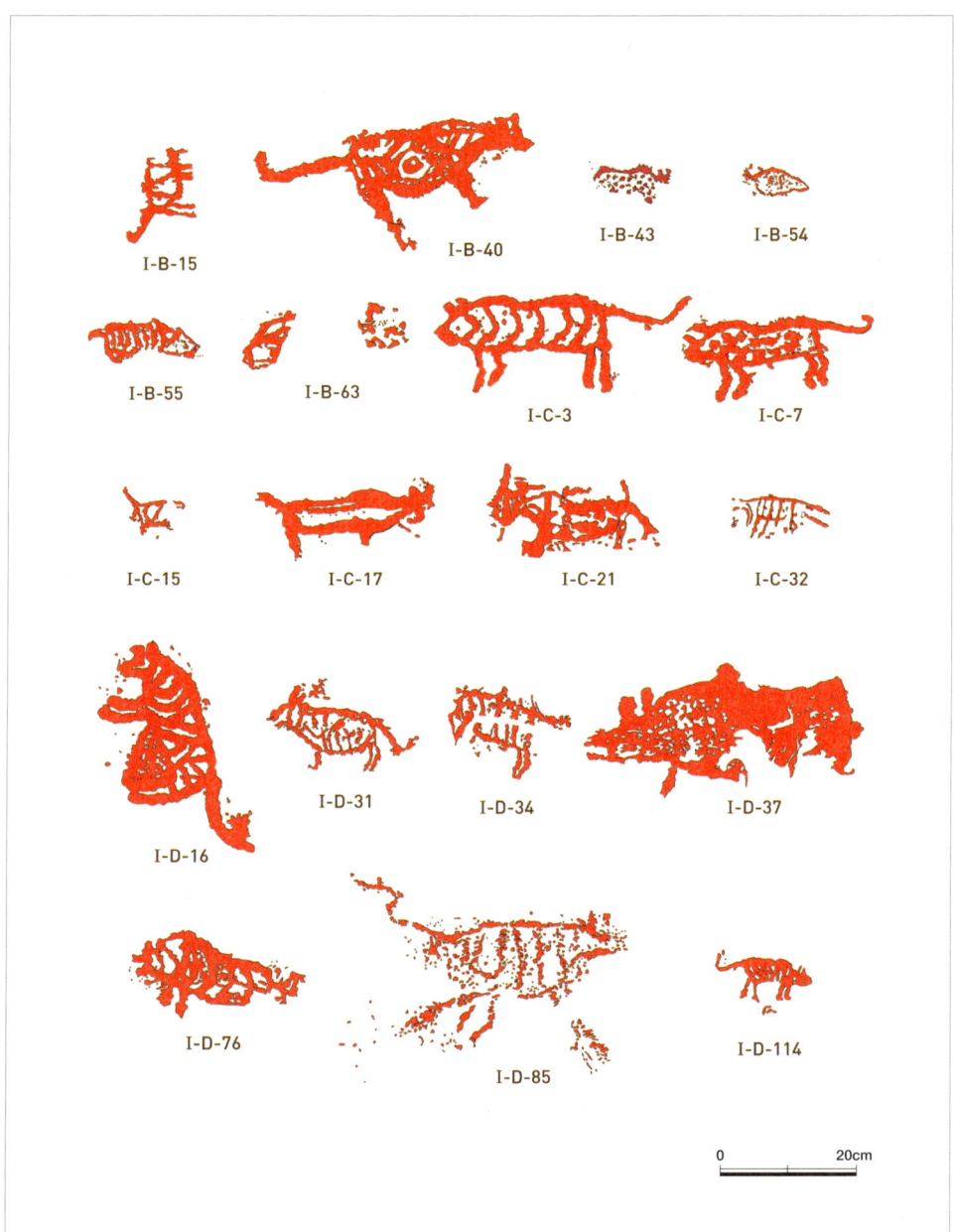

I-B-15

I-B-40

I-B-43

I-B-54

I-B-55

I-B-63

I-C-3

I-C-7

I-C-15

I-C-17

I-C-21

I-C-32

I-D-16

I-D-31

I-D-34

I-D-37

I-D-76

I-D-85

I-D-114

0   20cm

Fig. 30. Carnivora–terrestial (carnivora–earth) 1

Categories of Motifs in Bangudae Petroglyphs

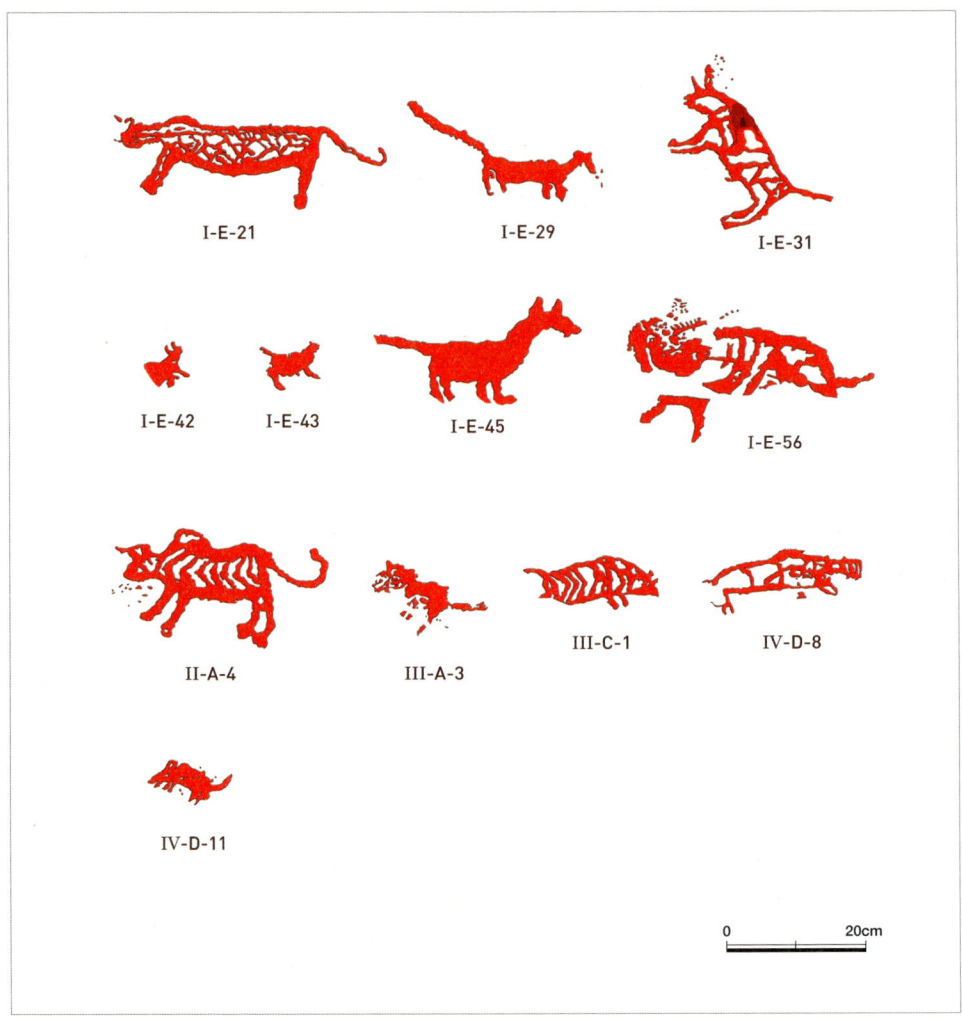

Fig. 31. Carnivora–terrestial (carnivora–earth) 2

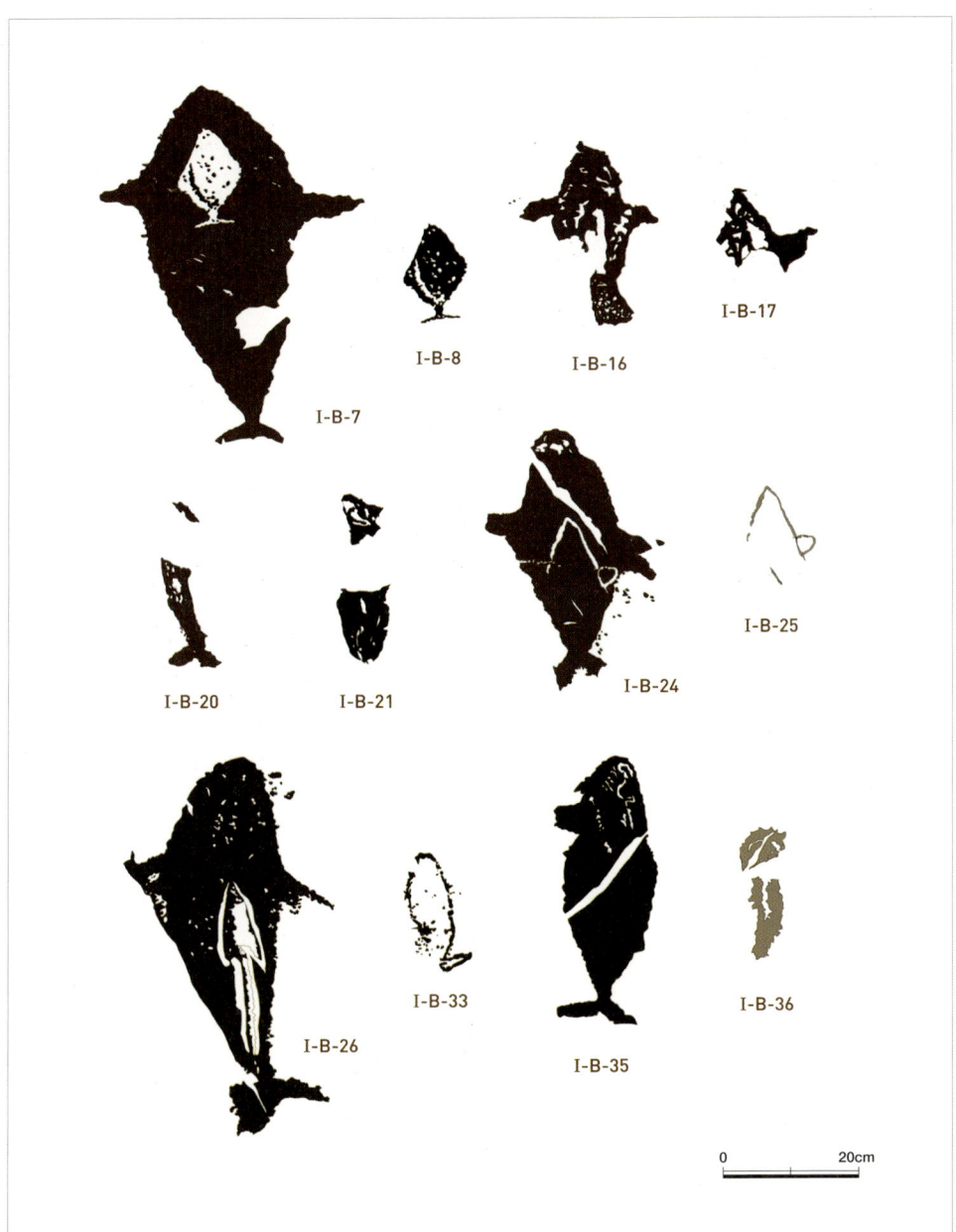

I-B-7

I-B-8

I-B-16

I-B-17

I-B-20

I-B-21

I-B-24

I-B-25

I-B-26

I-B-33

I-B-35

I-B-36

0   20cm

Fig. 32. Cetaceans (cetacea) 1

Categories of Motifs in Bangudae Petroglyphs

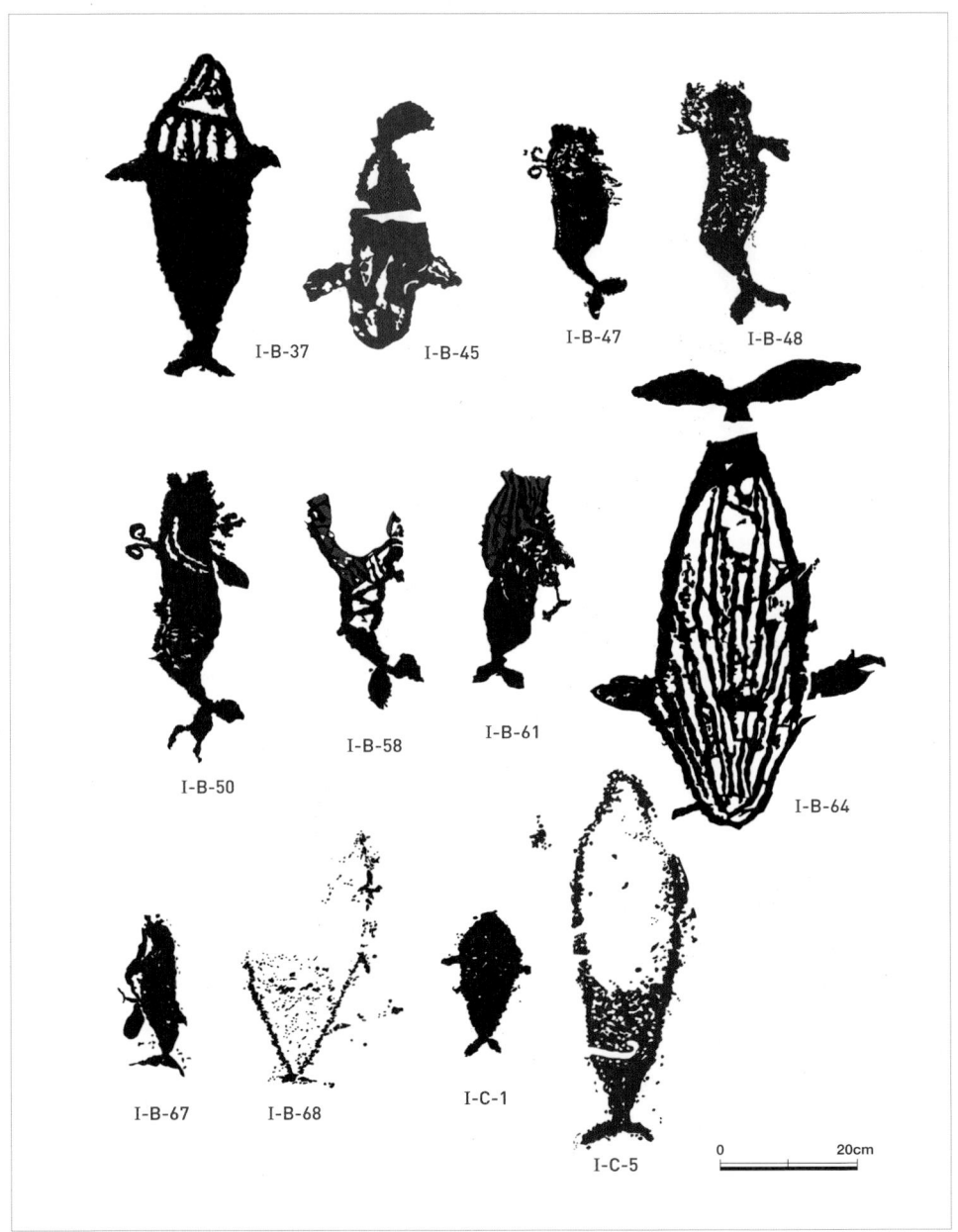

Fig. 33. Cetaceans (cetacea) 2

The Bangudae Petroglyphs in Ulsan

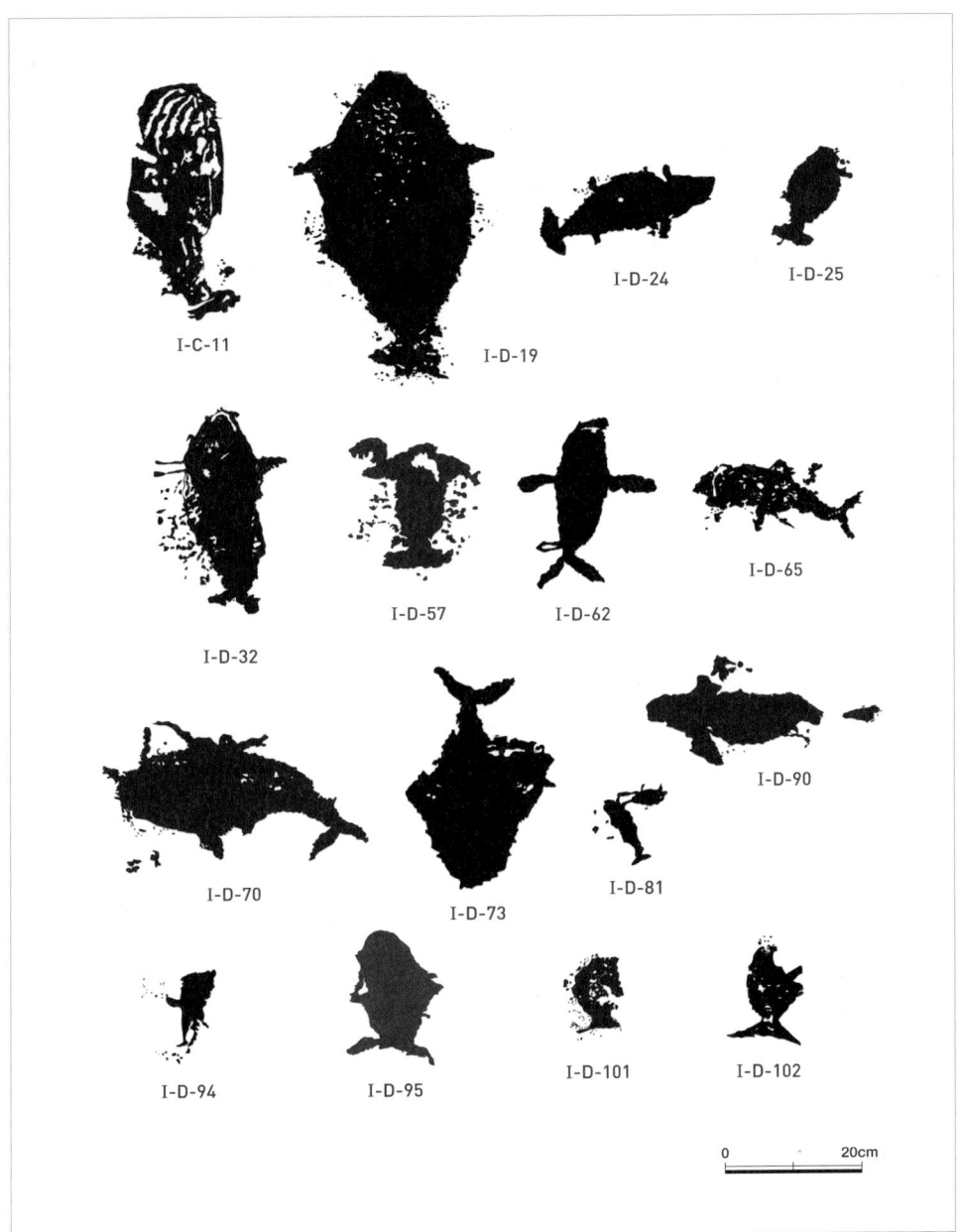

I-C-11

I-D-19

I-D-24

I-D-25

I-D-32

I-D-57

I-D-62

I-D-65

I-D-70

I-D-73

I-D-81

I-D-90

I-D-94

I-D-95

I-D-101

I-D-102

0　　　　　　20cm

Fig. 34. Cetaceans (cetacea) 3

Categories of Motifs in Bangudae Petroglyphs

81

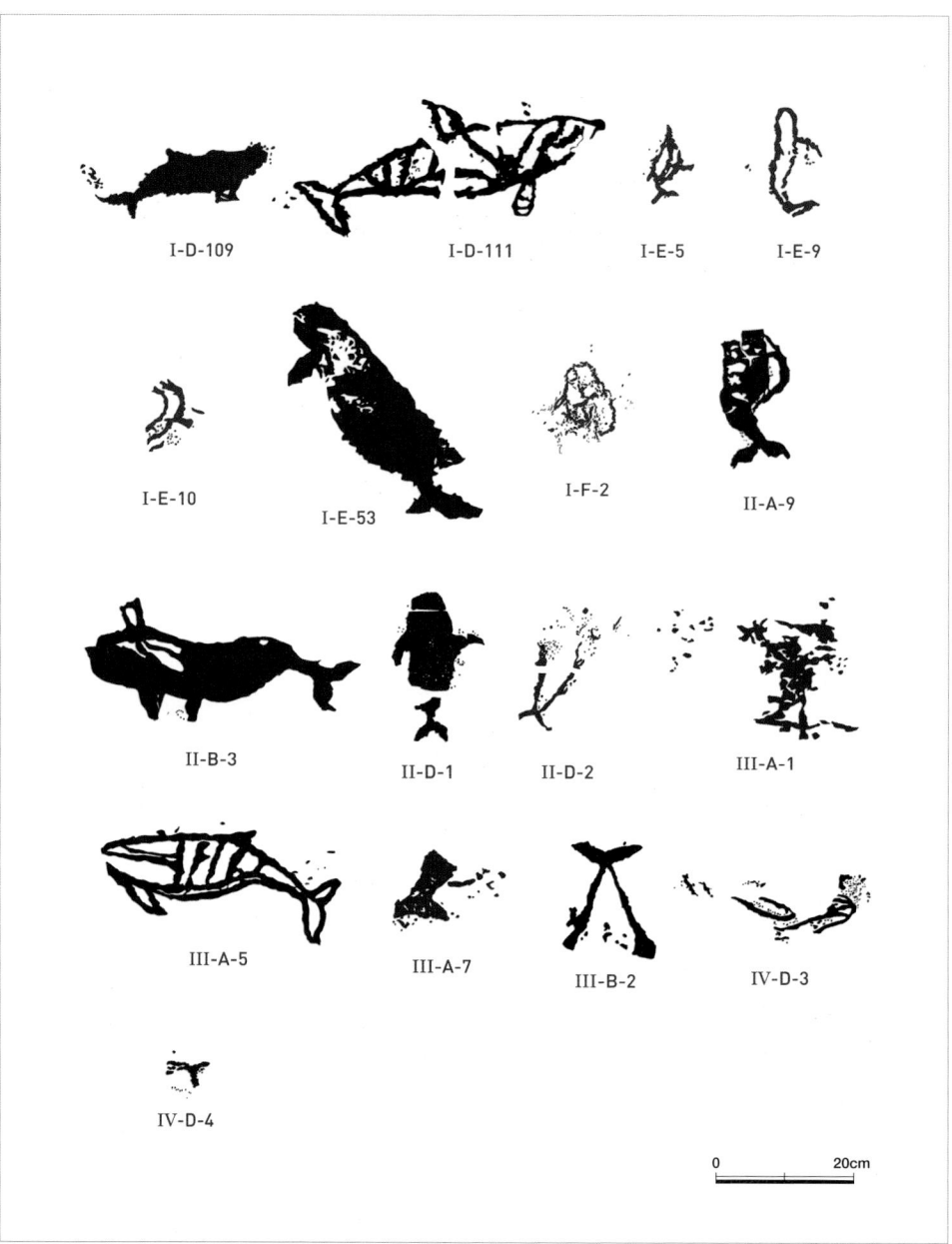

Fig. 35. Cetaceans (cetacea) 4

The Bangudae Petroglyphs in Ulsan

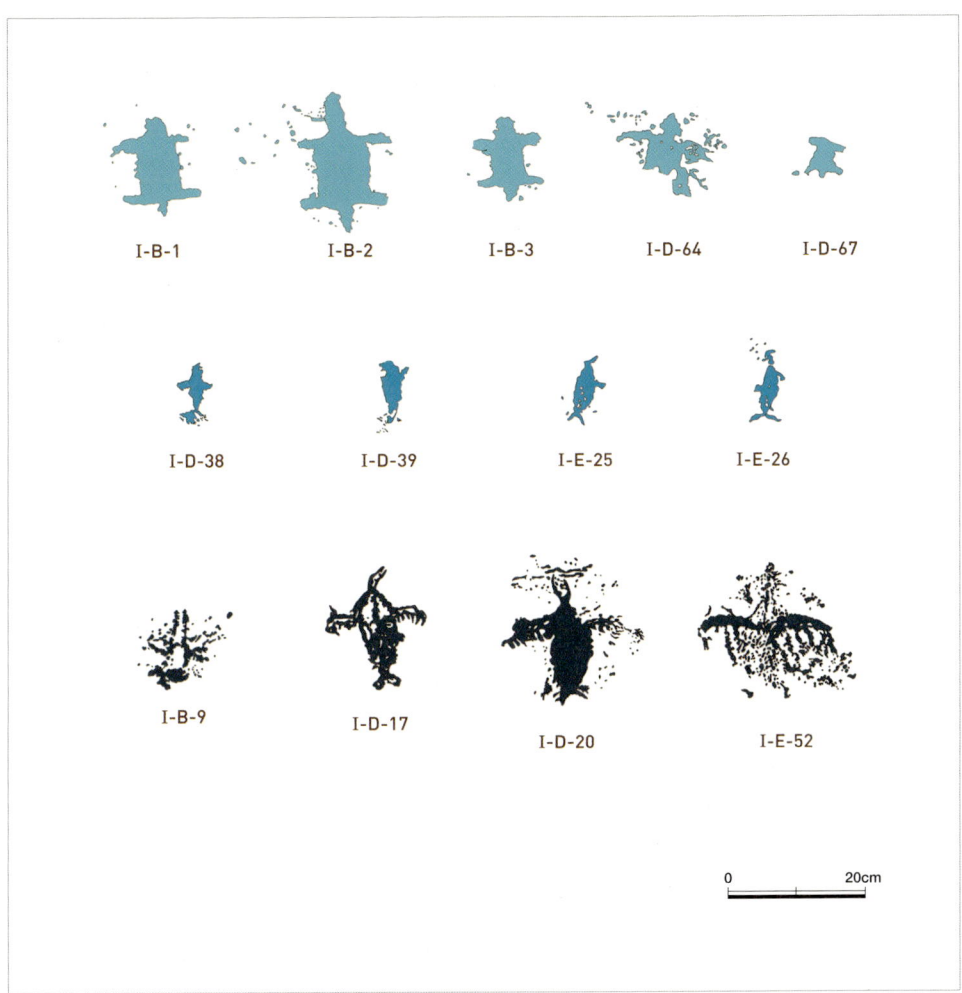

I-B-1 I-B-2 I-B-3 I-D-64 I-D-67

I-D-38 I-D-39 I-E-25 I-E-26

I-B-9 I-D-17 I-D-20 I-E-52

0   20cm

Fig. 36. Testudines (chelonia), carnivora–marine (pinnipedia), birds (aves)

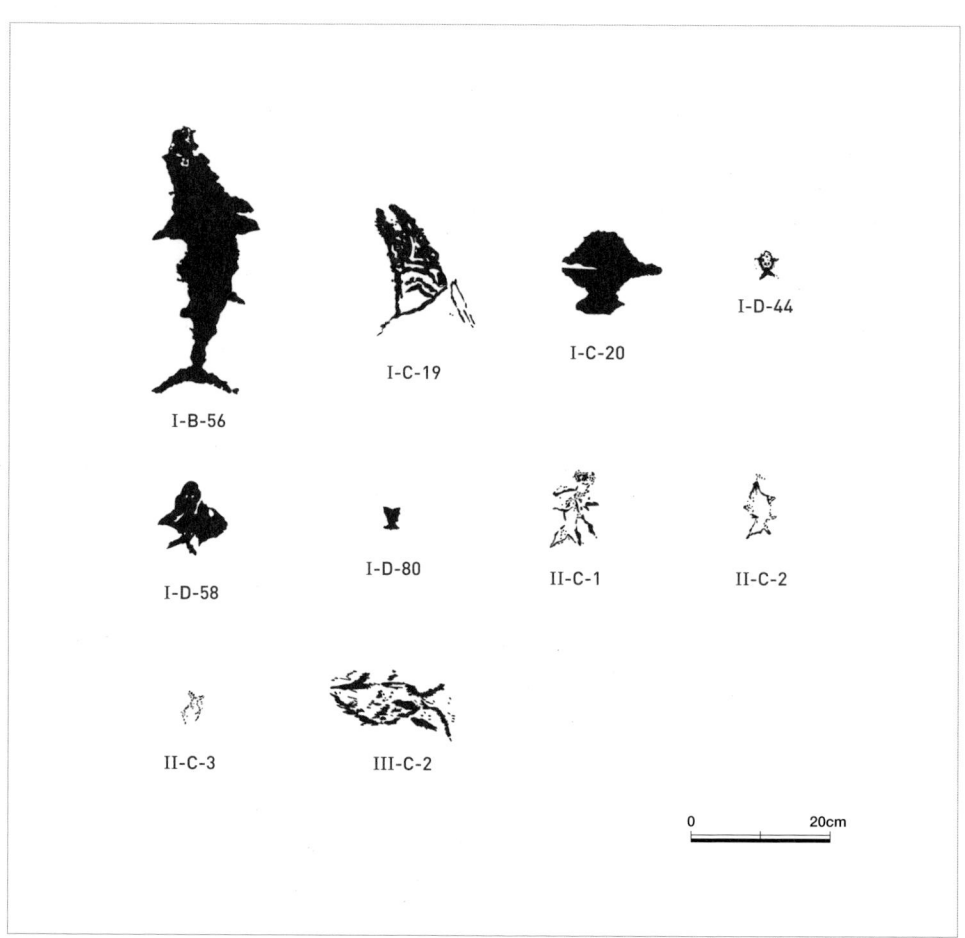

I-B-56

I-C-19

I-C-20

I-D-44

I-D-58

I-D-80

II-C-1

II-C-2

II-C-3

III-C-2

0   20cm

Fig. 37. Fish (piscis)

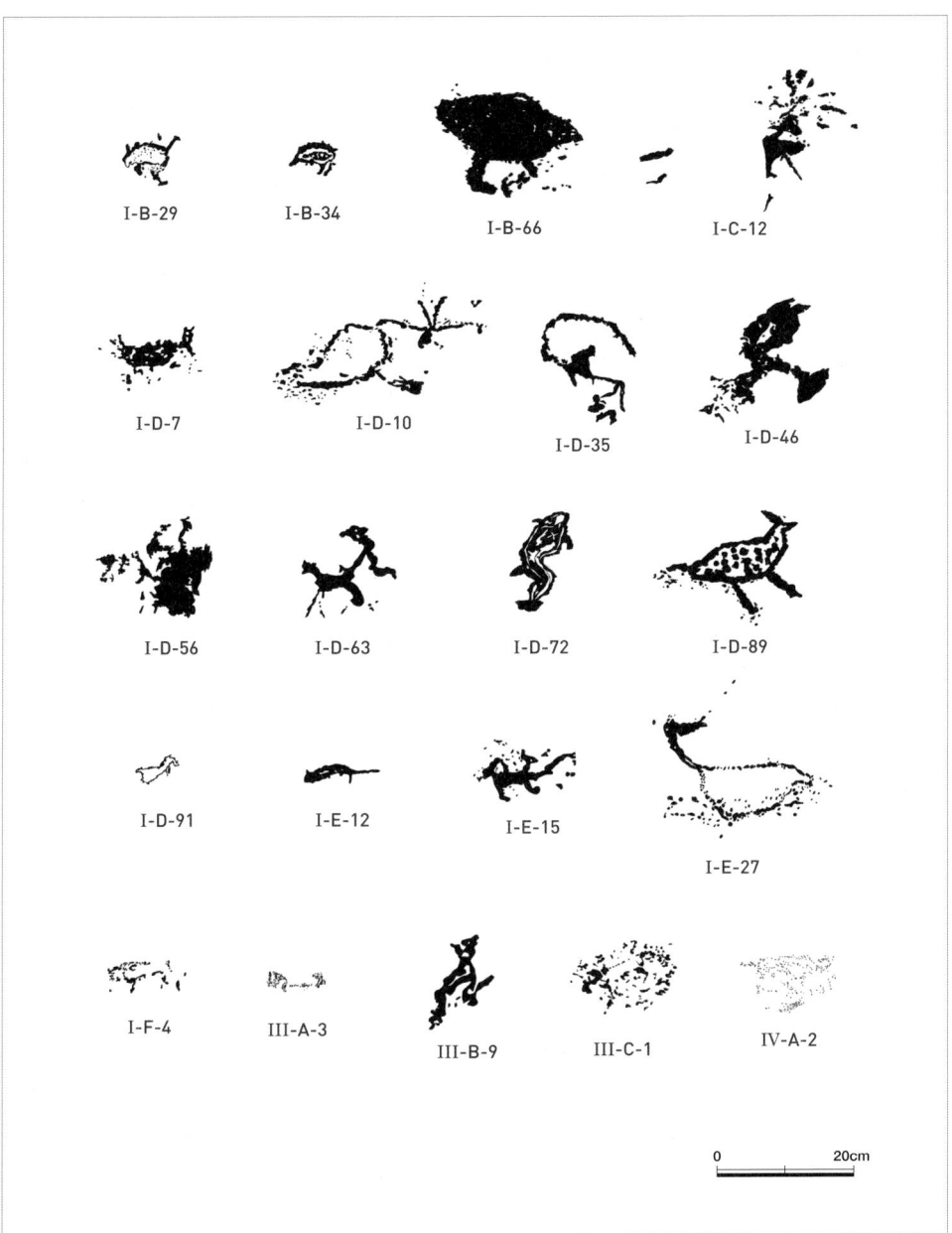

I-B-29

I-B-34

I-B-66

I-C-12

I-D-7

I-D-10

I-D-35

I-D-46

I-D-56

I-D-63

I-D-72

I-D-89

I-D-91

I-E-12

I-E-15

I-E-27

I-F-4

III-A-3

III-B-9

III-C-1

IV-A-2

0   20cm

Fig. 38. Unidentified species (unidentified)

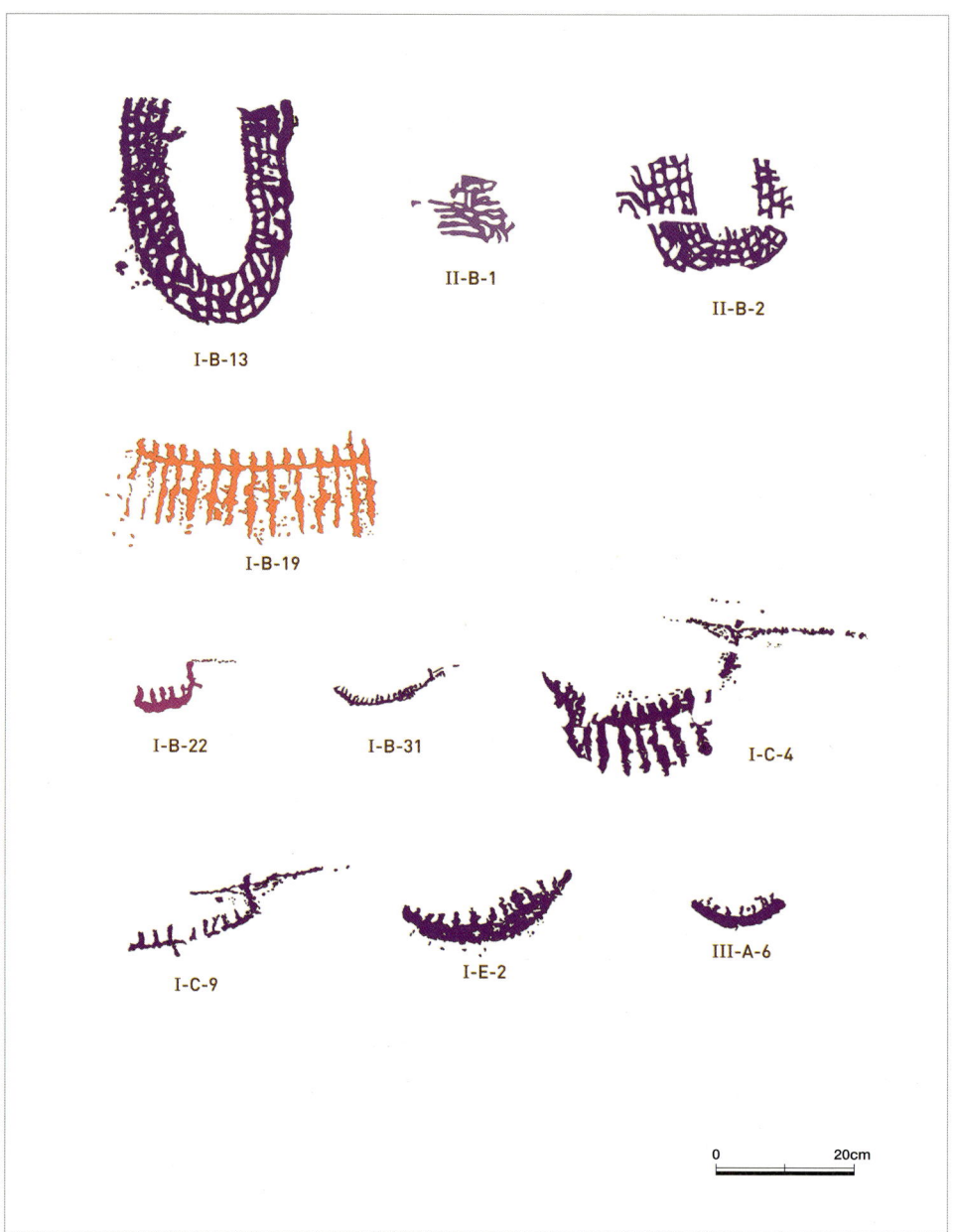

I-B-13

II-B-1

II-B-2

I-B-19

I-B-22

I-B-31

I-C-4

I-C-9

I-E-2

III-A-6

0   20cm

Fig. 39. Tools (tool figures)—nets (net), weir (fish trap), ships (boat)

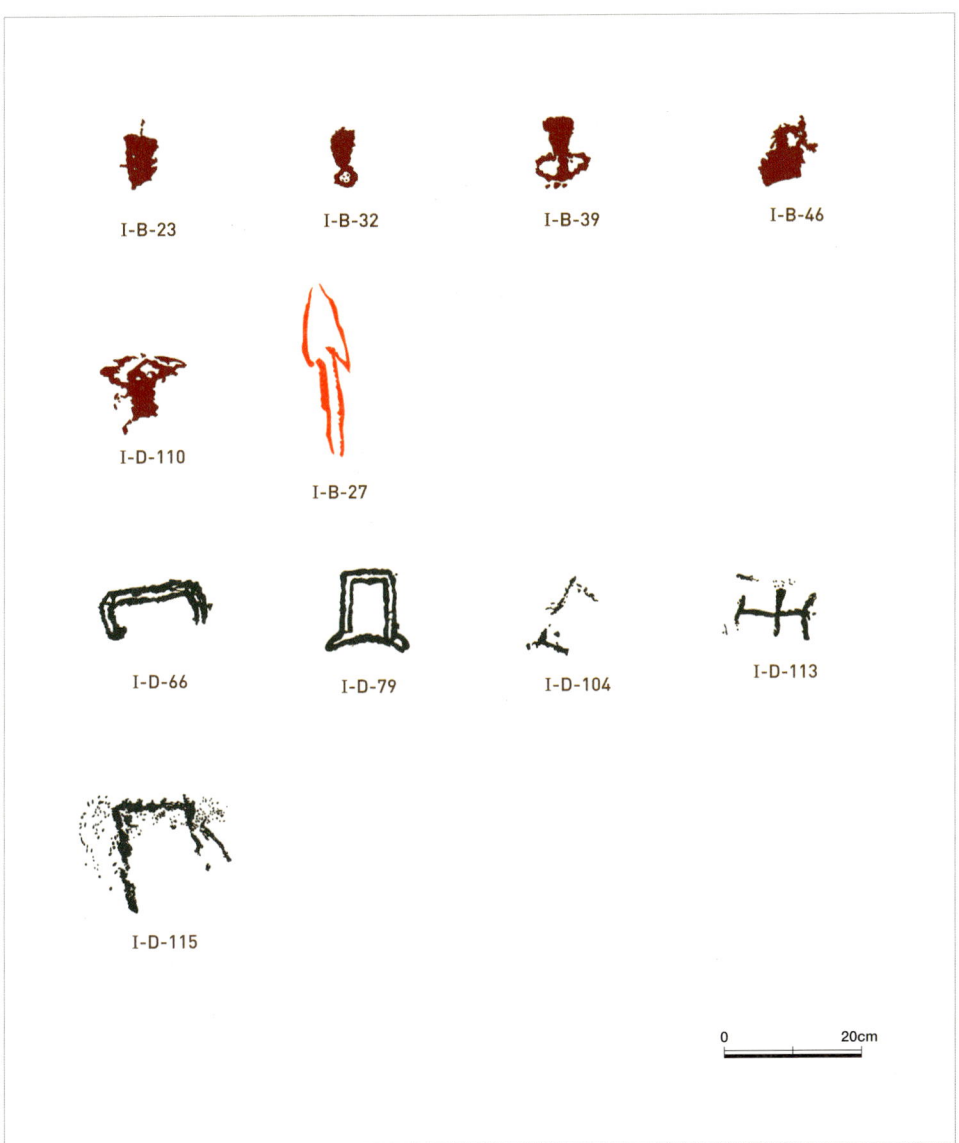

I-B-23

I-B-32

I-B-39

I-B-46

I-D-110

I-B-27

I-D-66

I-D-79

I-D-104

I-D-113

I-D-115

0   20cm

Fig. 40. Tools (tool figures)—floats (float), harpoons (fish spear), unidentified species (unidentified)

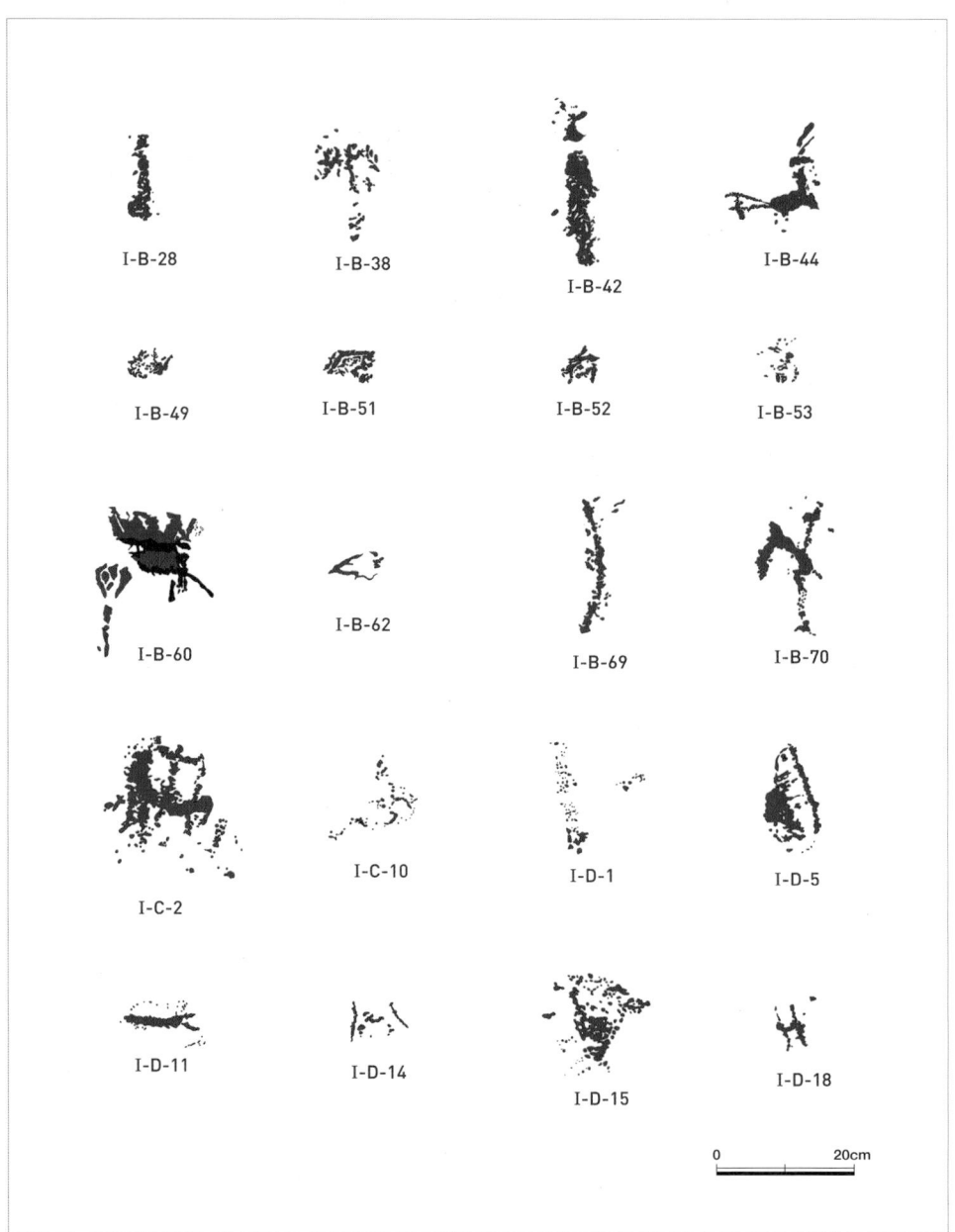

I-B-28

I-B-38

I-B-42

I-B-44

I-B-49

I-B-51

I-B-52

I-B-53

I-B-60

I-B-62

I-B-69

I-B-70

I-C-2

I-C-10

I-D-1

I-D-5

I-D-11

I-D-14

I-D-15

I-D-18

0   20cm

Fig. 41. Unidentified shapes (unidentified forms) 1 (73)

The Bangudae Petroglyphs in Ulsan

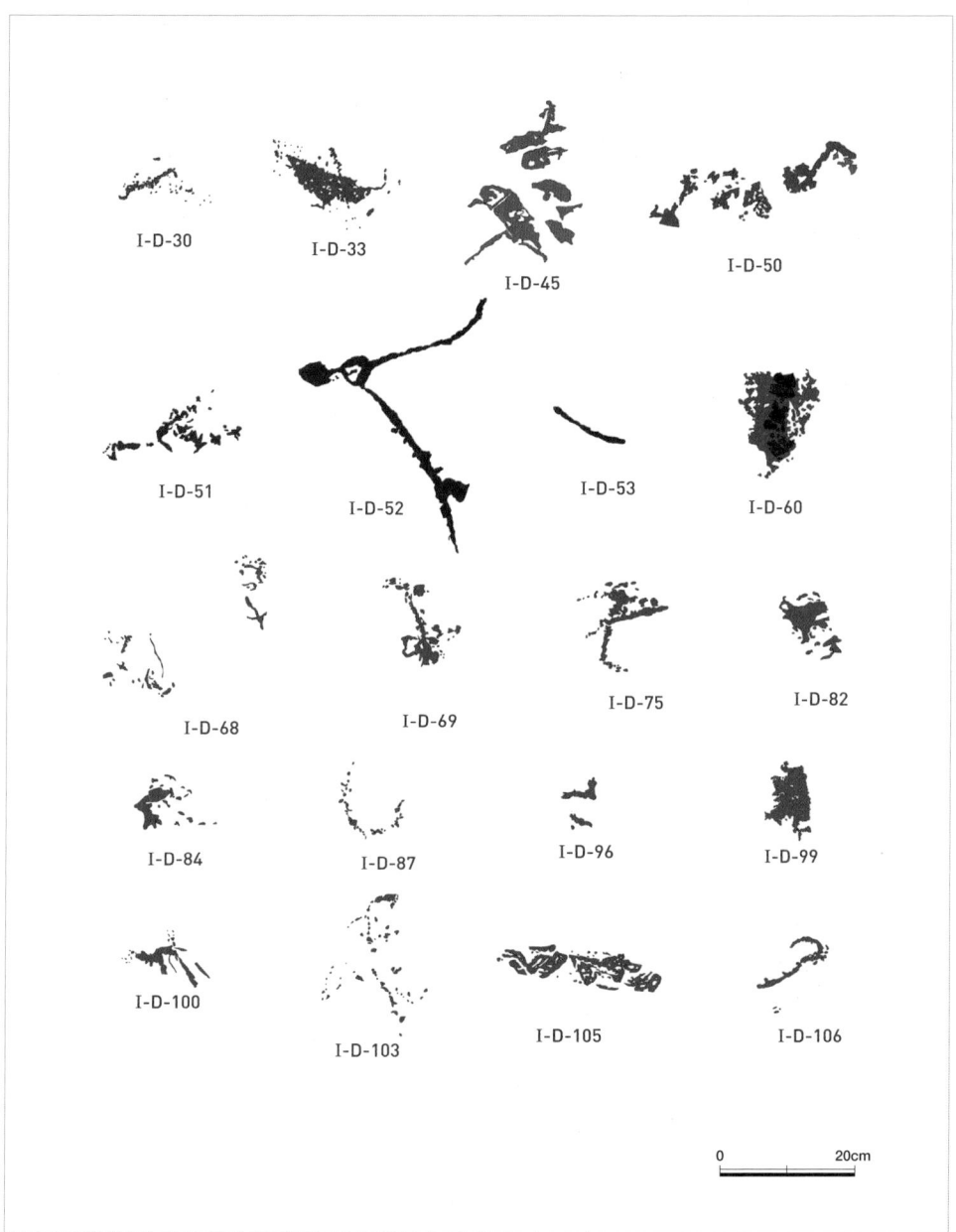

Fig. 42. Unidentified shapes (unidentified forms) 2 (73)

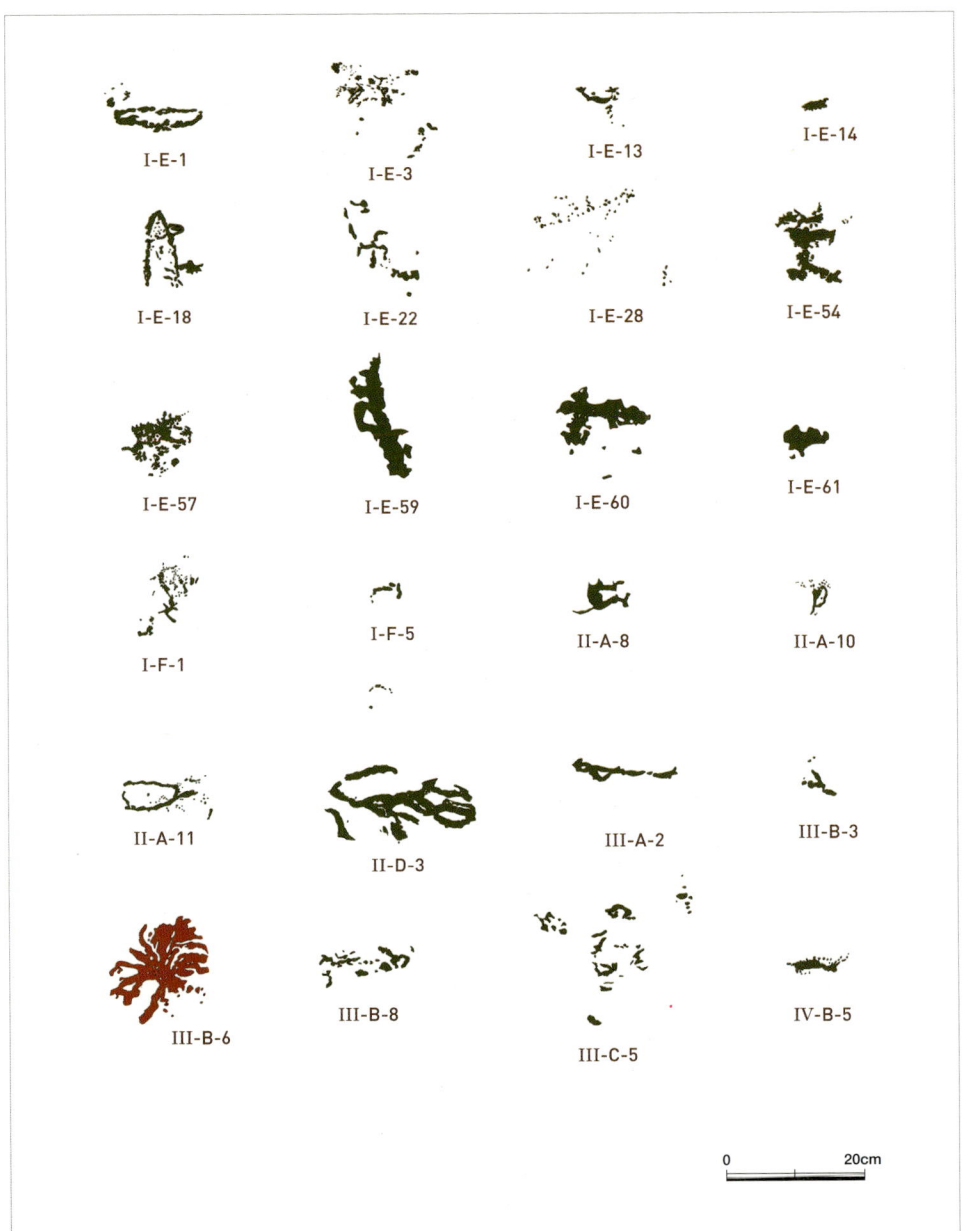

I-E-1

I-E-3

I-E-13

I-E-14

I-E-18

I-E-22

I-E-28

I-E-54

I-E-57

I-E-59

I-E-60

I-E-61

I-F-1

I-F-5

II-A-8

II-A-10

II-A-11

II-D-3

III-A-2

III-B-3

III-B-6

III-B-8

III-C-5

IV-B-5

0   20cm

Fig. 43. Unidentified shapes (unidentified forms) 3 (73)

The Bangudae Petroglyphs in Ulsan

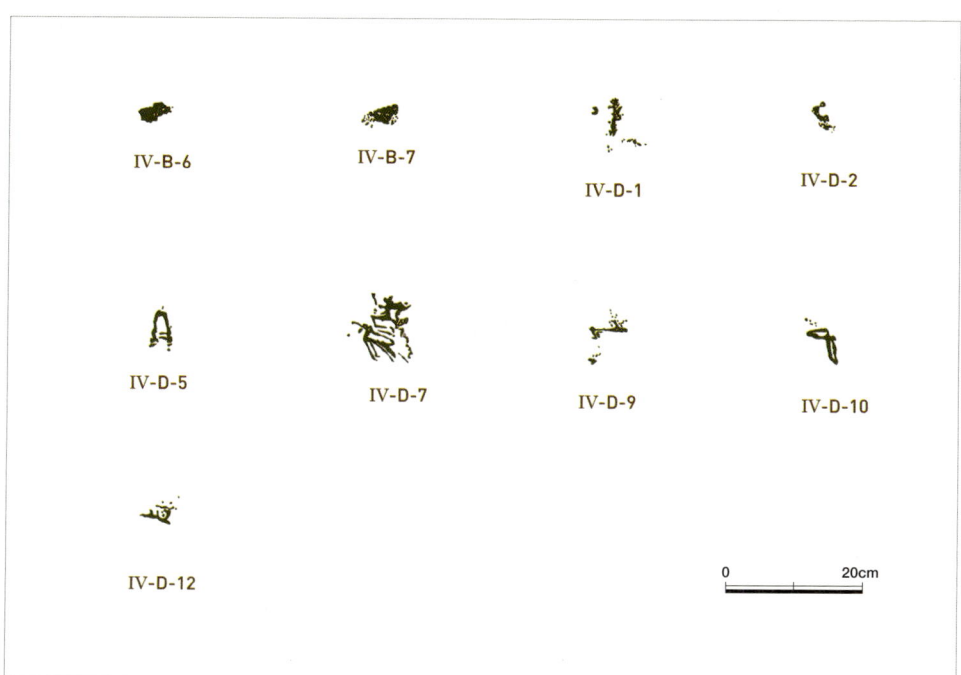

Fig. 44. Unidentified shapes (unidentified forms) 4 (73)

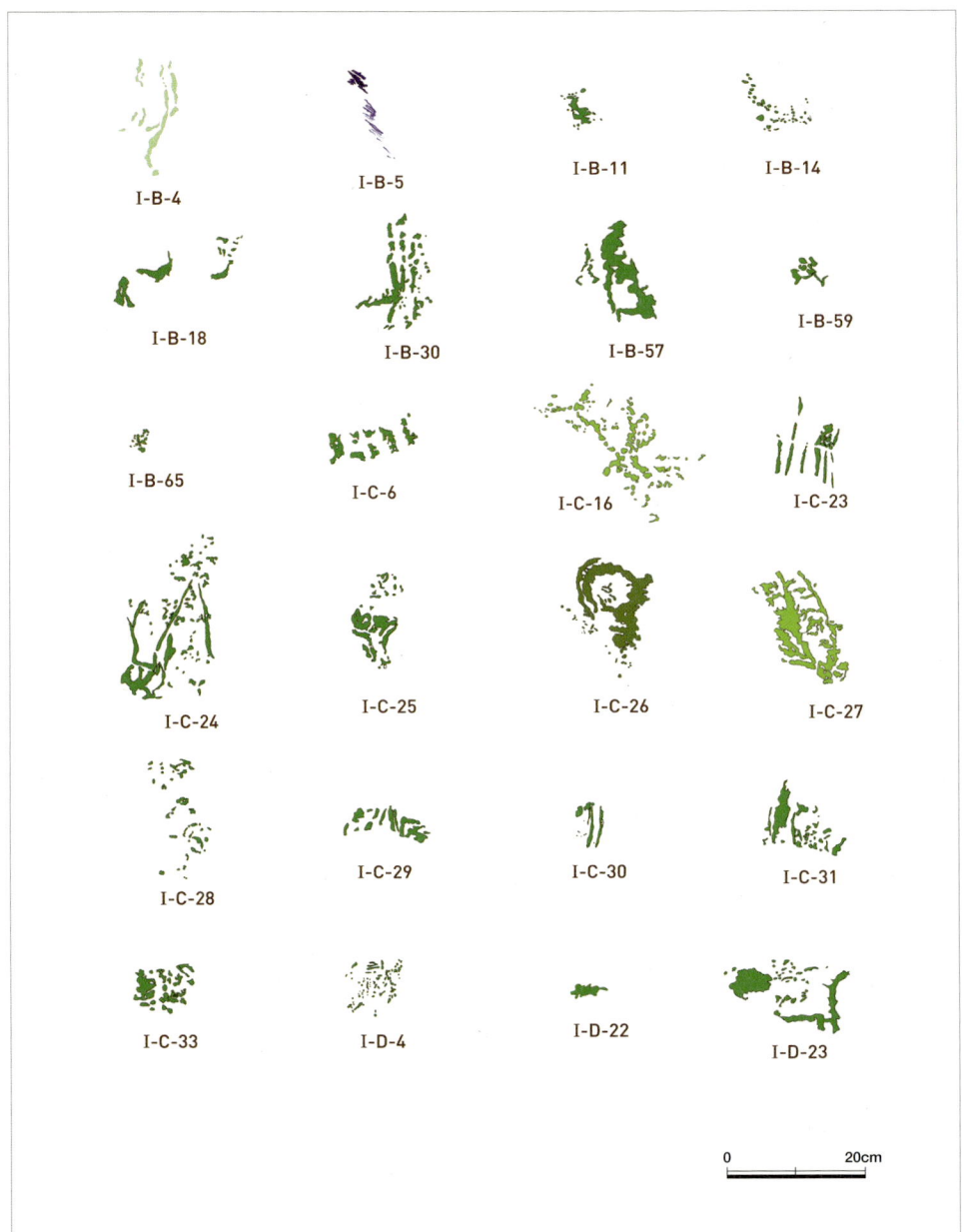

I-B-4

I-B-5

I-B-11

I-B-14

I-B-18

I-B-30

I-B-57

I-B-59

I-B-65

I-C-6

I-C-16

I-C-23

I-C-24

I-C-25

I-C-26

I-C-27

I-C-28

I-C-29

I-C-30

I-C-31

I-C-33

I-D-4

I-D-22

I-D-23

0   20cm

Fig. 45. Unidentifiable shapes (unrecognizable forms) 1 (41)

The Bangudae Petroglyphs in Ulsan

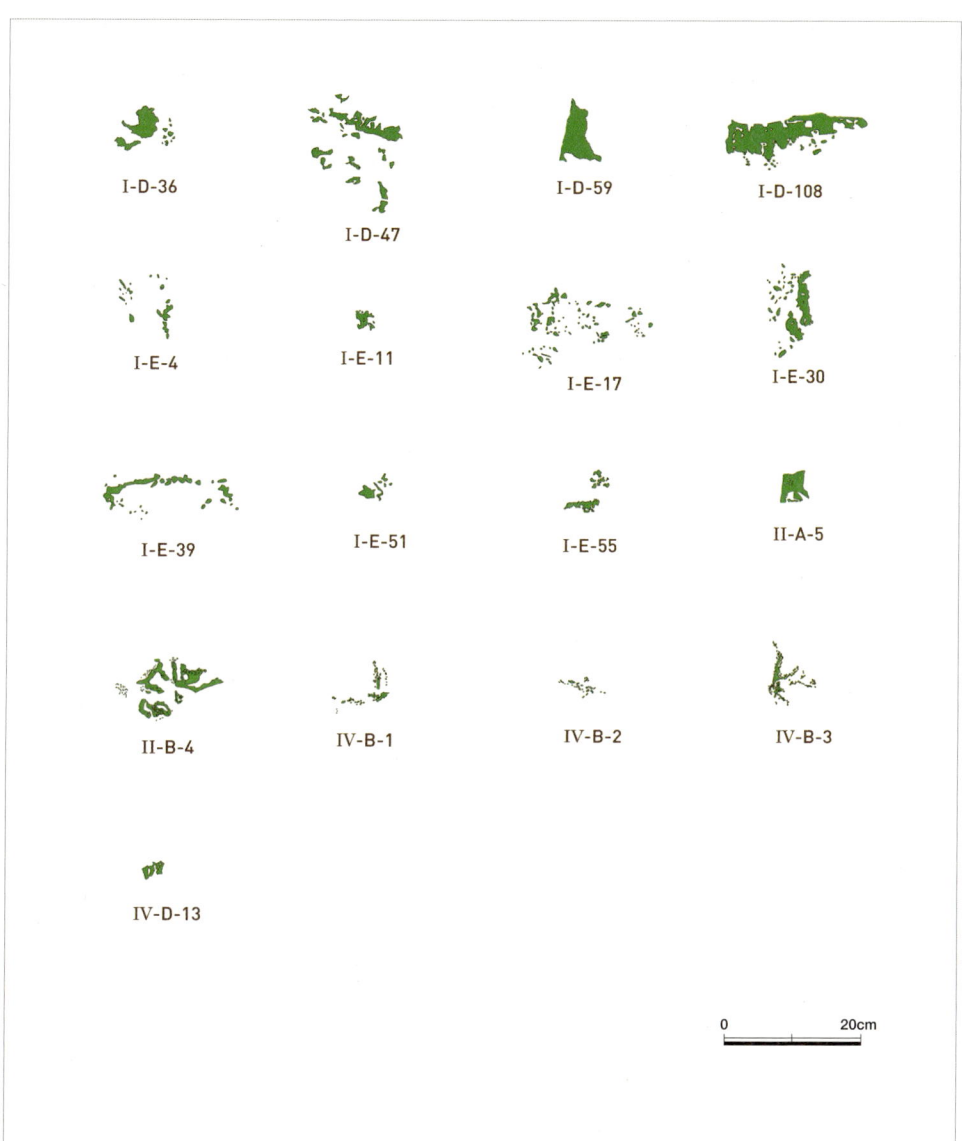

Fig. 46. Unidentifiable shapes (unrecognizable forms) 2 (41)

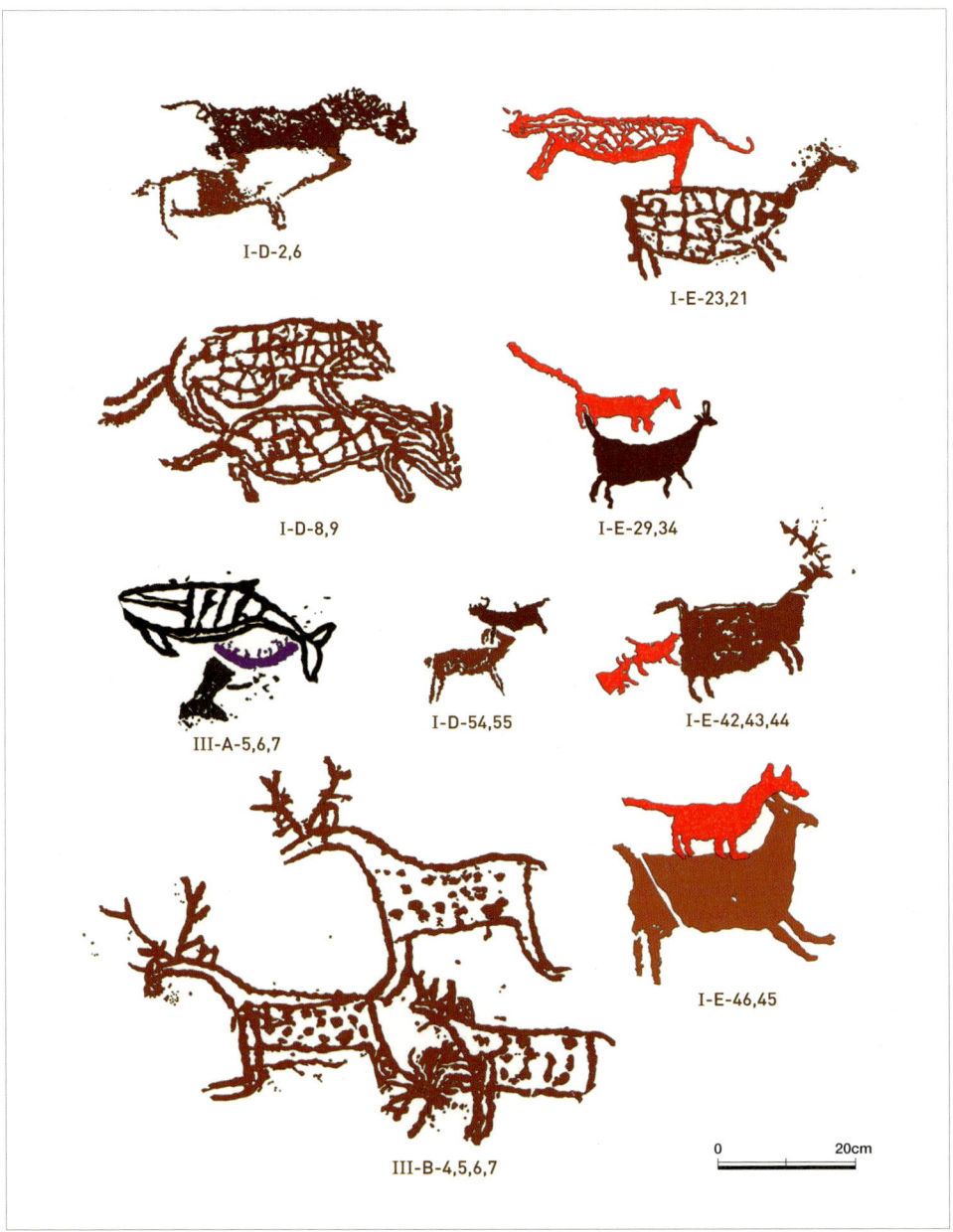

I-D-2,6

I-E-23,21

I-D-8,9

I-E-29,34

III-A-5,6,7

I-D-54,55

I-E-42,43,44

I-E-46,45

III-B-4,5,6,7

0   20cm

Fig. 47. Petroglyphs engraved at the same time

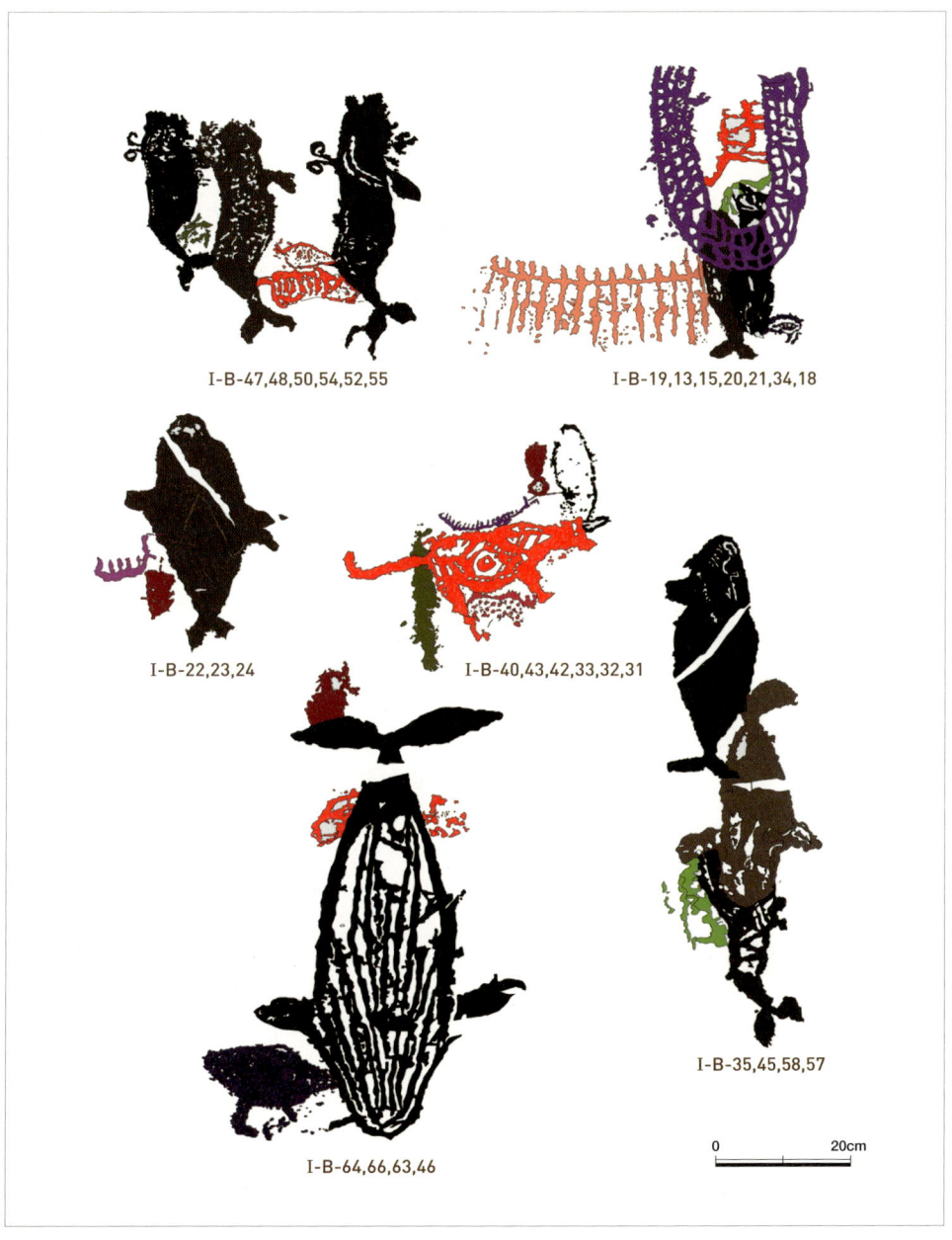

I-B-47,48,50,54,52,55

I-B-19,13,15,20,21,34,18

I-B-22,23,24

I-B-40,43,42,33,32,31

I-B-35,45,58,57

I-B-64,66,63,46

0   20cm

Fig. 48. Petroglyphs overlapped multiple times sequentially 1

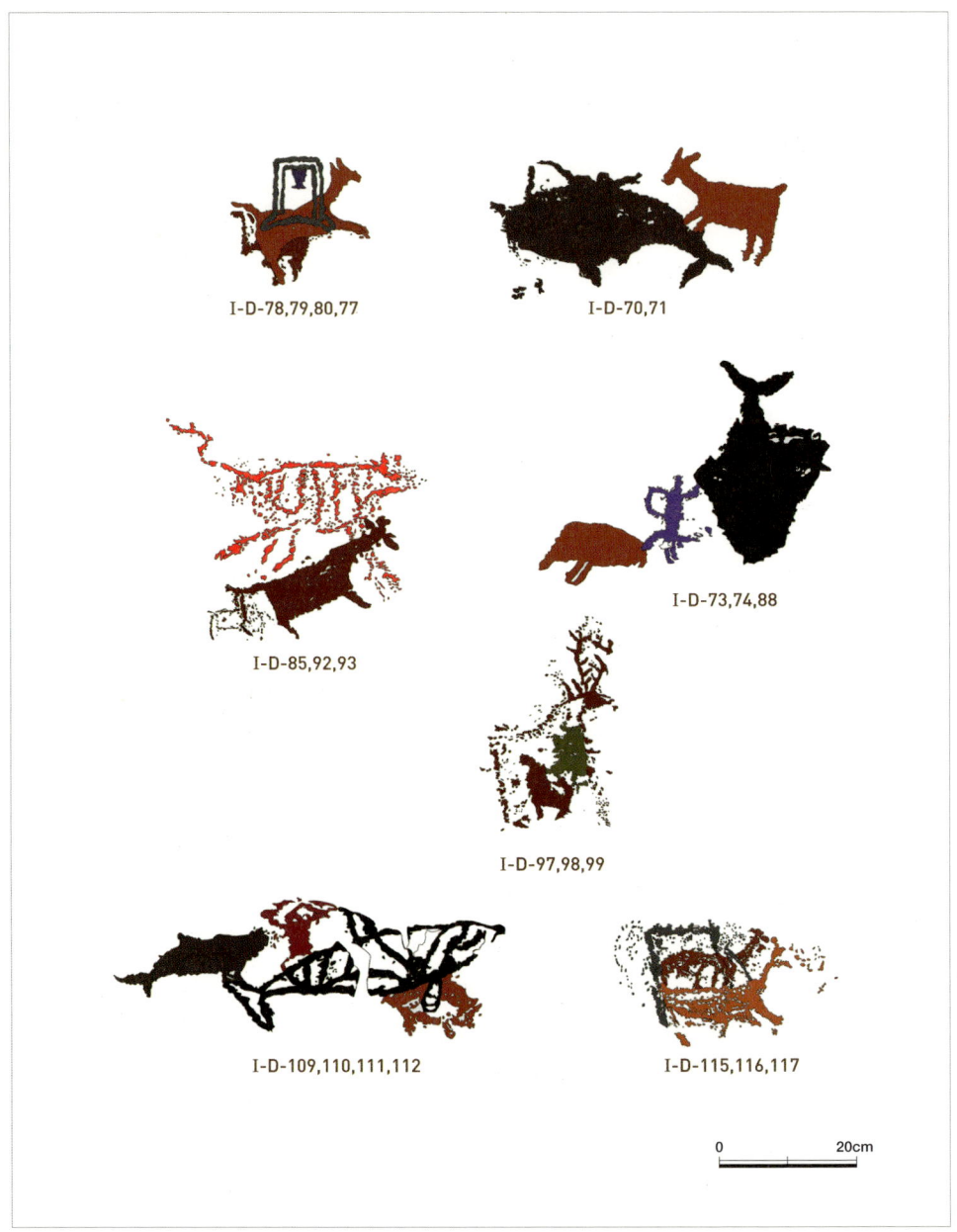

I-D-78,79,80,77

I-D-70,71

I-D-73,74,88

I-D-85,92,93

I-D-97,98,99

I-D-109,110,111,112

I-D-115,116,117

0   20cm

Fig. 49. Petroglyphs overlapped multiple times sequentially 2

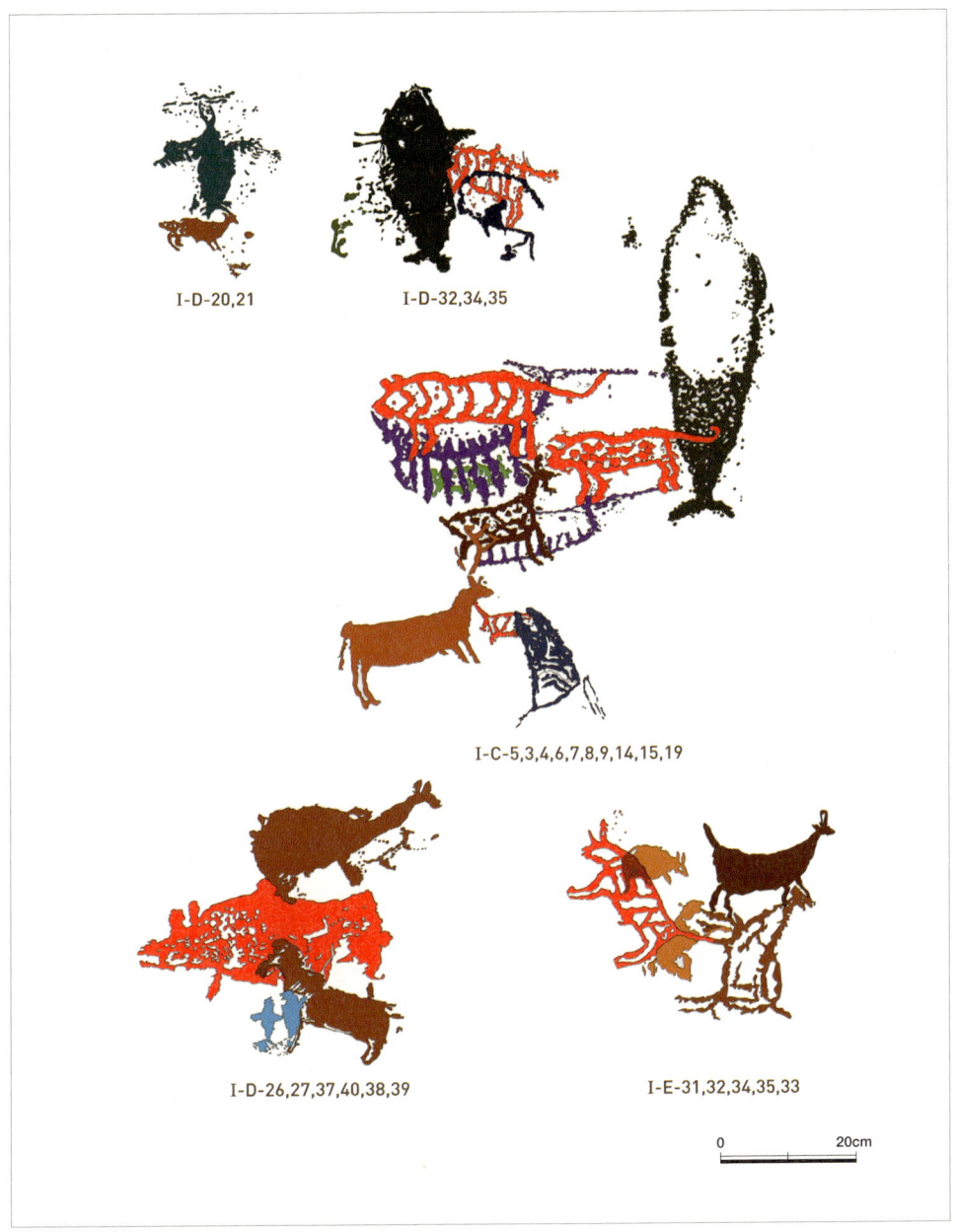

I-D-20,21   I-D-32,34,35

I-C-5,3,4,6,7,8,9,14,15,19

I-D-26,27,37,40,38,39   I-E-31,32,34,35,33

0   20cm

Fig. 50. Petroglyphs overlapped multiple times sequentially 3

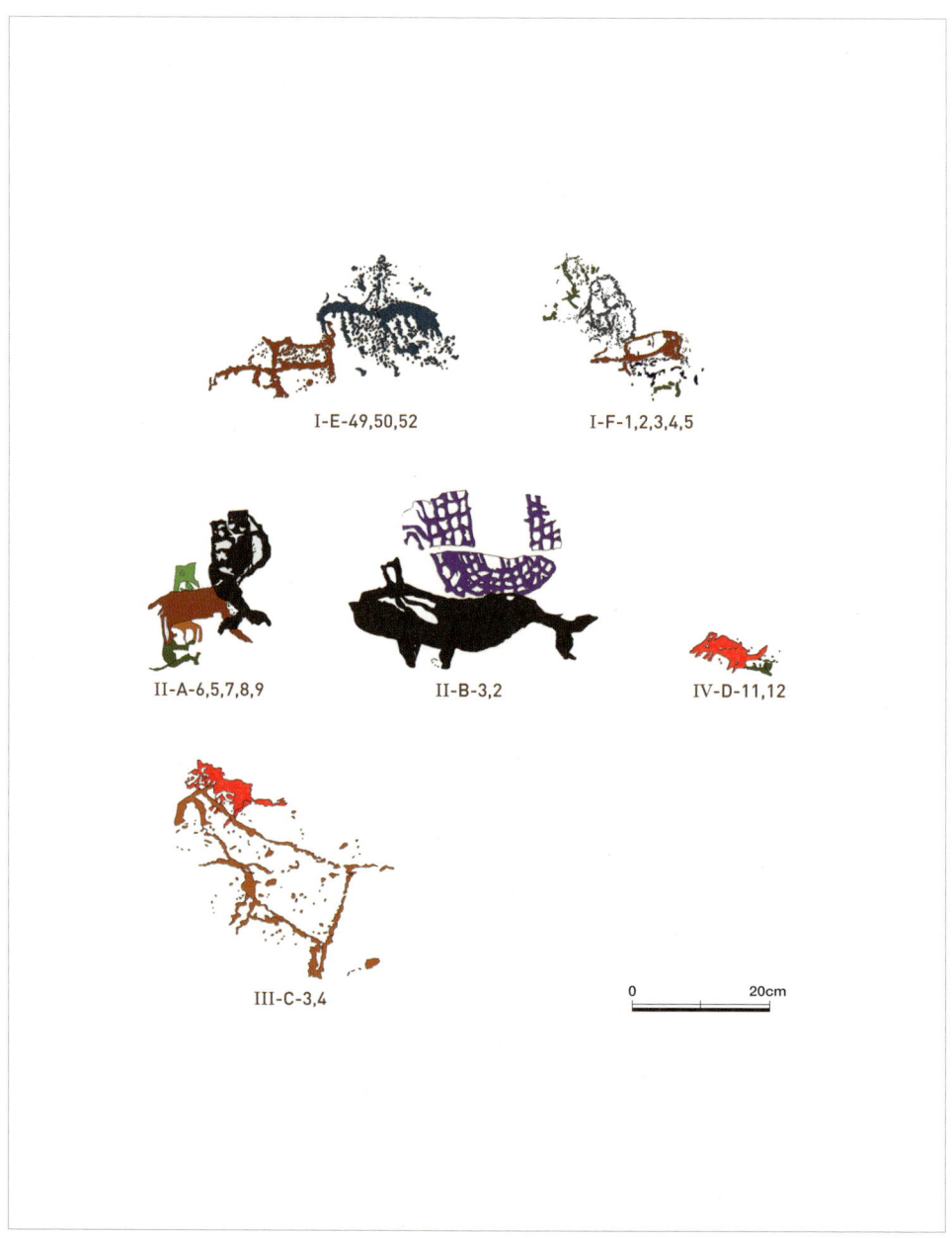

I-E-49,50,52

I-F-1,2,3,4,5

II-A-6,5,7,8,9

II-B-3,2

IV-D-11,12

III-C-3,4

0   20cm

Fig. 51. Petroglyphs overlapped multiple times sequentially 4

The Bangudae Petroglyphs in Ulsan

Conclusion

The detailed research on Bangudae Petroglyphs spanning five years allowed the University of Ulsan Bangudae Petroglyph Institute to confirm a total of 353 petroglyphs. The number of petroglyphs increased significantly from the previous numbers confirmed by the earlier three research reports. This is not only due to the more detailed research method but also to the attention put on the overlapping petroglyphs. The researchers also focused on the fact that the engravings took place more than four separate times and that people continued to add touches such as grinding, even after the age of petroglyphs was over.

The human act of engraving or painting images on rocks to last over time is found all across the world. Since the late Paleolithic Period rock engravings or paintings remain the longest artistic act and genre still continued by the aboriginal peoples of Kakadu National Park, northern Australia.

Petroglyphs and rock paintings result from the rock worship. The people who left Bangudae Petroglyphs were also aware that the act was distinct from a simple description of scenery or an experience. Engraving petroglyphs ensured that their religion and the world view survive throughout the time.

Bangudae Petroglyphs is the result of multiple efforts throughout the stretch of time. Distinct people of different livelihoods ranging from hunting to fishing came to the rock cliff at separate times to leave distinct marks. We cannot know when exactly the people who hunted on land and the people who hunted at sea each visited Bangudae. The degree of erosion on the early petroglyphs, the overlapping among the secondary, tertiary and quaternary petroglyphs, and the differences in the depths of the engravings as the technique shifted from line to face engraving only suggest that some time had passed between the petroglyphs of each period.

The majority of additional petroglyphs found by the Institution are either unidentifiable or unidentified shapes. In addition to the natural flaking of the rock surface due to erosion and the damage during the recent decades due to the repetition of flooding and drying, the early method of pecking makes it difficult to preserve well the form of the petroglyphs. The recent trend towards dating Bangudae Petroglyphs to the late Neolithic period is also meaningful.

The cetaceans (cetacea) that represent Bangudae Petroglyphs are understood to be proofs of the whaling practices of the early peoples of Ulsan Bay and Taewha hills from the late Neolithic Period to the Bronze Age. However, whether the various species of the cetacean (cetacea) that frequented the Ulsan Bay were game for a long period of time or the subject of worship, or whether it shifted from the object of worship to hunting need to be discussed further in the future. Depending on the time period and the life styles of the people, the various animals (zoomorphes) including cetaceans (cetacea) that occupied the mountains and the seas of Ulsan may have become food or the figure of worship.

Bangudae Petroglyphs show a variety of animals (zoomorphes) other than cetaceans (cetacea), deer (cervus nippon) and tigers (panthera tigris). The additional research findings and the increased understanding of prehistoric ecosystem and environment of Ulsan area may help identify the previously unidentified species of the petroglyphs. The identified animal species may also help provide evidence to the study of ecology and environment of prehistoric Ulsan. The human figures and tools would provide valuable resources in reconstructing the prehistoric and ancient history and culture of Ulsan. In order to make possible such research breakthrough, the academics of different fields must engage in interdisciplinary studies. A prerequisite to such effort would be an establishment of a research hub that facilitates international and domestic research cooperation. I hope that University of Ulsan Bangudae Petroglyph Institute and its research reports help provide foundation for such research breakthrough.

April, 2019

Dr. Jeon Hotae

Bangudae Petroglyph Institute Director, University of Ulsan

Bibliography

Books and Reports

강미희·윤봉선, 2016,『반구대암각화 바위에 새긴 고래이야기』, 도서출판 마루벌, 서울.

공주대학교, 2010,『반구대암각화 암면 보존방안 학술연구』, 울산광역시.

국립문화재연구소, 2011,『반구대 암각화』, 국립문화재연구소, 대전.

김호석, 2008,『한국의 바위그림』, 문학동네, 서울.

김혜림, 2009,『반구대암각화 관광자원화를 위한 전시관 기능연구』, 울산발전연구원.

문명대·이건청·이달희, 2016,『반구대암각화의 비밀』, UUP.

Cultural Heritage Administration, 2015,『코아계곡 암각화와 반구대암각화』.

Cultural Heritage Administration, 2016,『대곡천암각화군 역사문화사 비교연구』.

석조문화재보존과학연구회, 2003,『반구대암각화 보존대책 연구』, 울산광역시.

울산광역시, 2000,『반구대 암각화』.

울산광역시, 2008,『울산 반구대 암각화 學術(3D) 調査 用役 報告書』.

University of Ulsan Museum, 2000,『울산 반구대암각화』, 울산대학교 박물관 학술연구총서 5, University of Ulsan·Ulsan Metropolitan City.

University of Ulsan Museum·한국암각화학회·울산MBC, 2004,『울산 천전리 암각화의 재조명』, 2004 추계학술대회논문집.

University of Ulsan Bangudae Petroglyph Institute·한국암각화학회, 2013,『한국 암각화의 형태 분석론: 2013 추계학술회의논문집』.

University of Ulsan Bangudae Petroglyph Institute, 2016,『울산 반구대암각화 제작연대론』 울산대학교 반구대암각화유적보존연구소 한국암각화 학술연구총서 제 1 집.

University of Ulsan Bangudae Petroglyph Institute, 2016,『울산 반구대암각화 제작연대론』 울산대학교 반구대암각화유적보존연구소 한국암각화 학술연구총서 제 2 집.

University of Ulsan Bangudae Petroglyph Institute, 2016,『울산 반구대암각화 제작연대론』 울산대학교 반구대암각화유적보존연구소 한국암각화 학술연구총서 제 3 집.

University of Ulsan Foundation for Industry Cooperation, 2015,『대곡천암각화군의 세계 유산 등재를 위한 기반구축사업-보존·관리 및 활용』.

Ulsan Petroglyph Museum of Bangudae, 2013,『한국의 암각화 Ⅲ: 울주 대곡리 반구대암

각화」, 울산.

Ulsan Petroglyph Museum of Bangudae, 2017,「2017년 반구대암각화 국제학술대회 고래와 암각화 발표자료집」.

이코모스 코리아, 2012,「대곡천 암각화군의 유산적 가치 국제 세미나 논문집」.

이하우, 2011,「한국 암각화의 祭儀性」, 학연출판사, 서울.

이혜은 외, 2015,「세계유산등재추진을 위한 대곡천 암각화군의 세계유산적 가치도출」 Cultural Heritage Administration.

임세권, 1999,「한국의 암각화」, 대원사, 서울.

전호태, 2005,「울산의 암각화: 울산 대곡리 반구대암각화론」, University of Ulsan Press, 울산.

전호태, 2013,「울산 반구대암각화 연구」, 한림출판사, 서울.

정동찬, 1996,「살아있는 신화 바위그림」, 혜안, 서울.

제주교육박물관, 2017,「선사의 기적 한국의 암각화」, 제주.

한국역사민속학회, 1996,「한국의암각화」, 한길사, 서울.

황수영·문명대, 1984,「반구대암벽조각」, 동국대학교출판부, 서울.

허 권 외, 2012,「대곡천 암각화군 보존학술조사 연구용역」, Cultural Heritage Administration.

Bangudae Petroglyphs Institute, University Of Ulsan, 2013, Bangudae : Petroglyph Panels In Ulsan, Korea, In The Context Of World Rock Art, Hollym International Corp., USA.

Bangudae Petroglyphs Institute, University Of Ulsan, 2014, The Cheonjeon-Ri Petroglyphs In Ulsan, Hollym International Corp., USA.

Bangudae Petroglyphs Institute, University Of Ulsan, 2015, Petroglyphs Of Cheonjeon-Ri In Ulsan, Korea, In The Context Of World Rock Art, Hollym International Corp., USA.

Jeon Hotae, 2014, Bangudae Petroglyphs of Korea, Hollym International Corp., USA.

Lee Wonbok, 1998, The Rock Carvings of Pangudae, Koreana12, The Korea Foundation.

Thesis

강봉원, 2012,「반구대 암각화에 표출된 육지동물의 재인식-동물사육 문제와 편년의 재검토」「한국신석기연구」23:133-166, 한국신석기학회.

강봉원, 2013,「반구대 암각화 조사 방법에 대한 일고찰」「한국암각화연구」17:1-20, 한국암각화학회.

강봉원, 2015, 「반구대 암각화 편년의 재검토: 신석기시대 설을 중심으로」『울산 반구대 암각화 제작연대론』:35-62.

강봉원, 2016, 「반구대 및 천전리암각화의 편년과 고고학적 맥락 : 공반관계 및 교차편년 을 중심으로」『한국암각화디지털 박물관 기초연구』:65-84.

강봉원, 2016, 「대곡천일대 선사~역사시대 문화유산에 대한 검토: 반구대암각화의 편 년을 위한 고고학적 맥락을 중심으로」『울산 반구대암각화와 천전리 각석 연구』:81- 102.

강삼혜, 2014, 「대곡리암각화의 사슴상의 의미와 도상양식」『울산 반구대 대곡리 암각 화』:53-77, (사)한국미술사연구소.

강삼혜, 2016, 「대곡리암각화 사슴상의 의미와 도상 양식」『강좌미술사』 47:57-88, 한국 불교미술사학회(한국미술사연구소).

고경희, 2006, 「대곡리암각화에 나타난 신석기시대 한반도 의식생활문화」『韓國食生活 文化學會誌』 21, 한국식생활문화학회.

고재룡, 1997, 「대곡리 반구대암각화의 조형성에 관한 연구」 부산대학교 교육대학원 석 사학위 청구논문.

김권구, 1999, 「울주 대곡리 반구대암각화의 이해와 연구방향에 대하여」『울산연구1』, 울 산대학교박물관.

김권구, 2015, 「반구대암각화 신석기시대 조성시기설의 논거비판」『울산 반구대암각화 제작연대론』:63-81.

김건수, 2000, 「울산 암각화에 나타난 어로문화와 경제단계 연구」『울산암각화 발견 30 주년기념 암각화국제학술대회 논문집』:21-32, 예술의전당·울산광역시.

김성혜, 1988, 「경남 울주 반구대암각화의 형태에 나타난 조형형식에 관한 小考」 이화여 자대학교 교육대학원 석사학위 청구논문.

김수진, 2003, 「반구대암각화의 훼손시기와 훼손현상 진단분석」 반구대암각화 보존대책 연구.

김숙희, 2004, 「울산 반구대 바위그림의 신화적 상징-인물상, 동물상, 도구상을 중심으 로-」 공주대학교 교육대학원 석사학위 청구논문.

金榮美, 1993, 「韓國 先史岩刻畵의 形象에 대한 硏究」 홍익대학교 대학원 석사학위청구 논문.

김원룡, 1980, 「울주 반구대암각화에 대하여」『한국고고학보』 9:6-22, 한국고고학회.

김은경, 2016, 「울주 대곡리 반구대암각화와 고래제의」 고려대학교 대학원 석사학위청구 논문.

金貞培, 1997,「東北亞속의 韓國의 岩刻畵」『한국사연구』99.100, 한국사연구회.

김정배, 2015,「대곡리암각화의 문화사적 의미」『울산 반구대암각화제작연대론』:107-124.

김정옥, 2007,「반구대암각화 연구」동아대학교 교육대학원 석사학위 청구논문.

김종일, 2015,「장기 지속적 관점에서 본 반구대암각화의 제작과 그 사회적 의미」『울산 반구대암각화제작연대론』:169-185.

김지수, 2016,「댐의 축조로 인한 하천 퇴적환경 변화 : 울주군 반구대 암각화 지역의 퇴적층에 대한 사례연구」경상대학교 대학원 석사학위 청구논문.

김태욱, 2001,「울산 대곡리암각화에 대한 연구사적 고찰」『白山學報』60, 백산학회.

김현권, 2014,「대곡리암각화 인물상의 의미와 도상연구」『울산 반구대 대곡리암각화』:29-41, (사)한국미술사연구소.

김현권, 2016,「대곡리 반구대암각화 인물상의 의미와 도상 해석」『강좌미술사』47:35-56, 한국불교미술사학회(한국미술사연구소).

김호석, 2004,「반구대암각화 연구-고래그림의 사실성을 중심으로-」『한국암각화연구』5, 한국암각화학회.

김호석, 2006,「울산 대곡리 반구대암각화의 현상과 보존책」『한국암각화연구』9:13-30, 한국암각화학회.

김호석, 2006,「한국암각화의 도상과 조형성 연구」동국대학교 대학원 박사학위 청구논문.

김호석, 2006,「울산 대곡리 반구대암각화 제작 순서에 대한 고찰」『동악미술사학』7, 동악미술사학회.

김호석, 2006,「울산 대곡리암각화의 육지동물에 대한 형태적 특성 고찰」『백산학보』74, 백산학회.

김화원, 1993,「반구대암각화의 문화양태에 대한 시론」고려대학교 교육대학원 석사학위 청구논문.

나경수, 2012,「반구대암각화의 신화학적 해석 가능성」『한국암각화연구』16:5-19, 한국암각화학회.

문명대, 1973,「울산의 선사시대 암벽각화」『문화재』7:33-40, 문화재관리국.

문명대, 1973,「한국의 선사시대 암각화」『공간』77, 공간사.

문명대, 1977,「한국의 선사미술」『독서신문』45:41-49, 독서신문사.

문명대, 1990,「한국의 선사미술」『한국사상사대계I』, 한국정신문화연구소.

문명대, 2000,「울산 암각화의 발견경위와 연구 성과 회고」『울산암각화발견30주년기념 암각화국제학술대회논문집』:9-19, 예술의 전당·울산광역시.

문명대, 2010,「울산 반구대암각화 발견의 회고와 전망」『세계의 바위그림, 그 해석과 보존」:27-45, 동북아역사재단.

문명대, 2013, 「대곡천암각화의 발견」『한국의 암각화 Ⅲ : 울주 대곡리 반구대암각화』:16-33. 울산암각화박물관.

문명대, 2014, 「대곡리암각화의 의미와 기법과 양식을 통한 편년연구」『울산 반구대 대곡리 암각화』:11-27, (사)한국미술사연구소.

문명대, 2015, 「반구대 대곡리암각화의 신석기시대 편년연구」『울산 반구대암각화 제작연대론』: 23-33.

문명대, 2016, 「대곡리암각화의 의미와 기법과 양식에 의한 신석기시대 편년 연구」『강좌미술사』47:11-33, 한국불교미술사학회(한국미술사연구소).

박구병, 2003, 「반구대암각화에 나타난 경류와 포경」『수산업사연구』10.

박상호, 1997, 「한국 선사시대 암각화의 조형적 의미」영남대학교 교육대학원 석사학위 청구논문.

박영숙 외 2명, 2016, 「울산 반구대 암각화 인근 트렌치 퇴적물 내 규조의 환경 특성」『韓國地球科學會誌』37:11-20, 한국지구과학회.

박영희, 2016, 「반구대암각화와 천전리 각석의 상관관계에 관한 연구」『울산 반구대암각화와 천전리 각석연구』:63-79.

박정근, 2000, 「한국의 암각화 연구 성과와 문제점」『先史와 古代』15, 한국고대학회.

박정근, 2014, 「한국 암각화의 성격」『울주 대곡천 암각화군 국제심포지엄』:27-38. 이코모스 코리아.

방국진, 2009, 「한국 암각화의 특징연구」경기대학교 전통예술대학원 석사학위 청구논문.

서영대, 2008, 「한국 암각화의 신앙과 의례」『한국암각화연구』11·12:23-36, 한국암각화학회.

서영대, 2015, 「울산 반구대암각화의 종교사적 의미」『울산 반구대암각화제작연대론』:125-138.

손호선, 2012, 「반구대암각화의 고래 種」『한국암각화연구』16:21-32, 한국암각화학회.

손호선, 2013, 「반구대암각화의 고래」『한국의 암각화 Ⅲ : 울주 대곡리 반구대암각화』:188-201 울산암각화박물관.

송광익, 1978, 「한국 선사암각화에 관한 일연구」계명대학교 교육대학원 석사학위 청구논문.

송화섭, 1991, 「한국 암석각화와 그 의례에 대한 고찰」『한종만박사 회갑기념논문집』, 한국사상사, 원광대학교.

송화섭, 1994, 「韓國岩刻畵の源流と特徵」『還太平洋文化』8, 日本環太平洋學會.

송화섭, 2012,「북방 수렵유목문화 관점에서 본 반구대암각화」『한국암각화연구』16: 33-50, 한국암각화학회.

송화섭, 2016,「한국 암각화의 조성 주체와 제작 배경-해양지리적 관점을 중심으로-」『울산 반구대암각화와 천전리 각석연구』:1-21.

송화섭, 2016,「한국 암각화의 디지털콘텐츠 구축과 선사시대 생활상 복원」『인문콘텐츠』43:41-71, 인문콘텐츠학회.

신은정, 2014,「대곡리암각화 보존의 새로운 방안」『울산 반구대 대곡리 암각화』:11-27, (사)한국미술사연구소.

신은정, 2016,「대곡리 반구대암각화 보존현황과 과제」『강좌미술사』47:127-141, 한국불교미술사학회(한국미술사연구소).

신현경, 2006,「반구대암각화의 고래그림에 있어서 제례적 기능에 대한 고찰과 현대적의의」『동양예술』11, 한국동양예술학회.

이군우, 1998,「우리나라 암각화의 표현형식 및 그 내용에 관한 연구: 울주 대곡리 반구대암각화 중심으로」동국대학교 교육대학원 석사학위청구논문.

이기길, 1991,「울주 대곡리 바위 새긴 그림」『박물관휘보』1, 서울시립대박물관.

이상목, 2004,「울산 대곡리 반구대 선사유적의 동물그림: 생태적 특성과 계절성을 중심으로」『한국고고학보』52.

이상목, 2012,「대곡천 암각화군 현황과 세계유산의 보존관리사례 및 연구 동향」『대곡천 암각화군의 유산적가치 국제세미나』:41-53, ICOMOS-KOREA.

이상목, 2015,「반구대암각화 제작연대 규명에 따른 방법론적 고찰」『울산 반구대암각화 제작연대론』:83-105.

이상목, 2017,「반구대암각화와 선사시대 고래사냥」『2017년 반구대암각화 국제학술대회 고래와 암각화 발표자료집』:127-130.

이상우, 2017,「문화유산의 원형적 가치와 그 현대적 활용 -반구대암각화의 신화적 가치를 중심으로」『嶺南學』61:185-214, 경북대학교 영남문화연구원.

이상헌, 1994,「천전리각석과 대곡리 암각화의 보존에 대한 제언」『울산대학교 인문과학연구소 학술토론회』5 '천전리각석과 대곡리암각화의 중요성과 보존방안'.

이상헌, 2003,「국내 암각화의 훼손양상과 지질학적 보존대책」『한국암각화연구』4: 71-91, 한국암각화학회.

이석훈, 2003,「반구대암각화 암석의 풍화」『반구대암각화보존대책연구』.

이 선, 2012,「대곡천의 자연환경과 경관」『대곡천암각화군의 유산적가치 국제세미나』:129-140, ICOMOS-KOREA.

이정은, 2002, 「울주 대곡리암각화 형상에 관한 연구: 사슴형상을 중심으로」 계명대학교 교육대학원 석사학위 청구논문.

이찬희, 2012, 「울산 반구대암각화의 손상도 및 사면안정성 평가」 『대곡천 암각화군의 유산적 가치 국제세미나』:85-103, ICOMOS-KOREA.

이찬희·전유근·조영훈·서만철, 2012, 「울산 반구대암각화의 손상도 및 사면안정성평가」 『보존과학회지』 28, 한국문화재보존과학회.

이하우, 2007, 「반구대암각화의 제작 층에 대한 연구」 『한국상고사학보』 58:39-76, 한국 상고사학회.

이하우, 2009, 「한국 선사암각화의 제의표현에 관한 연구」 경주대학교대학원 박사학위청 구논문.

이하우, 2012, 「대곡천암각화군의 미술사적 특징과 가치」 『대곡천암각화군의 유산적가 치 국제세미나』:104-128, ICOMOS-KOREA.

이하우, 2013, 「암각화연구 기초자료의 검토-반구대암각화를 중심으로-」 『한국암각화연구』 17:21-44, 한국암각화학회.

이하우, 2015, 「암각화에서 샤먼표현의 형태적 속성」 『한국암각화연구』 19:77-97, 한국 암각화학회.

이하우, 2016, 「암각화 동물표현의 심상적 현상」 『한국암각화연구』 20:69-96, 한국암각 화학회.

이하우, 2016, 「대곡천암각화군의 제작 기법연구」 『울산 반구대암각화와 천전리 각석 연 구』:23-62.

이하우, 2016, 「한국 암각화자료의 디지털 가공방법에 관한 연구」 『한국암각화디지털박 물관 기초연구』:85-103.

임세권, 1984, 「우리나라 선사암각화의 연대에 관하여」 『남사 정재각박사 고희기념 동양 학논총』:517-542, 동양학논총편찬위원회.

임세권, 1994, 「韓國 先史時代 岩刻畵의 性格」 단국대학교 대학원 박사학위 청구논문.

임세권, 2013, 「반구대암각화의 역사적 의미」 『내일을 여는 역사』 53, 내일을 여는 역사 재단.

임장혁, 1991, 「대곡리 암벽각화의 민속학적 고찰」 『한국민속학』 24:171-195.

장명수, 1996, 「한국 암각화의 편년」 『한국의 암각화』:179-227, 한길사, 서울.

장명수, 1997, 「울산 대곡리 암각화인들의 생업과 신앙」 『인하사학』 5:65-146, 인하대학교.

장명수, 1999, 「암각화를 통해본 우리나라 선사인들의 신앙사유」 『한국암각화연구』 1: 27-65.

장명수, 1999, 「울주 대곡리 반구대암각화에 나타난 신앙의식」『울산연구』 1:67-100, 울산대학교 박물관.

장명수, 2000, 「한국 암각화의 유형과 특성」『학예연구』 1, 국민대학교박물관.

장명수, 2000, 「한국선사시대 암각화 신앙의 전개양상」『한국암각화연구』 2:5-45, 한국 암각화학회.

장명수, 2001, 「한국 암각화의 문화상에 대한 연구」 인하대학교 대학원 박사학위 청구논문.

장명수, 2001, 「한국 암각화의 편년에 대한 검토」『학예연구』 2, 국민대학교 박물관.

장명수, 2007, 「한국 암각화의 문화적 특성」 고대 동북아 암각화 비교연구 학술심포지엄 발표 요지문.

장명수, 2007, 「한국 암각화의 형식 분류와 문화특성」『한국암각화연구』 10:1-28.

장석호, 1986, 「반구대암각화의 조형성 연구」 계명대학교 대학원 석사학위 청구논문.

장석호, 2007, 「국보 제285호 대곡리암각화의 도상해석학적 연구」『선사와 고대』 27:131-163.

장석호, 2010, 「메타언어-바위그림의 공간과 제재의 상징성-대곡리암각화를 중심으로-」『세계의 바위그림, 그 해석과 보존』:165-179, 동북아역사재단.

장석호, 2014, 「대곡리암각화의 세계유산적 가치」『울주 대곡천 암각화군 국제심포지엄』:41-53. 이코모스 코리아.

장석호, 2017, 「울산 대곡리암각화 속에 표현된 고래 형상」『2017년 반구대암각화 국제학술대회 고래와 암각화 발표자료집』:75-76.

장지선, 2006, 「한국 암각화의 조형적 특징에 관한 연구-울산지역을 중심으로-」 경희대학교 교육대학원 석사학위 청구논문.

전호태, 1996, 「울주 대곡리·천전리암각화」『한국의 암각화』:45-95, 한길사.

전호태, 2000, 「울산 반구대암각화 보존론」『한국암각화연구』 2:47-67, 한국암각화학회.

전호태, 2000, 「울산 반구대암각화 편년론」『울산사학』 10:1-37, 울산대학교 사학회.

전호태, 2001, 「울산 반구대암각화 실측형상 재분류 및 새김새 재검토」『울산사학』 9:1-56, 울산대학교 사학회.

전호태, 2012, 「한국의 선사 및 고대 초기예술과 반구대암각화」『역사와 경계』 85, 부산경남사학회.

전호태, 2012, 「한국 암각화 유적의 현황과 연구과제」『울산사학』 16:1~102, 울산사학회.

전호태, 2015, 「울산 반구대암각화의 종교문화사적 가치와 편년」『울산 반구대암각화 제작연대론』:1-21.

전호태, 2015, 「울산 반구대암각화 편년론의 추이와 전망」『울산사학』 19:1-38.

전호태, 2016, 「한국 암각화 전시교육 디지털 아카이브 구축을 위한 기본 개념설정 및 시행방안 연구」『고문화』87:33-63, 한국대학박물관협회.

전호태, 2016, 「한국 암각화 디지털 전시 및 교육프로그램 개발방향 연구」『글로벌문화콘텐츠』25:137-157, 글로벌문화콘텐츠학회.

전호태, 2016, 「한국 암각화 디지털 박물관 전시 콘텐츠 연구」『인문콘텐츠』43:25-40, 인문콘텐츠학회.

전호태, 2016, 「한국 암각화 전시교육 디지털 아카이브 구축 기초연구」『한국암각화디지털 박물관 기초연구』:7-36.

전호태, 2016, 「울산 반구대암각화와 천전리 각석 연구의 추이와 전망」『울산사학』20:1-37, 울산사학회.

정병모, 2014, 「대곡리암각화 호랑이상의 의미와 도상연구-민화의 시원양식에 대한 논의-」『울산 반구대 대곡리 암각화』:43-51, (사)한국미술사연구소.

정동찬, 1986, 「우리나라 선사 바위그림의 연구」, 연세대학교 대학원 석사학위 청구논문.

정동찬, 1988, 「울주 대곡리의 선사바위그림 연구」『손보기박사 정년기념 고고인류학논총』:389-434.

조홍제, 2010, 「대곡천 암각화군의 공학적 진단과 보존방안의 제안」『터널과 지하 공간』20, 한국암반공학회.

주수완, 2014, 「대곡리암각화 고래상과 포경선의 의미와 도상양식」『울산 반구대 대곡리 암각화』:79-93, (사)한국미술사연구소.

주수완, 2016, 「반구대암각화 고래도상의 미술사적 의의」『강좌미술사』47:89-107, 한국불교미술사학회(한국미술사연구소).

천진기, 2000, 「울산 암각화를 통해본 동물숭배, 생식신앙, 민속의례와 세계관」『울산암각화 발견 30주년기념국제학술대회논문집』:43-61, 울산광역시·예술의전당.

하인수, 2012, 「동삼동패총과 반구대암각화」『대곡천암각화군의 유산적 가치 국제 세미나』:151-172, ICOMOS-KOREA.

하인수, 2012, 「반구대암각화의 조성시기론-동삼동패총 자료를 중심으로-」『한국신석기연구』23, 한국신석기학회.

하인수, 2013, 「고고학적 맥락에서 본 반구대암각화-동삼동 패총을 중심으로」『한국의 암각화Ⅲ : 울주 대곡리 반구대암각화』:204-223, 울산암각화박물관.

한상훈, 2013, 「반구대암각화의 동물」『한국의 암각화 Ⅲ : 울주 대곡리 반구대암각화』:178-187.울산암각화박물관.

허 권, 2010, 「울산 암각화지역의 세계유산 등재추진의 현황과 과제」『세계의 바위그림,

그 해석과 보존」:237-253, 동북아역사재단.

허언욱, 2000, 「울산 암각화의 문화관광자원 개발문제」『울산암각화 발견30주년기념 암각화 국제학술대회논문집』:75-82, 예술의 전당·울산광역시.

허영섭, 2016, 「반구대암각화 어떻게 보존해야 하는가」『대한토목학회지』64:54-55, 대한토목학회.

황기원, 2006, 「경관으로 보는 울산 반구대암각화 유적」『美術史學硏究』252, 한국미술사학회.

황상일, 2010, 「반구대암각화의 주기적인 침수와 구성암석의 풍화 특성」『대한지리학회』45, 대한지리학회.

황상일, 2015, 「울산지역의 Holocene 자연환경 변화와 선사시대 태화강중류 및 하류부인간 생활」『울산반구대암각화제작연대론』:139-168.

황상일·윤순옥, 1995, 「반구대암각화와 후빙기 후기 울산만의 환경변화」『한국제4기학보』, 한국 제4기학회.

황용훈, 1975, 「한반도 선사시대암각의 제작기술과 형식분류」『고고미술』127, 한국미술사학회.

황용훈, 1977, 「한국 선사 암각 연구」경희대학교 대학원 박사학위 청구논문.

조파리 드 셸뤼, 2017, 「반구대암각화와 정주 수렵채집민들의 유산 알렝테스타에게 바치는 헌사」『2017년 반구대암각화 국제학술대회 고래와 암각화 발표자료집』:119-122.

체벤도르지 D., 2000, 「한반도와 동북아지역 암각화비교연구」『암각화학술대회논문집』:147-155, 예술의 전당·울산광역시.

Choi, H. Y., Kwak, S. J., Yoo, S. H., 2016, "The preservation value of the Bangudae Petroglyphs, the 285th Korean National Treasure", JOURNAL OF CULTURAL HERITAGE 18:1296-2074, Elsevier Science B.V., Amsterdam.

Jeon Hotae, 2013, "Art of Prehistoric and Ancient Korea and the Bangudae Petroglyphs", BANGUDAE: PETROGLYPH PANELS IN ULSAN, KOREA, IN THE CONTEXT OF WORLD ROCK ART:11-35, Hollym International Corp., USA.

Jeon Hotae, 2013, "THE CURRENT STATE OF KOREAN PETROGLYPHS", BANGUDAE: PETROGLYPH PANELS IN ULSAN, KOREA, IN THE CONTEXT OF WORLD ROCK ART:161-211, Hollym International Corp., USA.

Jun-hi Han, 2013, "THE BANGUDAE PETROGLYPH SITE AND PERSPECTIVES FOR ITS INSCRIPTION ON THE WORLD HERITAGE LIST", BANGUDAE: PETROGLYPH PANELS IN ULSAN, KOREA, IN THE CONTEXT OF WORLD ROCK

ART:139-159, Hollym International Corp., USA.

Esther Jacobson-Tepfer, 2013, "The Rock Art of Siberia as Regional Context for the Consideration of Bangudae", BANGUDAE: PETROGLYPH PANELS IN ULSAN, KOREA, IN THE CONTEXT OF WORLD ROCK ART:67-98, Hollym International Corp., USA.

Henri-Paul Francfort, 2013, "The Bangudae Rock Art Panel: A Structural View", BANGUDAE: PETROGLYPH PANELS IN ULSAN, KOREA, IN THE CONTEXT OF WORLD ROCK ART:99-110, Hollym International Corp., USA.

Paul G. Bahn, 2013, "The Bangudae Cetacean (cetacea) in the Context of World Rock Art", BANGUDAE: PETROGLYPH PANELS IN ULSAN, KOREA, IN THE CONTEXT OF WORLD ROCK ART:37-66, Hollym International Corp., USA.

Abstract

Ulsan Daegok-ri Bangudae Petroglyph (National Treasure No. 285) is a valued work in the world prehistoric art history. It is among the sites often brought up when discussing the flow of the world prehistoric art history. Bangudae Petroglyphs preserve the view of the world, nature, and life of the prehistoric people that relied mostly on hunting and gathering.

When Bangudae Petroglyphs were first found in 1971, the site had already been going through the yearly cycle of being submerged in water for a period of time and resurfacing after. In 1965, Sayeon Dam was built in the lower Daegok stream, causing the water levels to rise during the wet season and lower during the dry season. When the Buddhism Archaeological Research Team of Donguk University found the site, Bangudae Petroglyphs had already lost a part of the original natural surroundings.

The first academic report on Bangudae Petroglyphs was made in 1984 by the Donguk University Museum. In 2000, University of Ulsan Museum photographed various newly found surfaces in addition to the main rock surface which holds most of the petroglyphs and published a detailed report. The Ulsan Petroglyph Museum which opened in 2008 reviewed the existing reports and published a new report with additional field research in 2013.

Since its founding in October 2011, University of Ulsan Bangudae Petroglyph Conservation Research Center has continued to collaborate with domestic and international resaerch institutions to study petroglyphs as well as prehistoric art sites and artifacts. Every year, Bangudae Petroglyph Conservation Research Center releases the results as academic report for the use of domestic and international research institutions and academics. Ulsan Bangudae Petroglyphs, National Treasure

No. 285 is the fourth installment of its Korean petroglyph site detailed report series.

Since its founding, the Bangudae Petroglyph Conservation Research Center has been asked by the researchers to publish an official detailed report that can also be used in an international context. Although reports have been made three times, some petroglyphs require re-categorization while some additional discoveries lack reports. Such requests for a new report and a research book have continued to rise. When the research members conducted additional examinations, additional petroglyphs were discovered in the main and surrounding rock surfaces.

Under the principles applied to the third series of the existing academic research volumes, which is to provide organized information that could be used objectively to domestic and international scholars of prehistoric art, each petroglyph in this book has a unique number and a scale. In addition to variety of field photographs, we have included the aerial photographs from before the site's discovery to today, showing the changes in the environment. The detailed photographs of newly found petroglyph surfaces near the main rock surface are also included.

From autumn 2011, we have examined in details the changes in the sites for two years. Since the early 2013, the research team has visited as often as possible the actual site and the Research Center's blueprint workspace. Even after the late 2015 when the petroglyph comparison began in preparation of the new research report, the team continued to visit the Bangudae Petroglyphs and the Research Center. We have also paid attention to the changes in the site's surrounding environment.

As a result of five years of detailed examination, University of Ulsan Bangudae Petroglyph Conservation Research Center has confirmed 353 petroglyphs in Bangudae Petroglyphs. Compared to the previous three reports, the number of petroglyphs increased significantly. While this is also due to the more sophisticated methods but also because of the attention paid to the overlapping images during the research. The petroglyphs had been worked at least four times. The researchers also endeavored to read the traces of additional retouches on the petroglyph including grinding and such long after the engravings were done.

Human effort to engrave or draw certain figures to remain on the surfaces of rocks can be found all over the world. From peoples of the Late Paleolithic Period to the native peoples of the northern Australian Kakadu National Park, people have

Table 2. Classification of individual figures of the Bangudae Petroglyphs

Group		Humans (anthromorphes) – Full Body	Humans – Face	Animals: Mammals – Even-toed ungulates (artiodactyla)	Mammals – Carnivora-terrestrial (carnivora-earth)	Mammals – Carnivora-marine (pinnipedia)	Mammals – Cetacean (cetacea)	Birds (aves)	Reptiles – Testudine (chelonia)	Fish (piscis)	Unidentified species	Tools – Ships (boats)	Tools – Nets (net)	Tools – Weir (fish trap)	Tools – Floats (float)	Tools – Harpoons (fish spear)	Tools – Unidentified figures	Unidentified forms	Unrecognizable forms	Total
I	A	1																		1
I	B	2		3	6		22	1	3	1	3	2	1	1	4	1		12	9	71
I	C	1		4	6		3			2	3							2	12	33
I	D	5	2	29	7	2	17	2	2	3	9	1					5	26	7	117
I	E	3		21	7	2	4	1			1	2			1			12	7	61
I	F			1			1				1							2		5
I	**Sub Total**	12	2	58	26	4	47	4	5	6	17	5	1	1	5	1	5	54	35	**288**
II	D	1					2													3
II	C									3										3
II	B						1						2						1	4
II	A			4	1		1				1							4		11
II	**Sub Total**	1		4	1		4			3	1		2					4	1	**21**
III	C				1						1	1						2		5
III	B						1			1	1							3	1	7
III	A	1		4	1		3													9
III	**Sub Total**	1		4	2		4			1	2	1						5	1	**21**
IV	A				1						1									2
IV	B			1																1
IV	C			1														3	3	7
IV	D			1	2		2											7	1	13
IV	**Sub Total**			3	3		2				1							10	4	**23**
Total		14	2	69	32	4	57	4	5	10	21	6	3	1	5	1	5	73	41	**353**

Category totals: Humans (anthromorphes) = 16; Animals (zoomorphes) = 202; Tools (tool figures) = 21; Unidentified = 114.

continued the tradition of rock images which make petroglyphs one of the oldest artistic activities and genre.

Rock engravings or paintings are the result of the rock worship. The creators of Bangudae Petroglyphs were also aware as they were engraving figures on the rock that the act was distinct from a simple descriptions of the world they occupy or the experiences lived. The rock engraving was a way to show their faith and the world view and passing them down to the younger generations.

Bangudae Petroglyphs are the result of many engravings over a long stretch of period. Diverse groups of people whose livelihood ranged from hunting, fishing and beyond left traces on the rocks over different periods of time. We do not know how much time lies between those who left marks of hunting and those who engraved images of fishing. The erosion of the earlier petroglyphs, the overlapping of the second and the third engravings, and the differences in the depths of the marks as the artists shifted from line to plane engraving merely hint that some time had passed between each layers.

The majority of the additional petroglyphs found are either of miscellaneous or unrecognized shapes. While the natural erosion of rock surfaces and the recent water damages from the several decades of submersion and resurfacing contributed to such confusion, the very method of the dot engraving that is characteristic of the early petroglyphs led to the poor conservation. The recent trend of dating Bangudae to the Late Neolithic Period also is meaningful in such respect.

The cetacean (cetacea) engravings that visually represent Bangudae are understood to be the indication that the peoples of Ulsan Bay and Taewha River hills from the Late Neolithic to the Bronze Period participated in whaling. However, whether the people saw the various species of cetacean (cetacea) that passed through Ulsan Bay as long-lasting sources of meat or sometimes as the targets of worship needs to be discussed and researched in the future. Depending on the trend of the time and the livelihood of the people, various animals (zoomorphes) including cetaceans (cetacea) may have become food or the objects of worship.

Bangudae Petroglyphs show diverse animals (zoomorphes) not limited to cetaceans (cetacea), deer (cervus nippon) and tigers (panthera tigris). Increased knowledge of prehistoric ecosystem in Ulsan and the additional research may help name currently unidentified animals (zoomorphes). The animal figures in the petroglyph may as well provide helpful information for those studying prehistoric ecology in Ulsan. A new understanding of people and tools would aid reconstructing Ulsan's prehistoric and ancient historic culture. For such future, the collaborative interdisciplinary research among different fields is a must. Establishing and running a research hub that may activate domestic and international collaboration is the foundation. We hope that University of Ulsan Bangudae Petroglyph Conservation Research Center's Bangudae Petroglyph detailed examination and report becomes the ground for solving various tasks and opening new possibilities.

April, 2019

Dr. Jeon Hotae

Bangudae Petroglyph Institute Director, University of Ulsan

Appendix

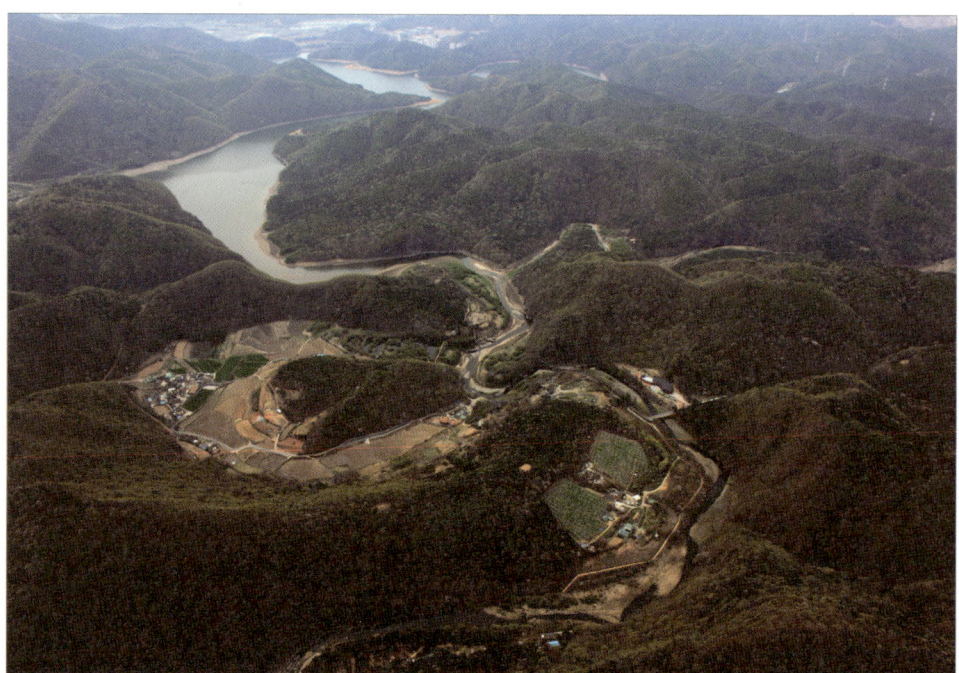

Photo 6. A complete view of the Daegok Stream

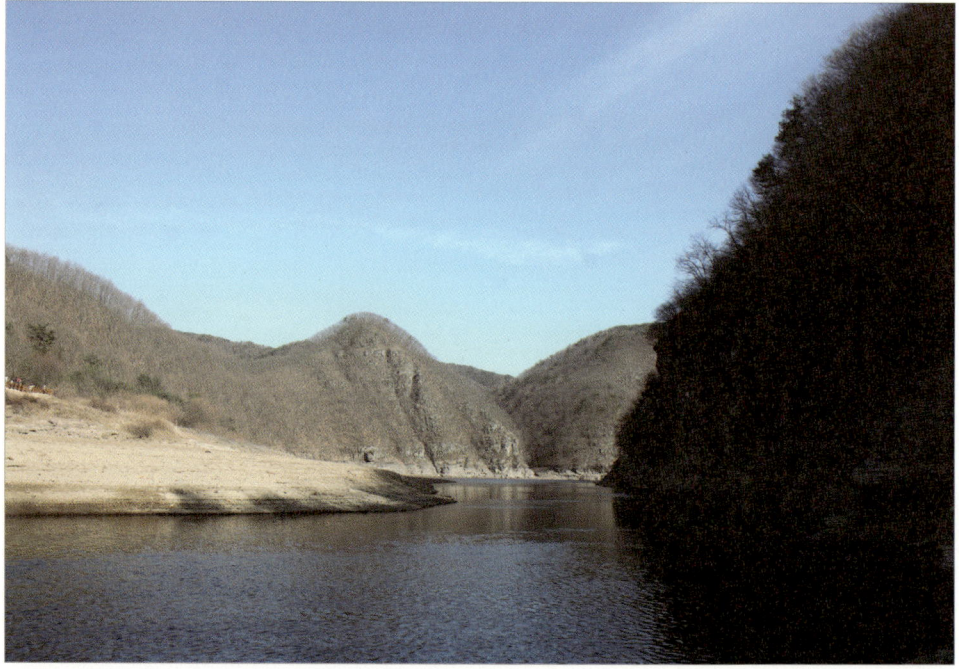

Photo 7. A view of the Daegok Stream (the upper→the lower)

The Bangudae Petroglyphs in Ulsan

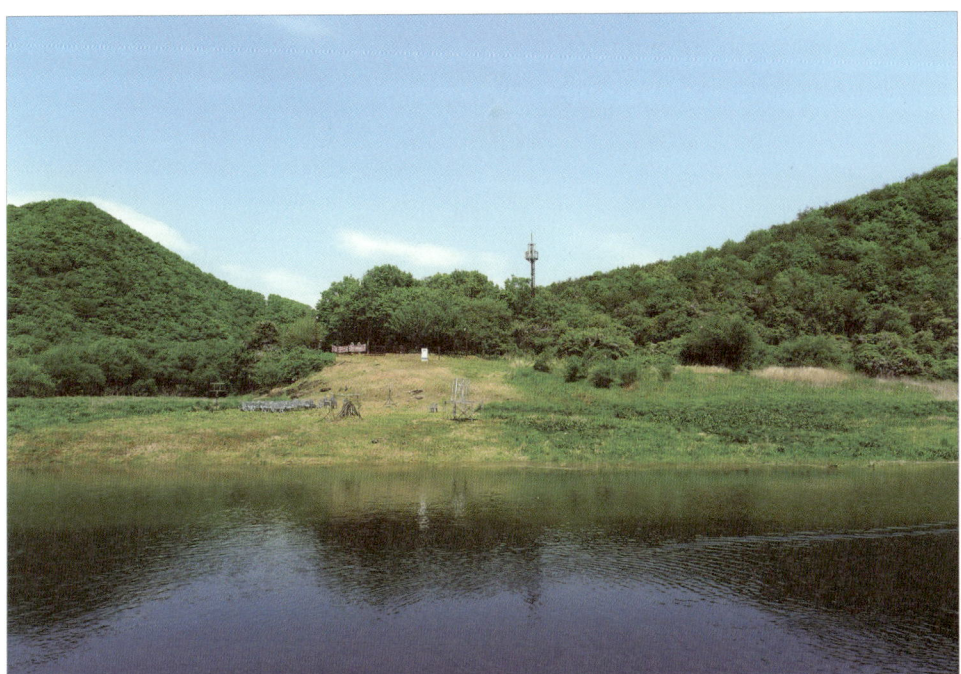

Photo 8. A complete view of the Bangudae Petroglyphs

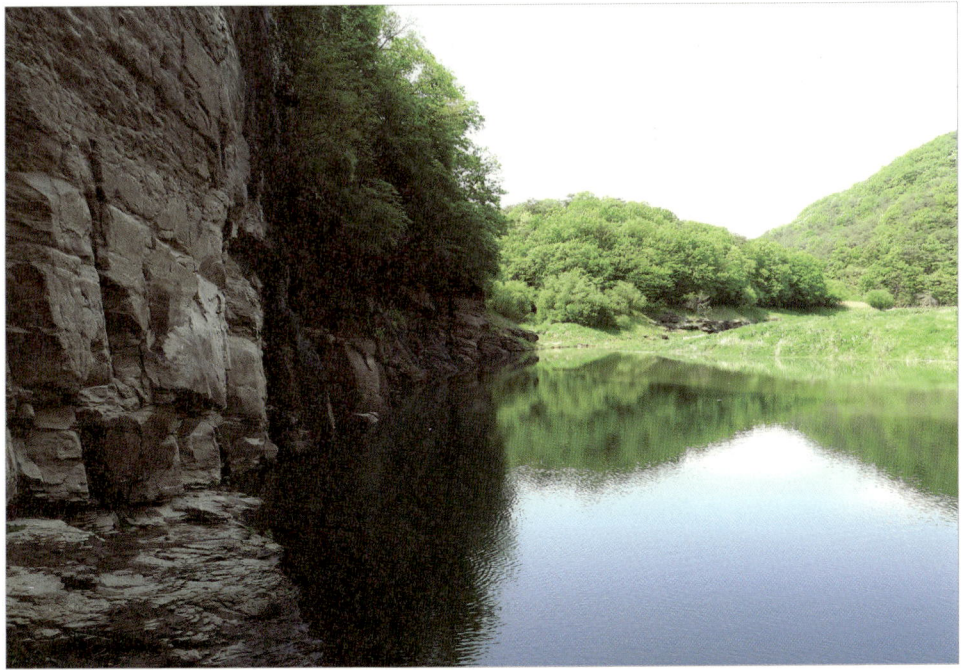

Photo 9. The upper reaches of the Bangudae Petroglyphs

Appendix

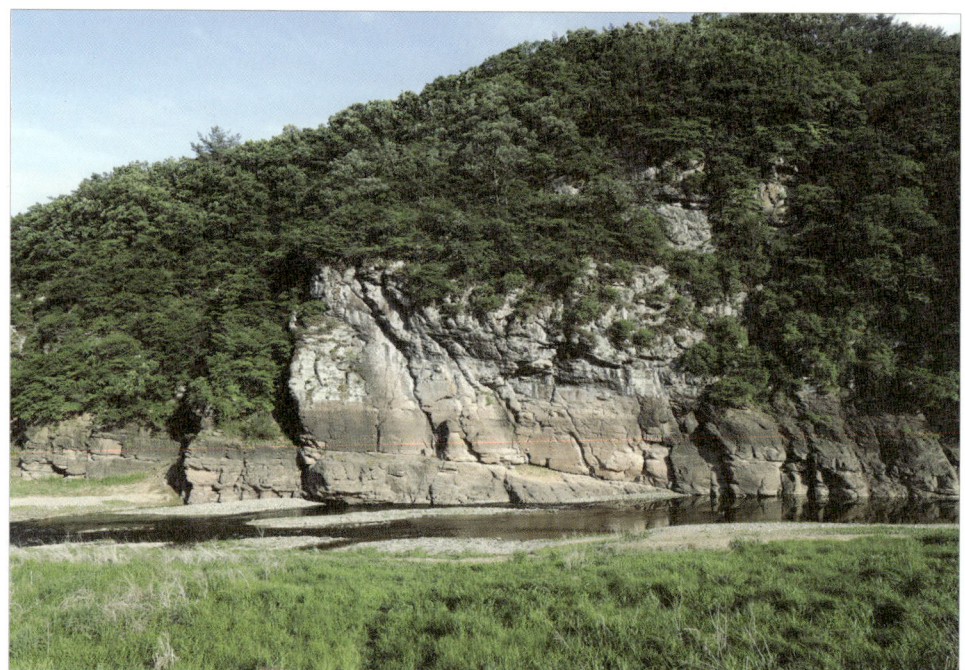

Photo 10. A distant view of the Bangudae Petroglyphs

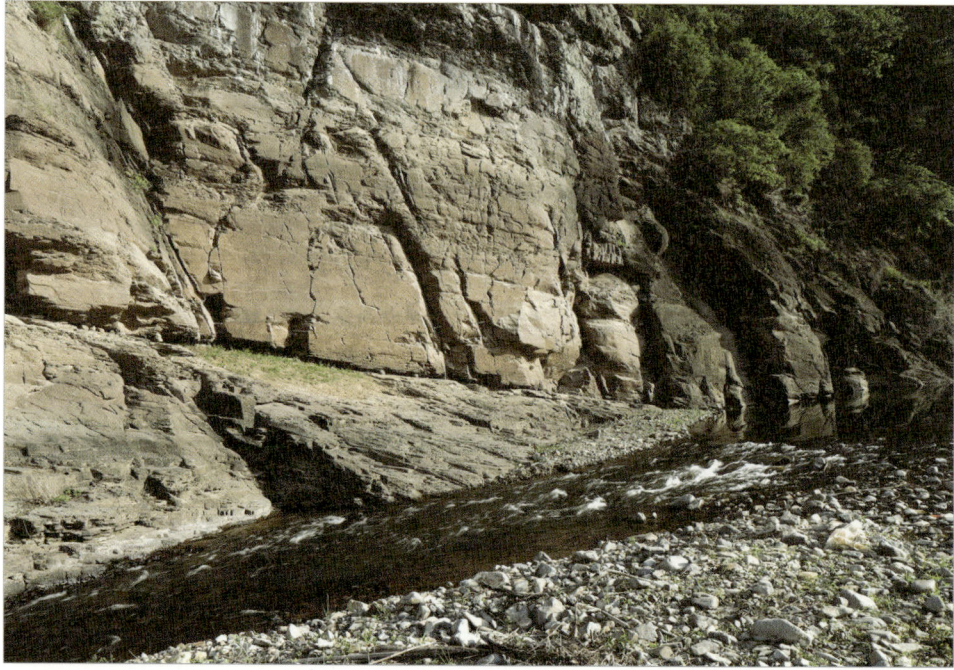

Photo 11. A distant view of the Bangudae Petroglyphs

The Bangudae Petroglyphs in Ulsan

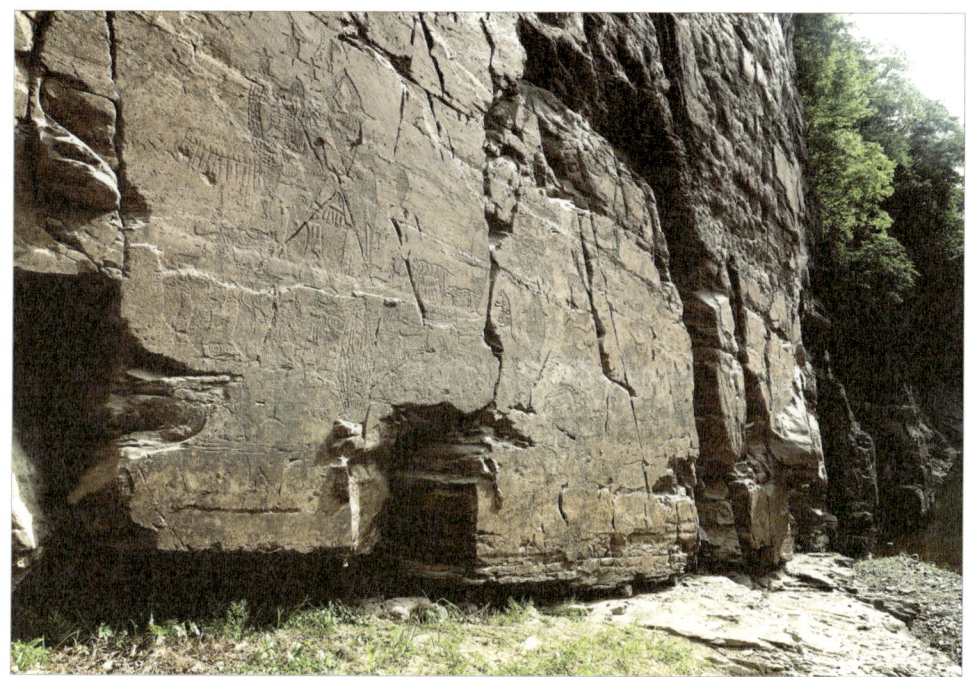

Photo 12. A complete view of surface Ⅰ (east→west)

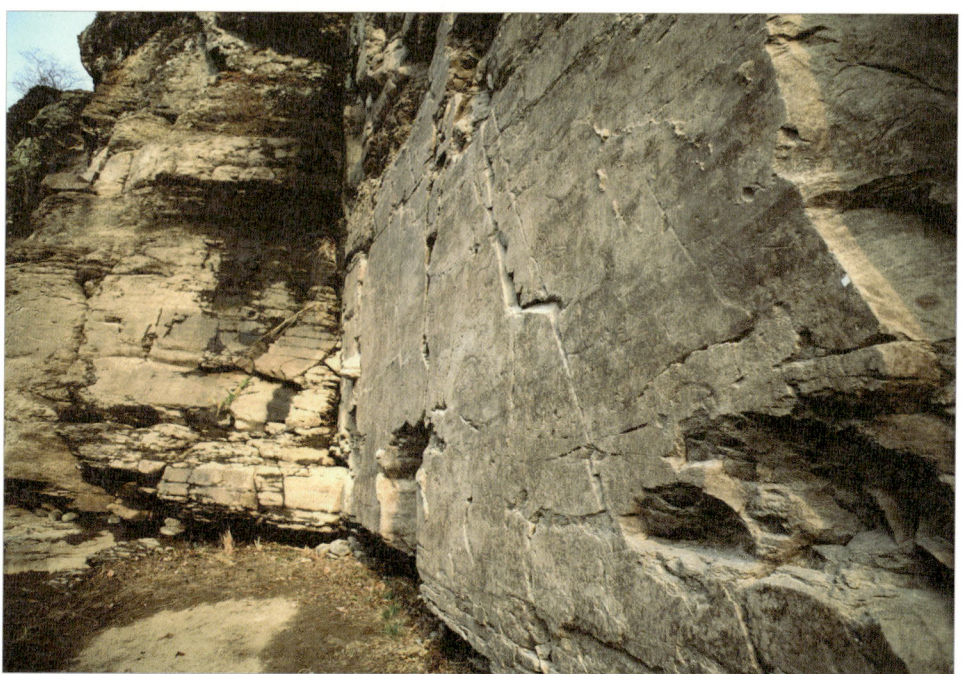

Photo 13. A complete view of surface Ⅰ, Ⅱ (west→east)

Appendix

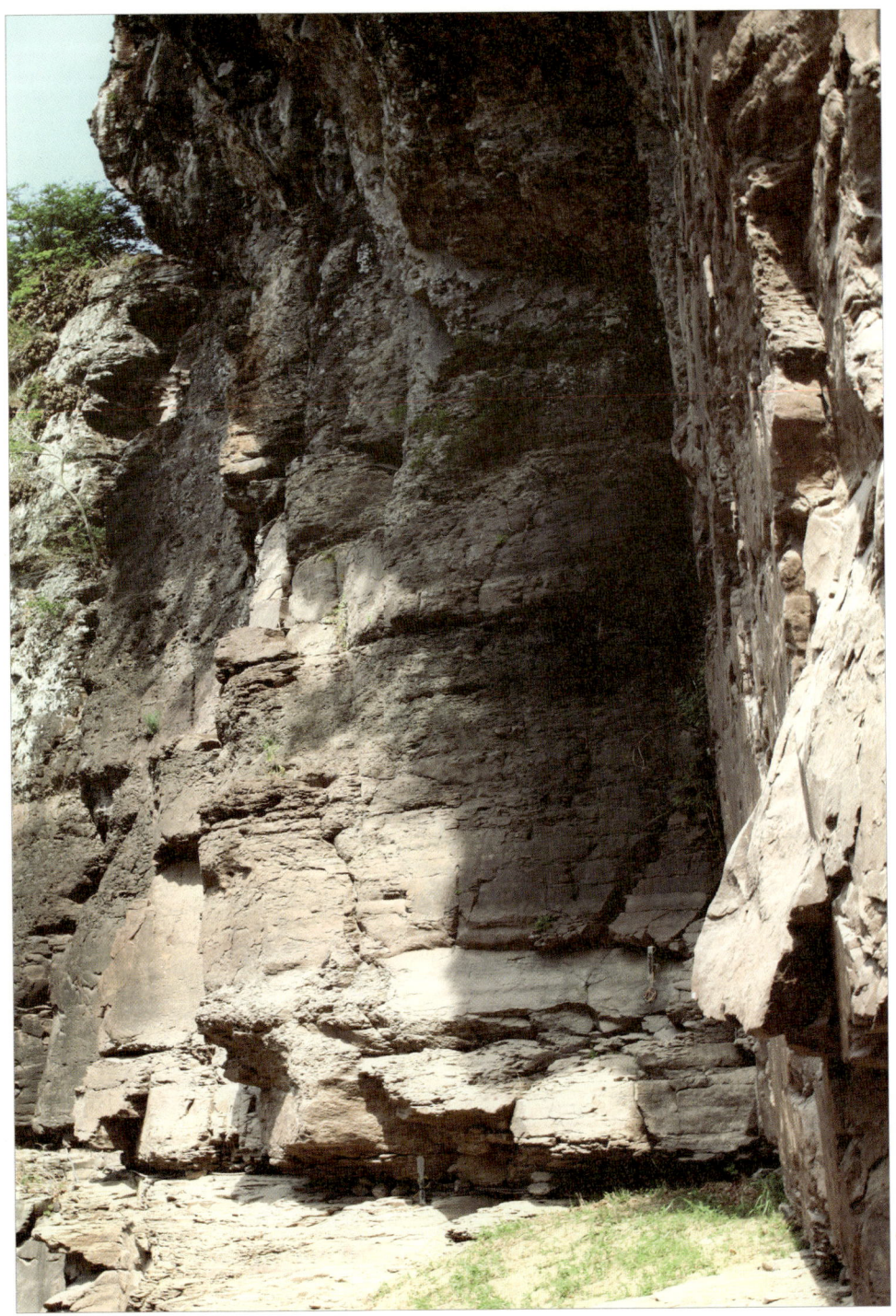

Photo 14. A complete view of surface II, IV

The Bangudae Petroglyphs in Ulsan

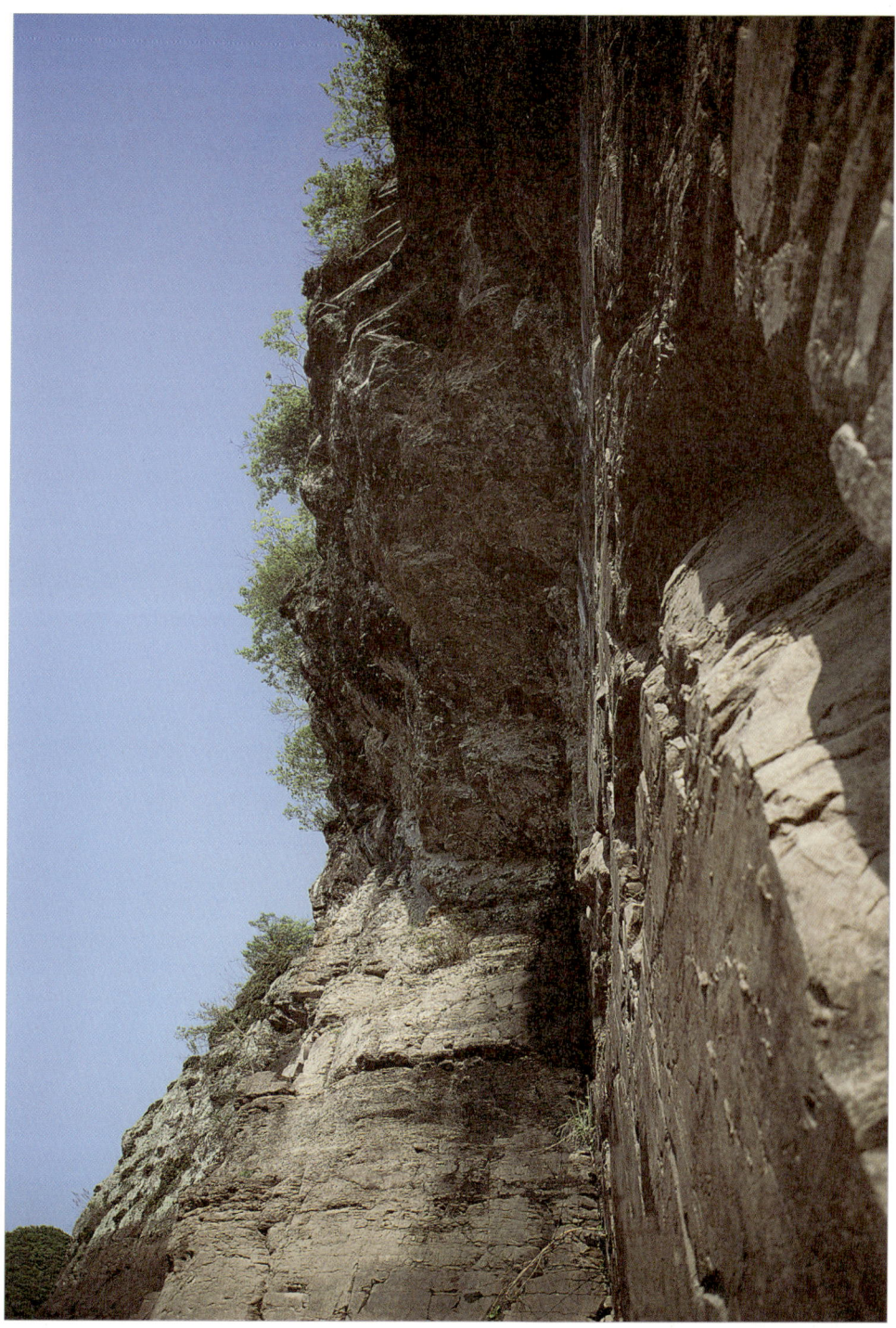

Photo 15. The upper part of the Bangudae Petroglyphs

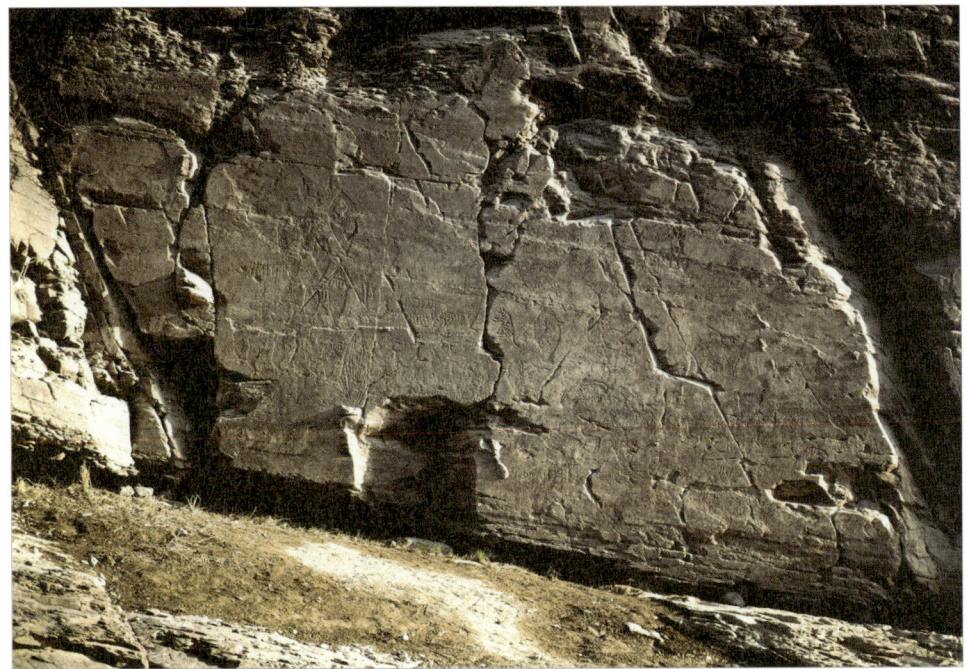

Photo 16. A complete view of surface Ⅰ

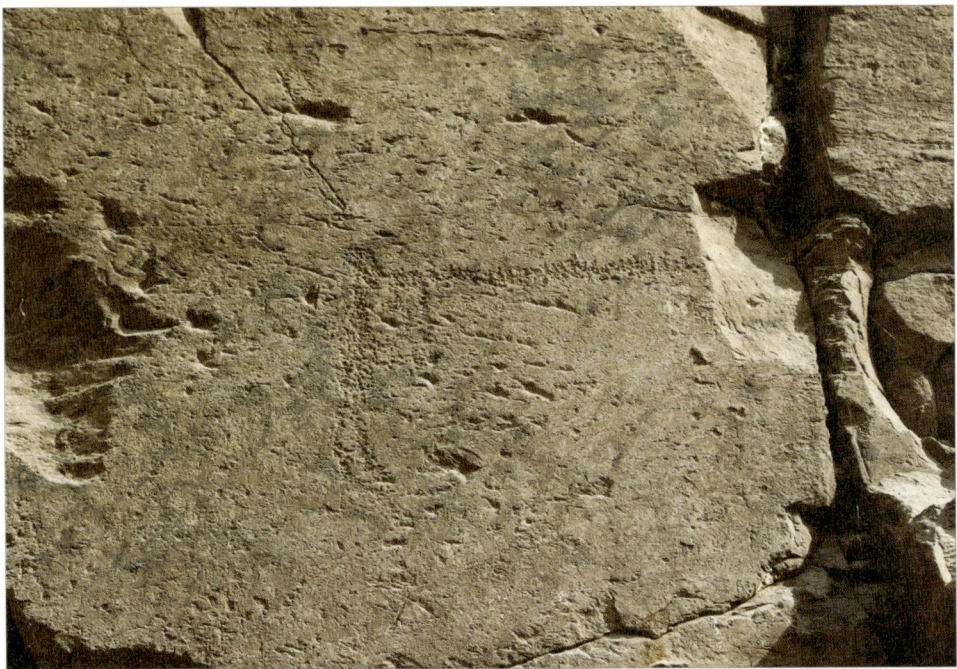

Photo 17. Surface Ⅰ–A, humans (anthromorphes)

The Bangudae Petroglyphs in Ulsan

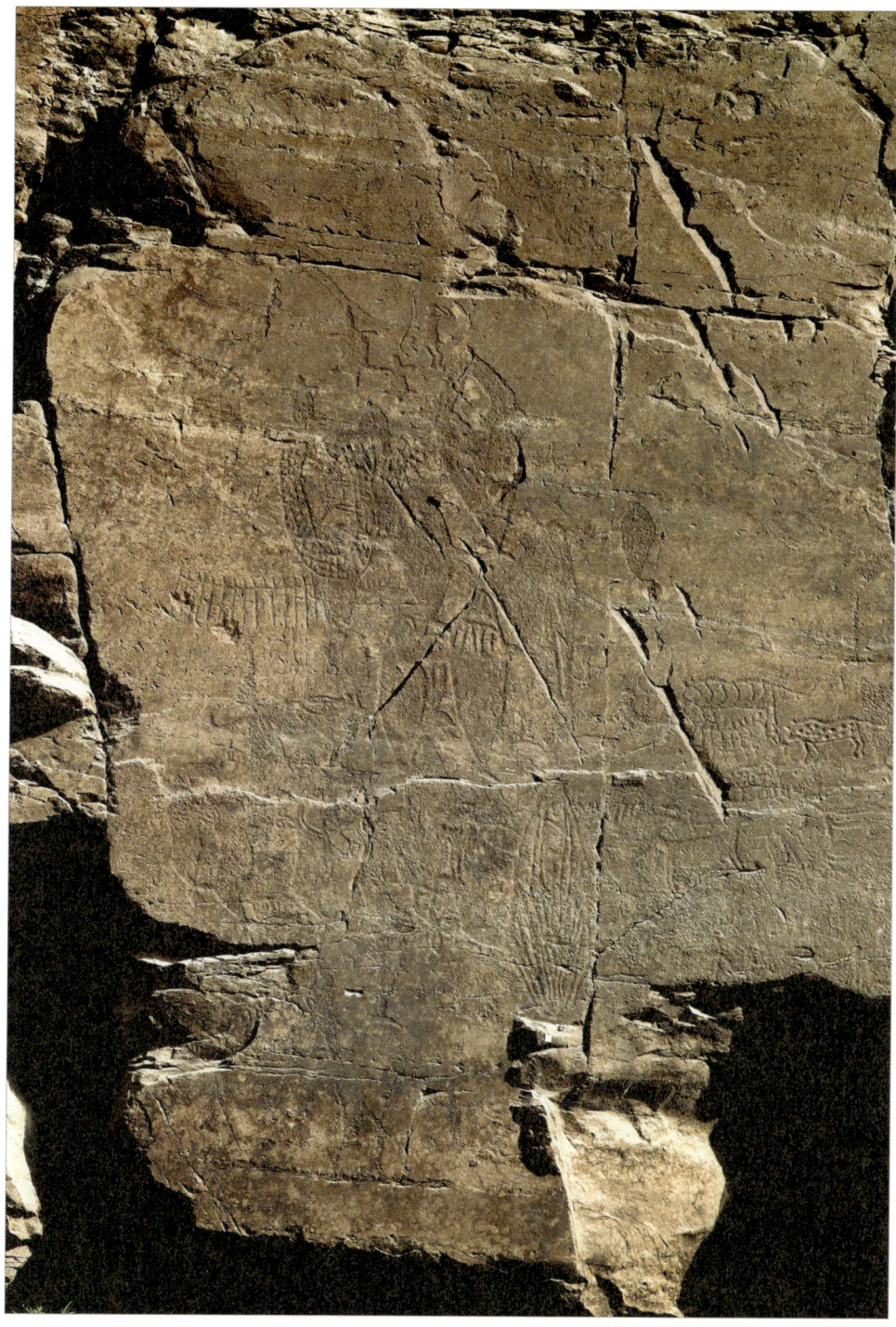

Photo 18. Area of surface I (east)

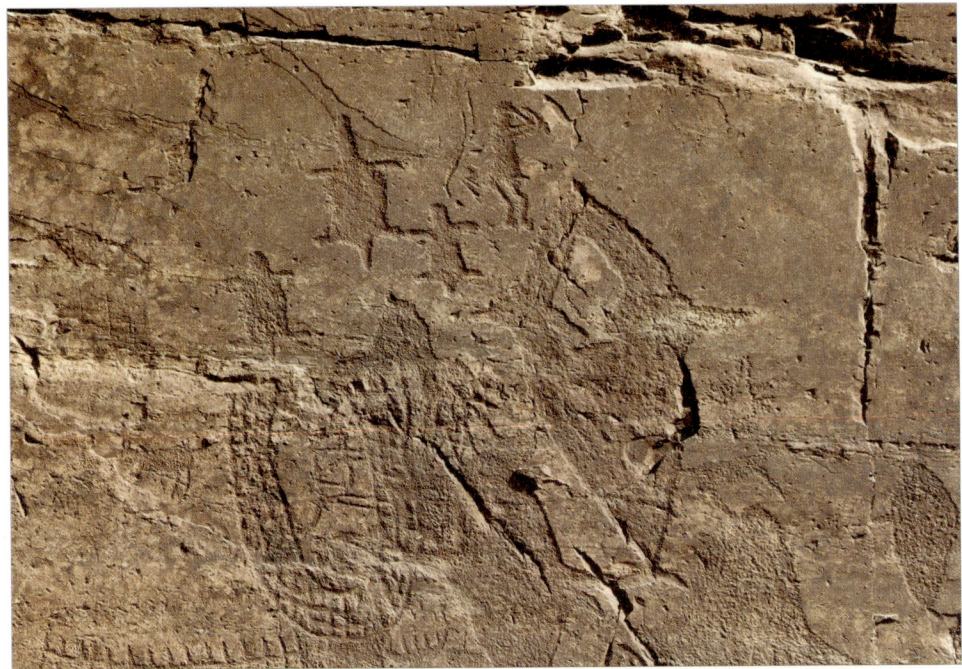

Photo 19. Area of surface I–B (top)

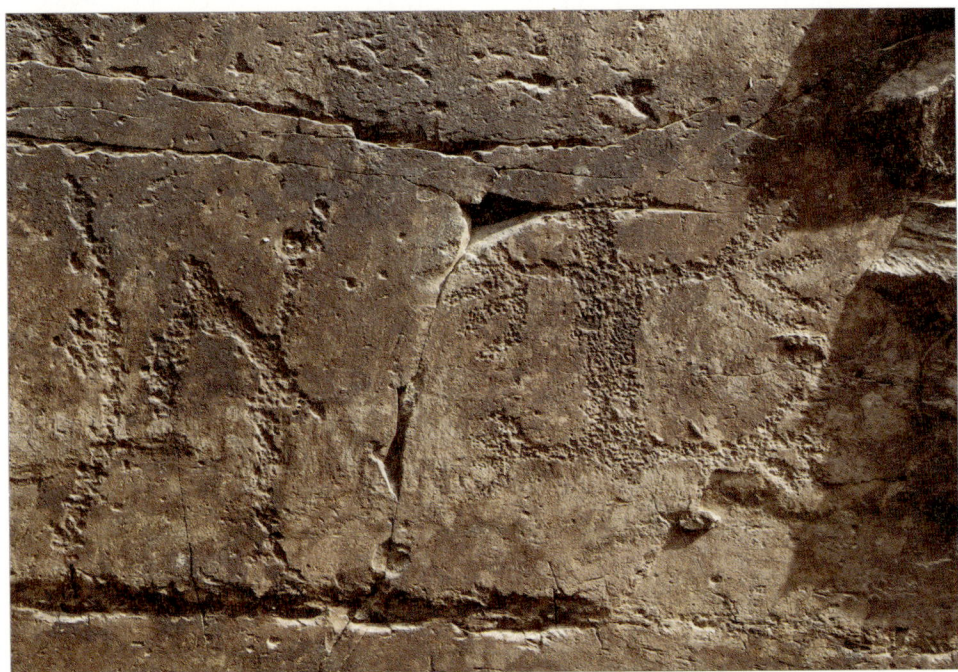

Photo 20. Surface I–B, humans (anthromorphes) and unidentified (unidentified figures)

The Bangudae Petroglyphs in Ulsan

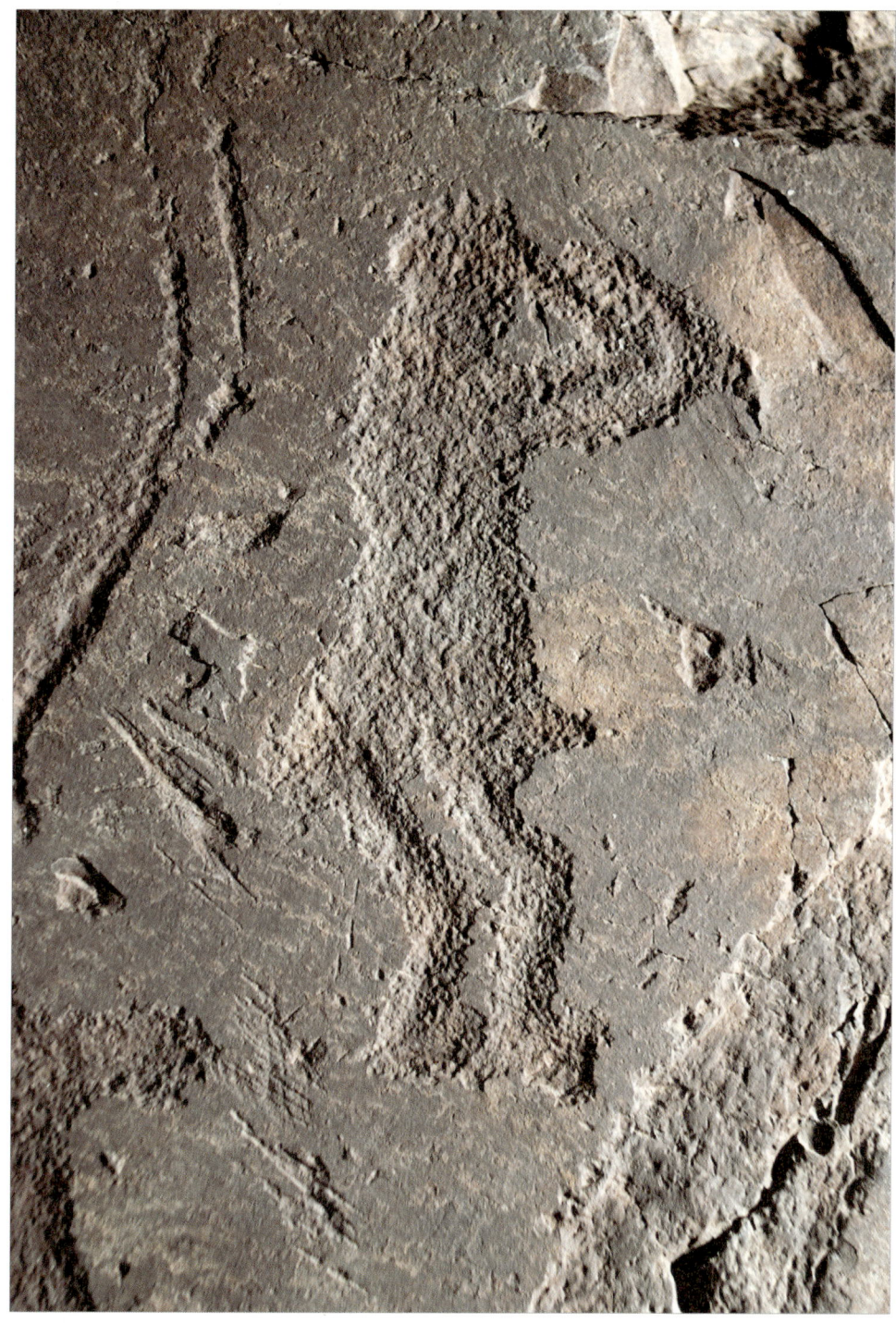

Photo 21. Surface I–B, humans (anthromorphes)

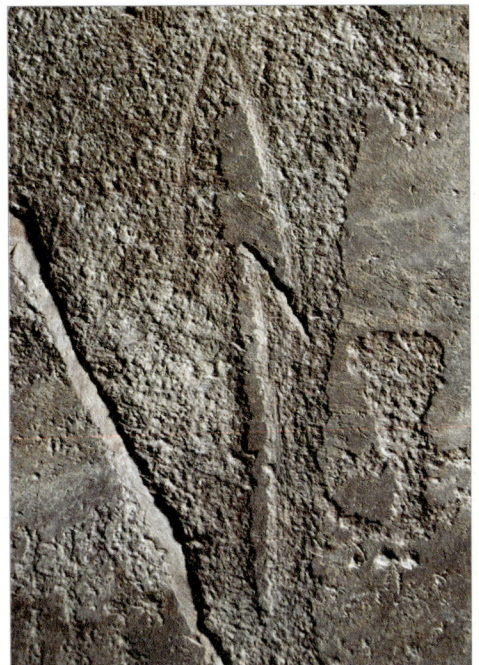

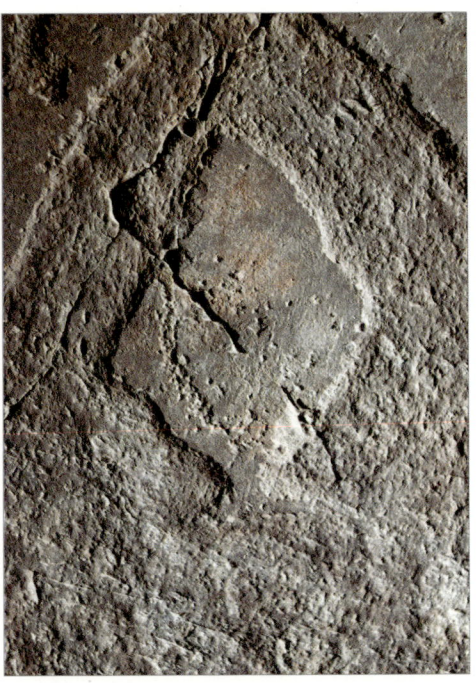

Photo 22. Surface I–B, harpoons (fish spear) and floats (float)

Photo 23. Surface I–B, cetacean (cetacea)

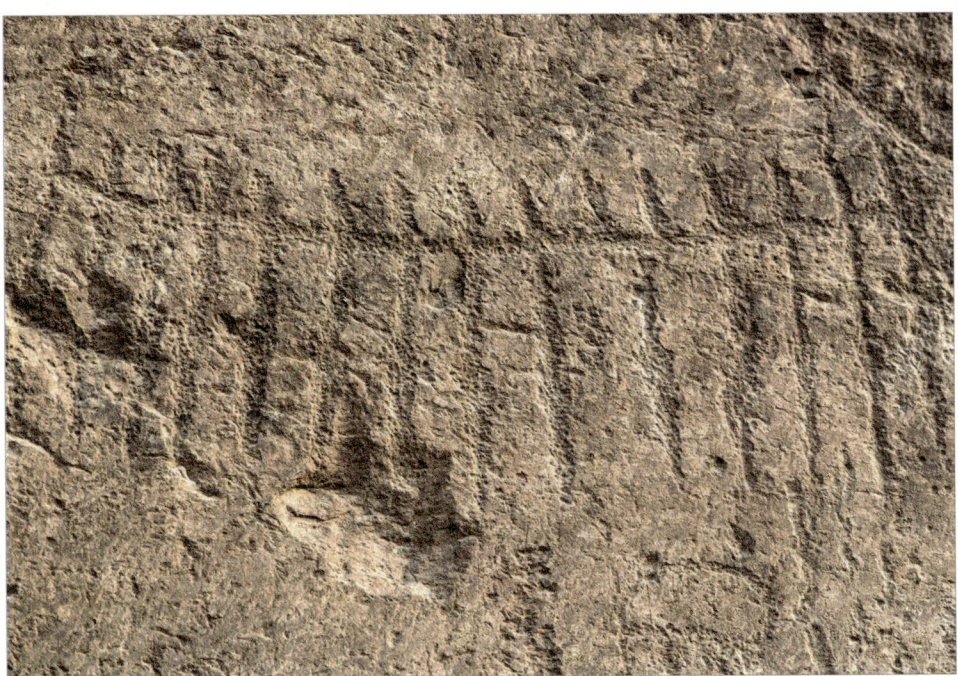

Photo 24. Surface I–B, weir (fish trap)

The Bangudae Petroglyphs in Ulsan

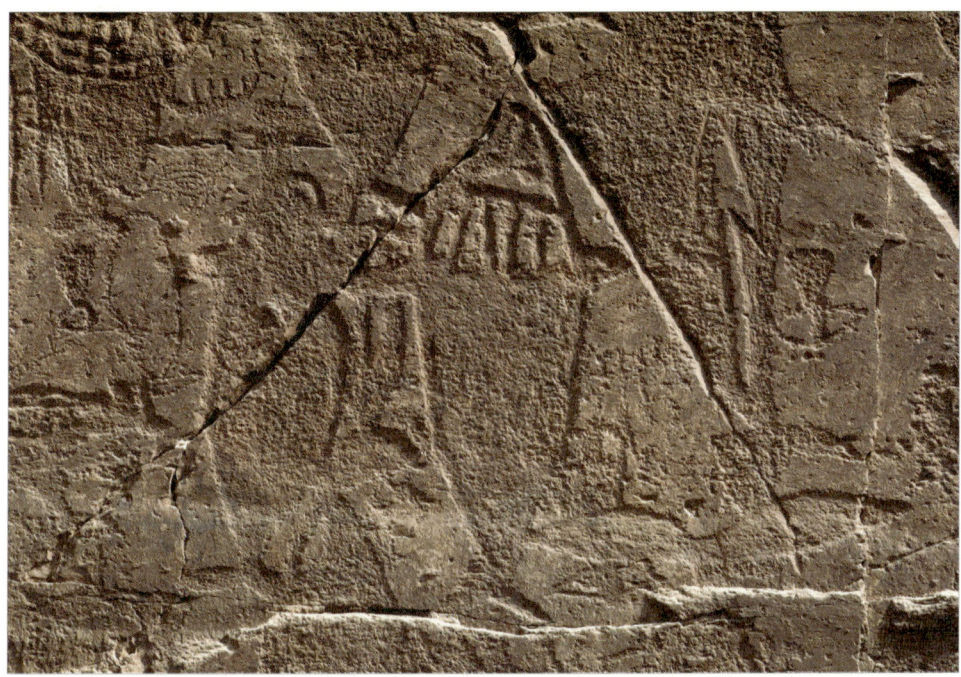

Photo 25. Surface I–B, cetacean (cetacea)

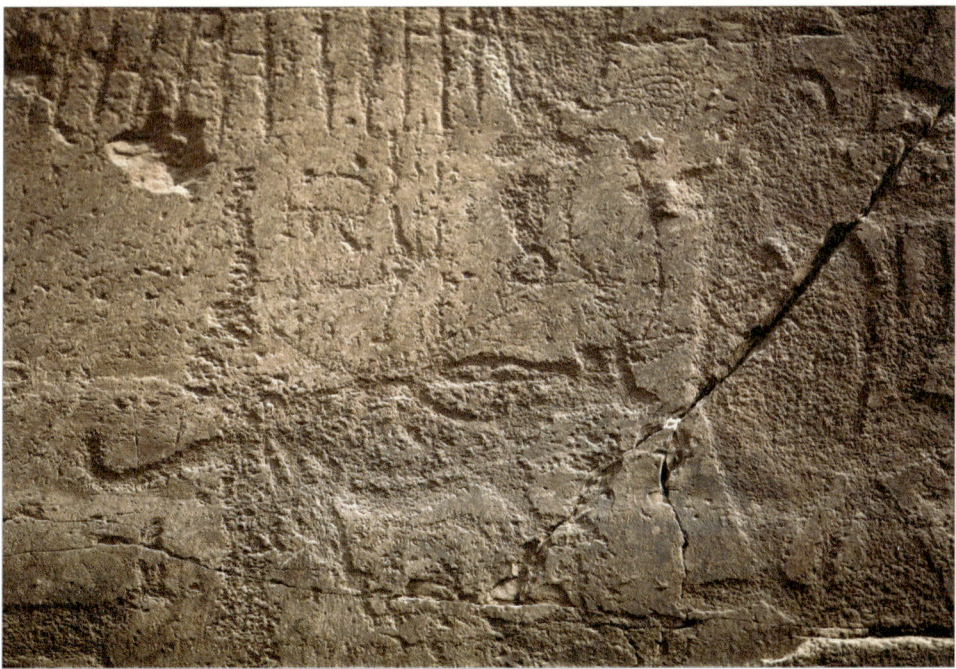

Photo 26. Surface I–B, whaling ships; cetacean (cetacea); tiger (panthera tigris)

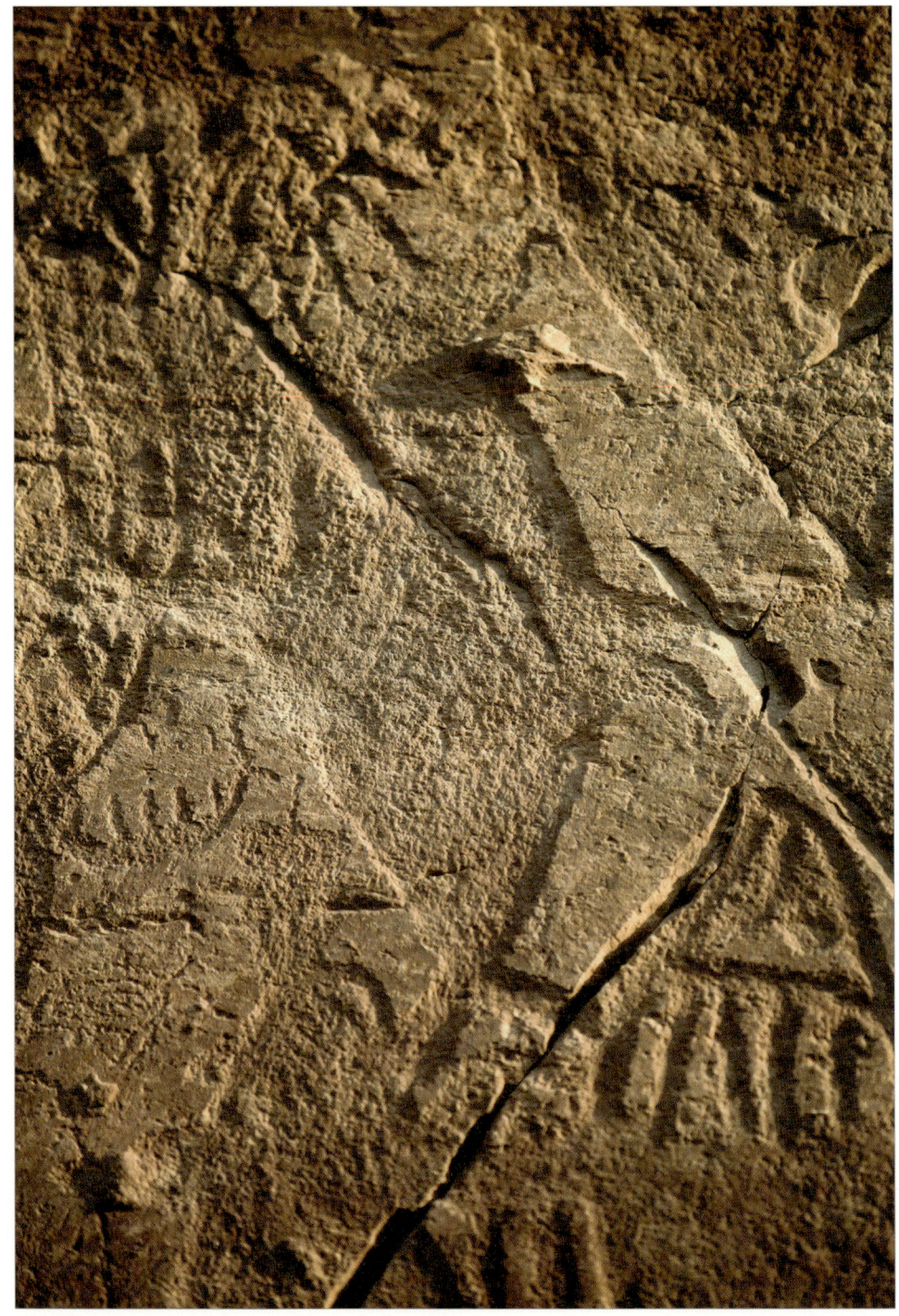

Photo 27. Surface I–B, whaling ships and cetaceans (cetacea)

The Bangudae Petroglyphs in Ulsan

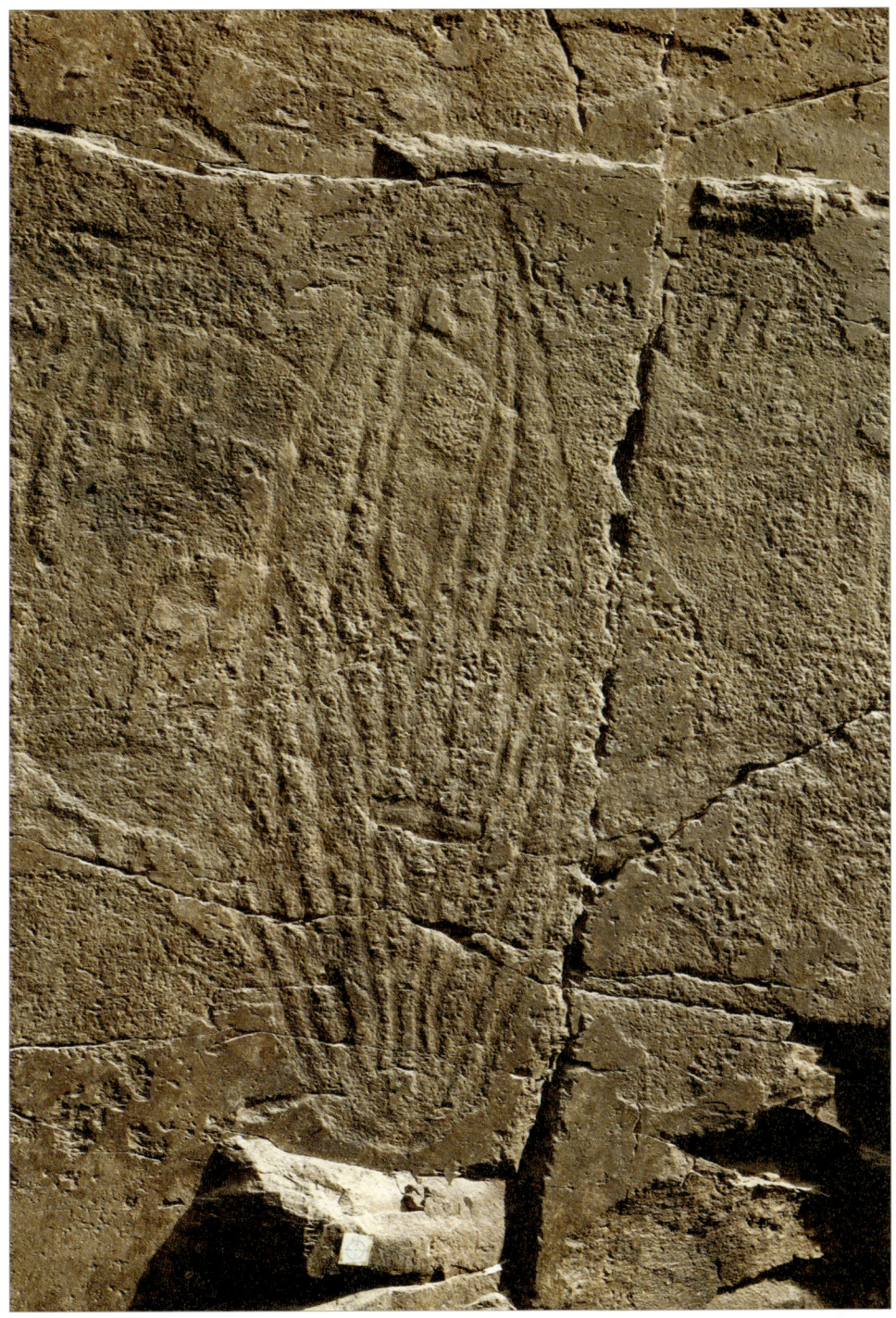

Photo 28. Surface I–B, cetaceans (cetacea)

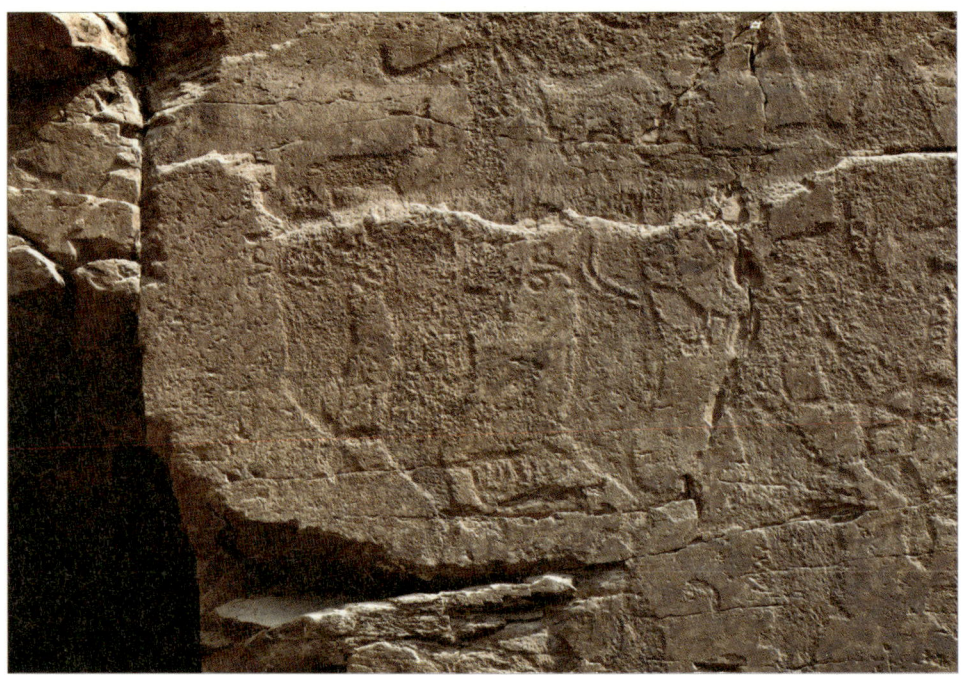

Photo 29. Surface I–B, cetaceans (cetacea)

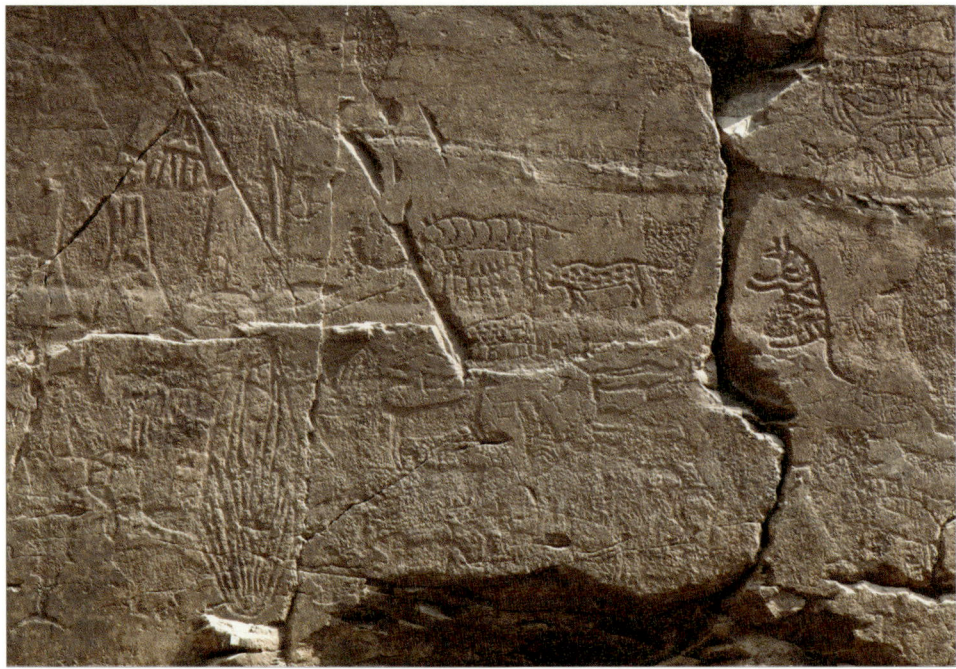

Photo 30. *Left*, Bottom part of surface I–B; *right*, upper part of surface I–C

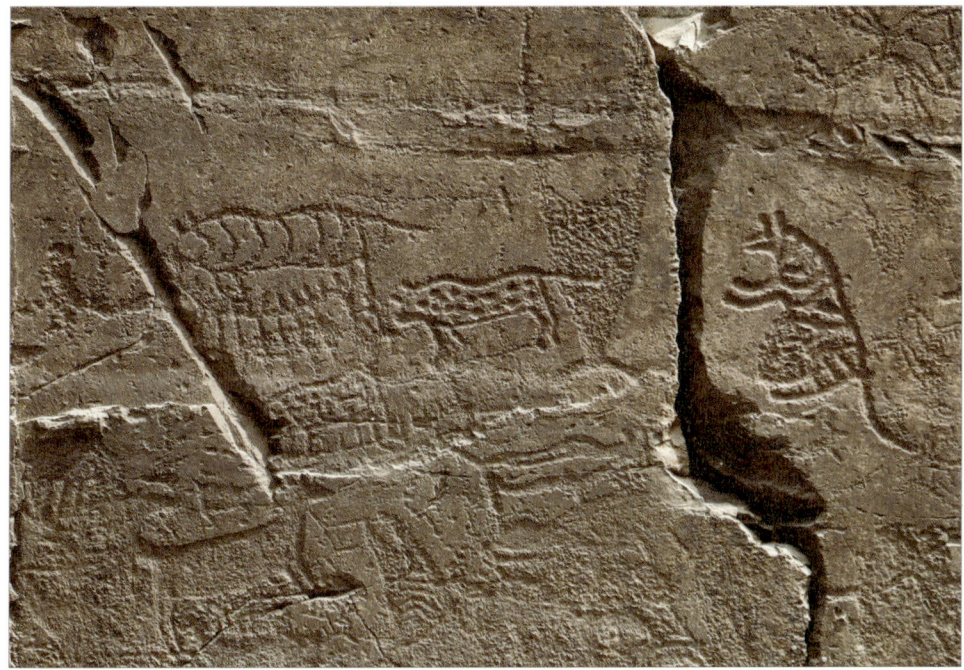

Photo 31. Area of surface I–C

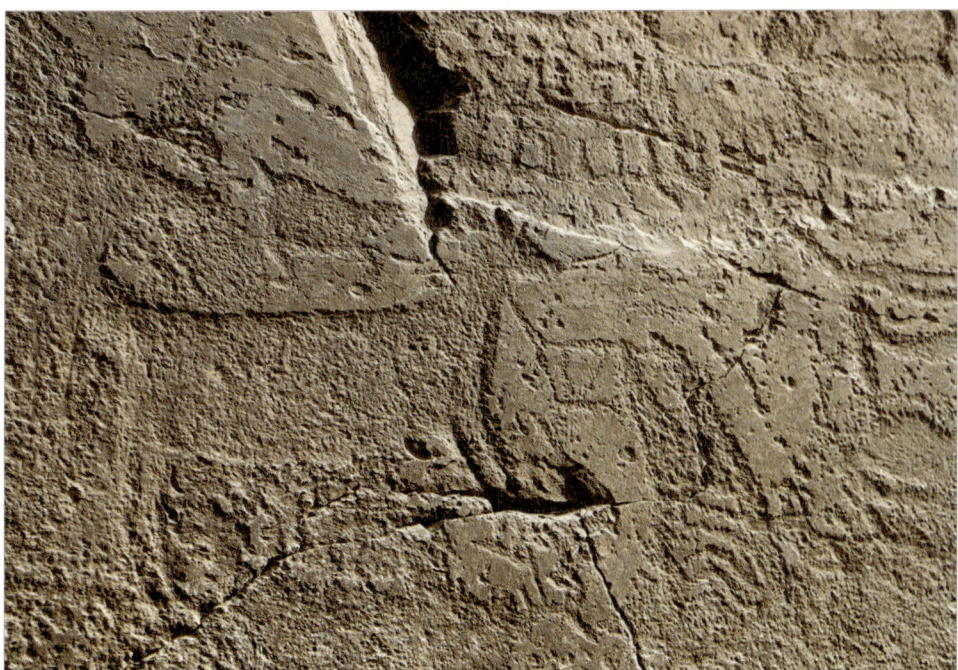

Photo 32. Surface I–C, deer (cervus nippon)

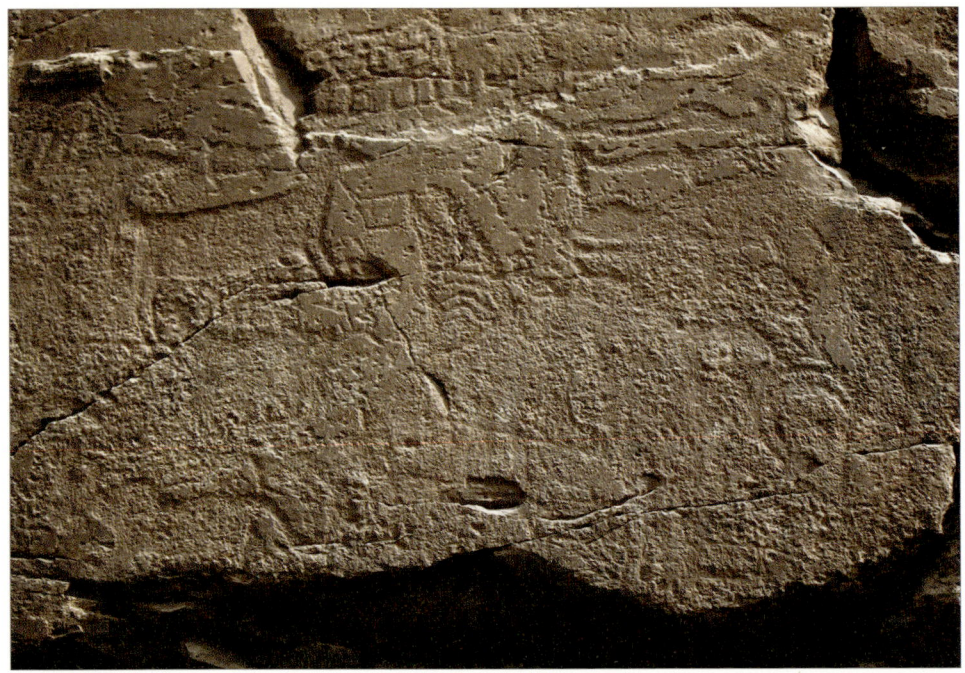

Photo 33. Surface I–C, humans (anthromorphes) and animals (zoomorphes)

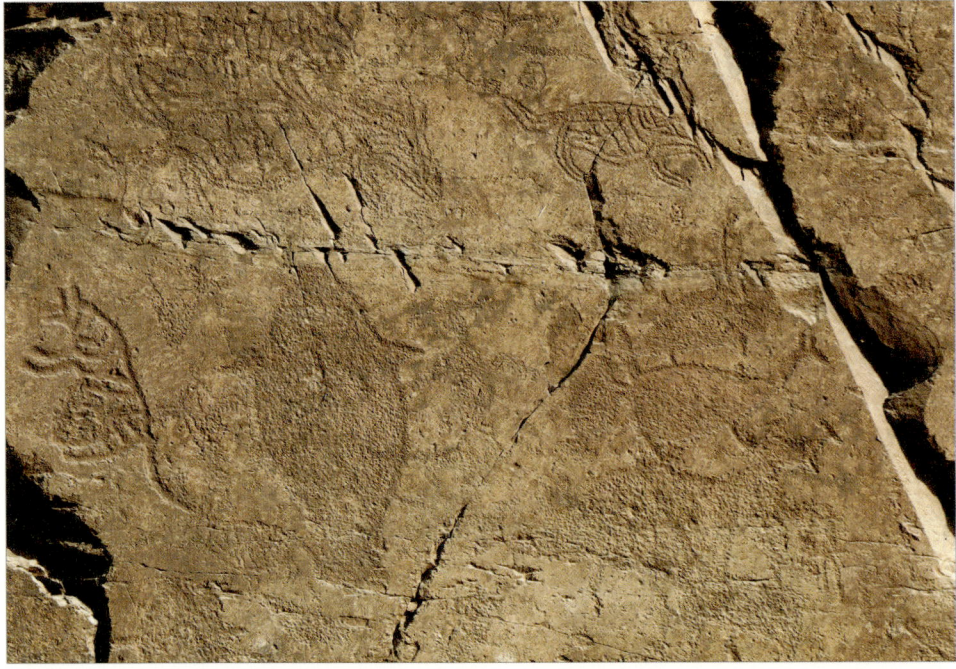

Photo 34. Surface I–D, tigers (panthera tigris); cetacean (cetacea); cormorants (phalacrocorax capillatus)

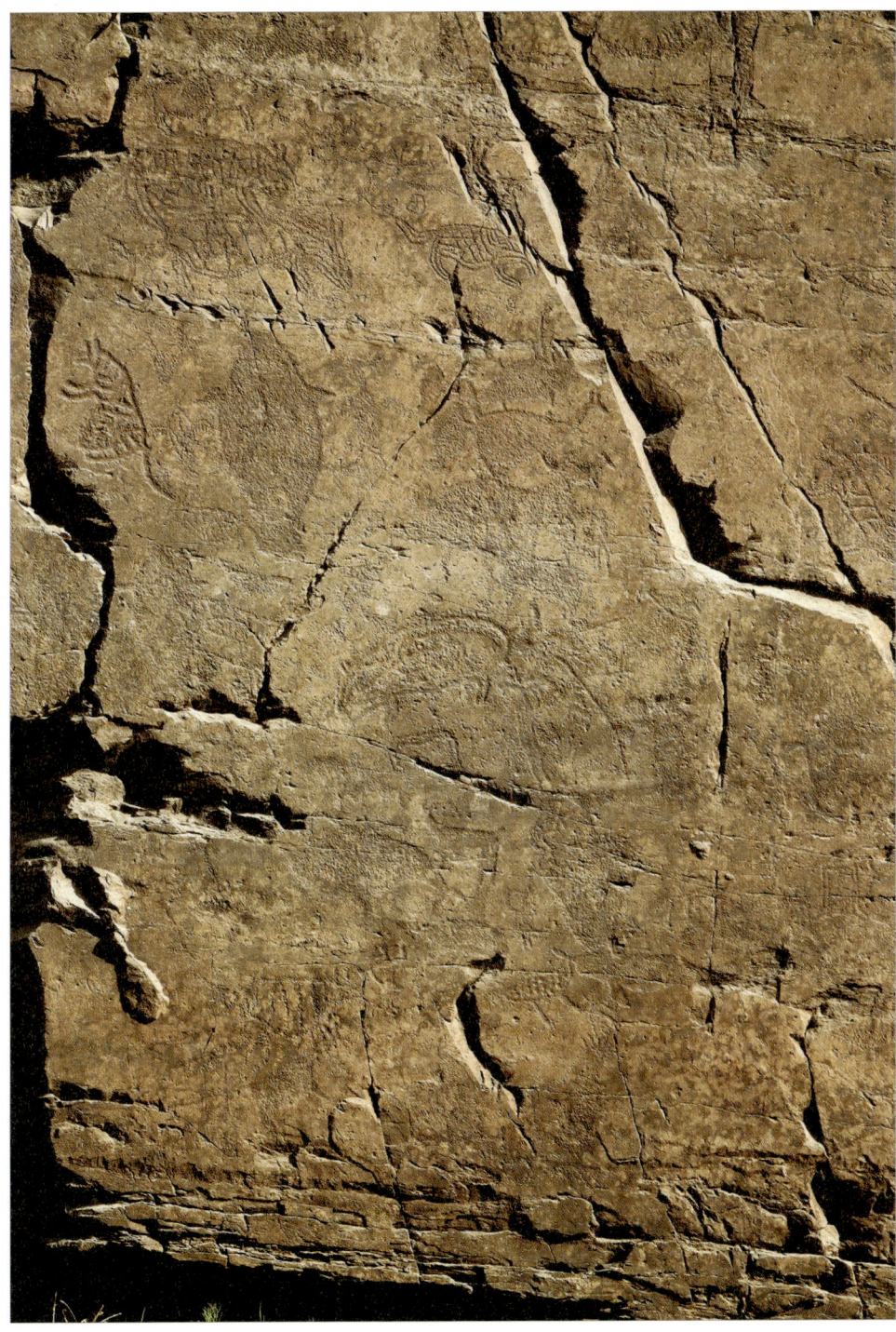

Photo 35. A front view of surface I–D

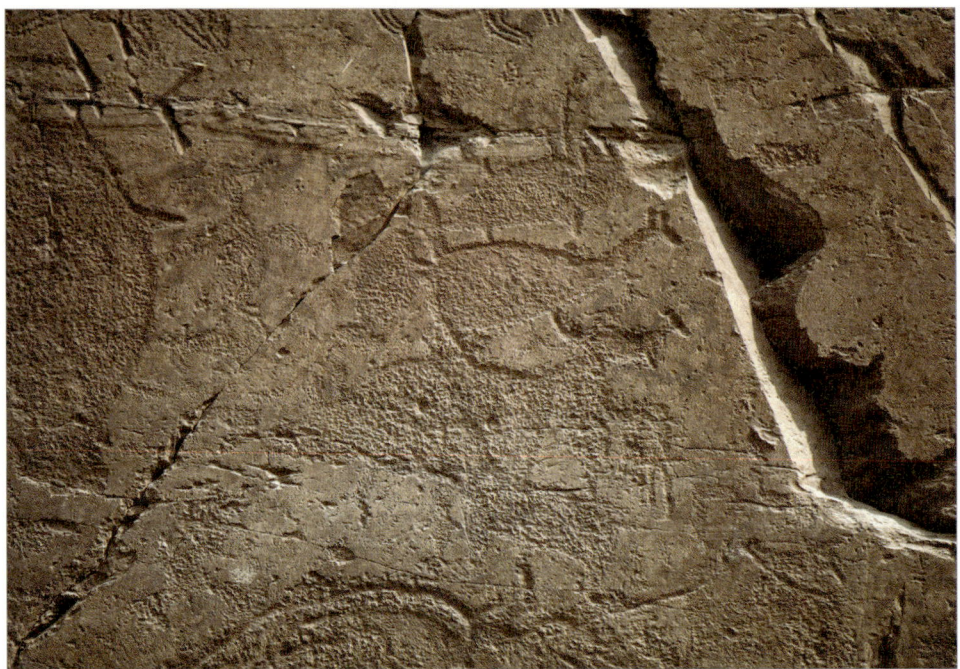

Photo 36. Surface I–D, hunters and animals (zoomorphes)

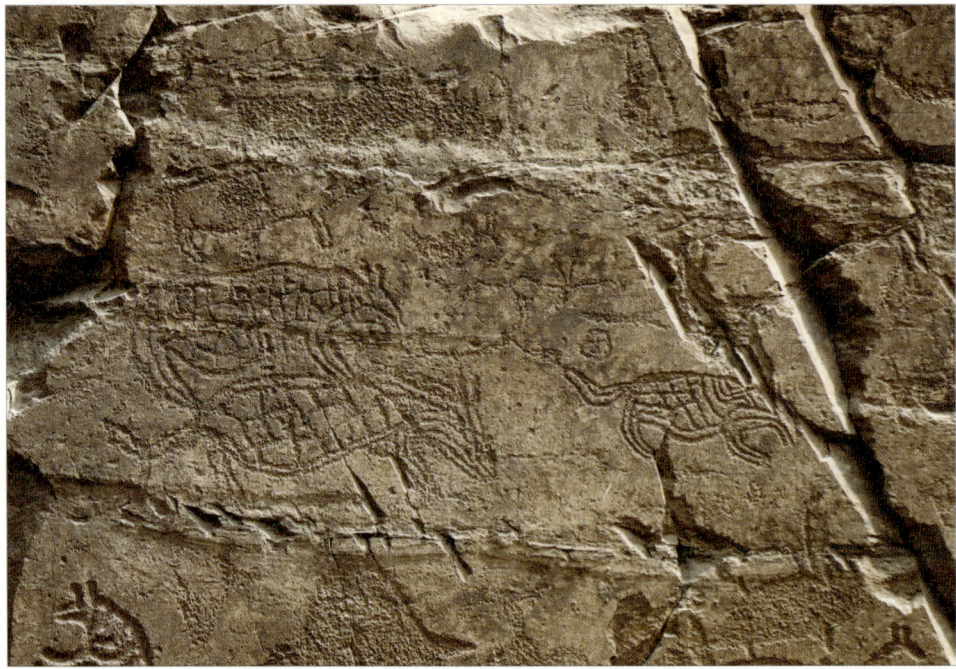

Photo 37. Surface I–D, human faces and animals (zoomorphes)

The Bangudae Petroglyphs in Ulsan

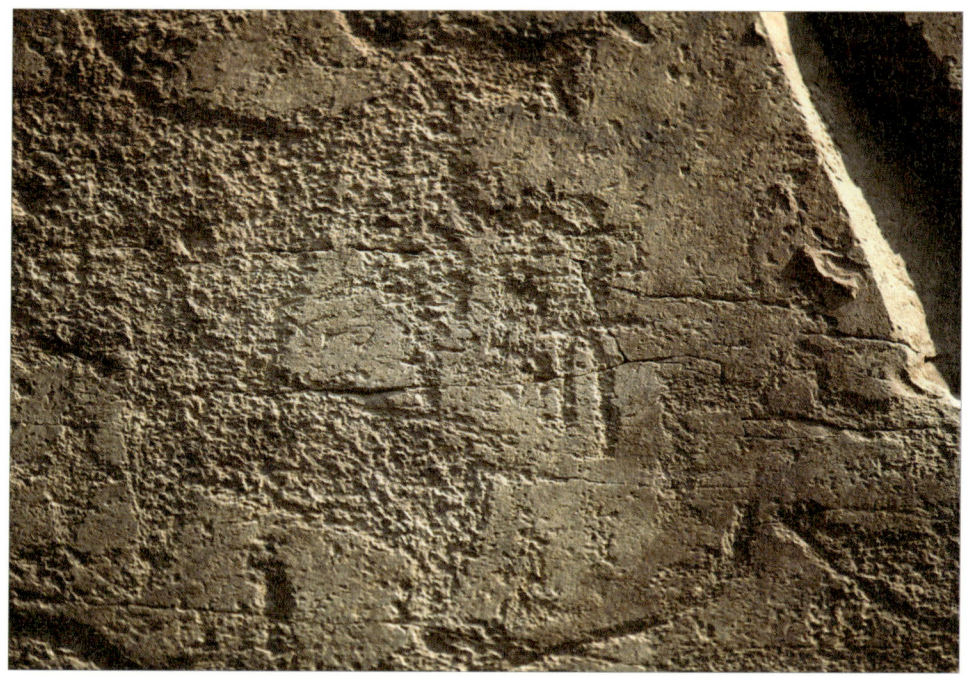

Photo 38. Surface I–D, humans (anthromorphes) and animals (zoomorphes)

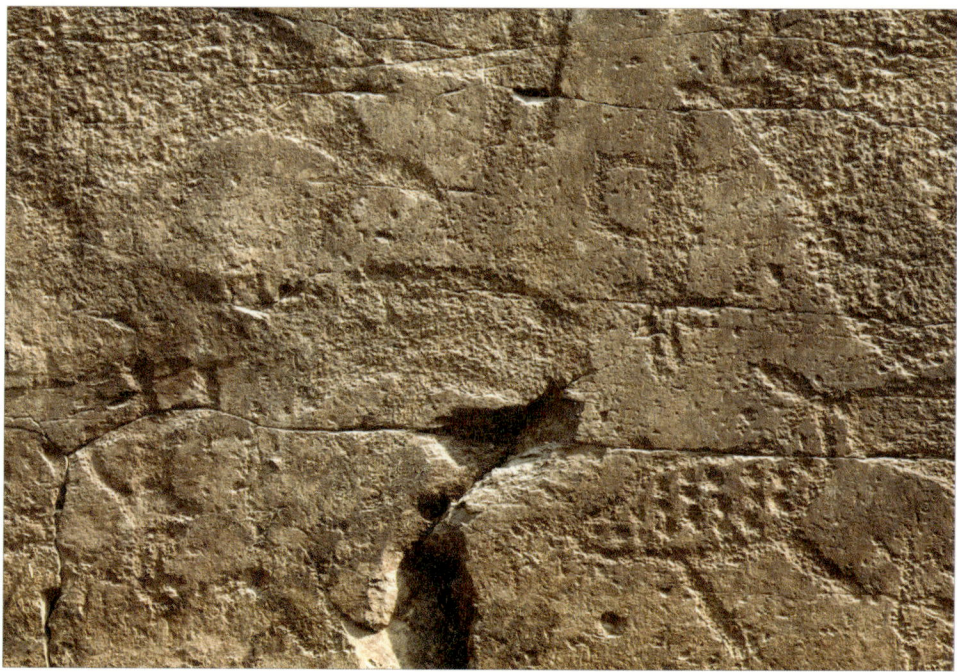

Photo 39. Surface I–D, humans (anthromorphes) and animals (zoomorphes)

Appendix

137

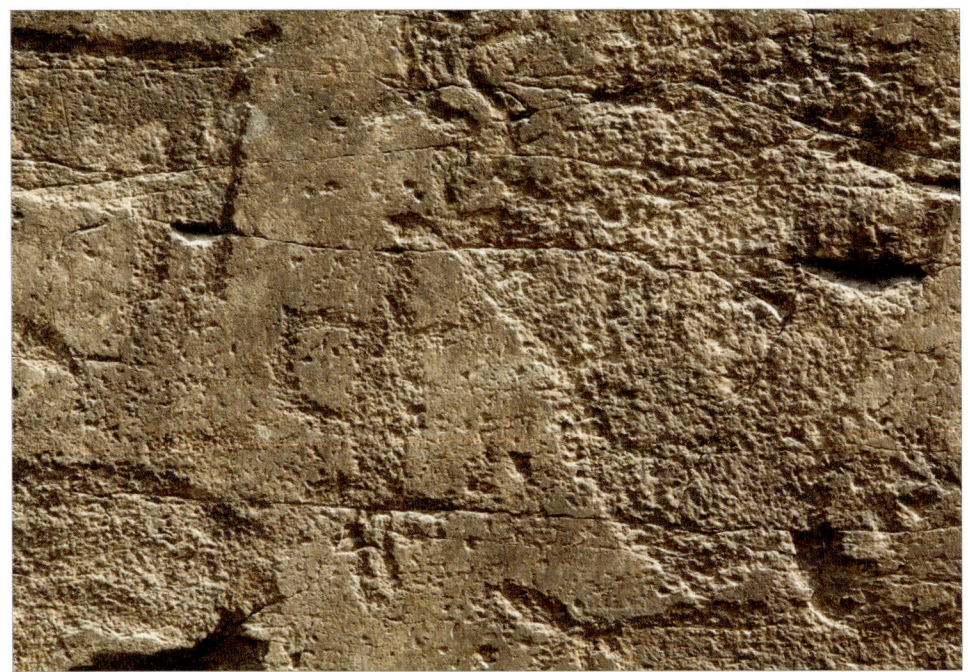

Photo 40. Surface I–D, humans (anthromorphes) and animals (zoomorphes)

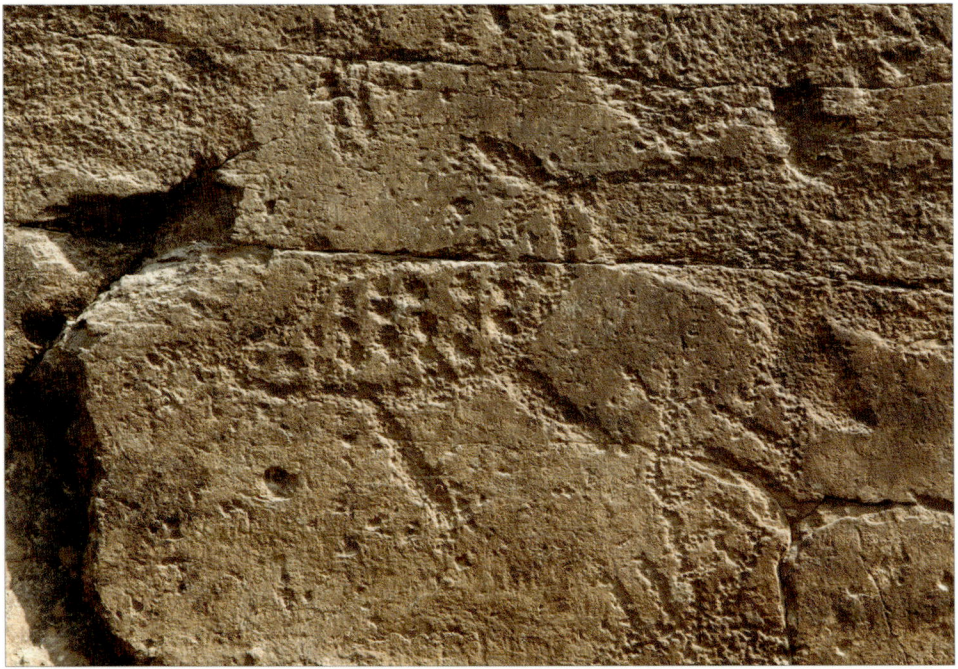

Photo 41. Surface I–D, unidentified animals

The Bangudae Petroglyphs in Ulsan

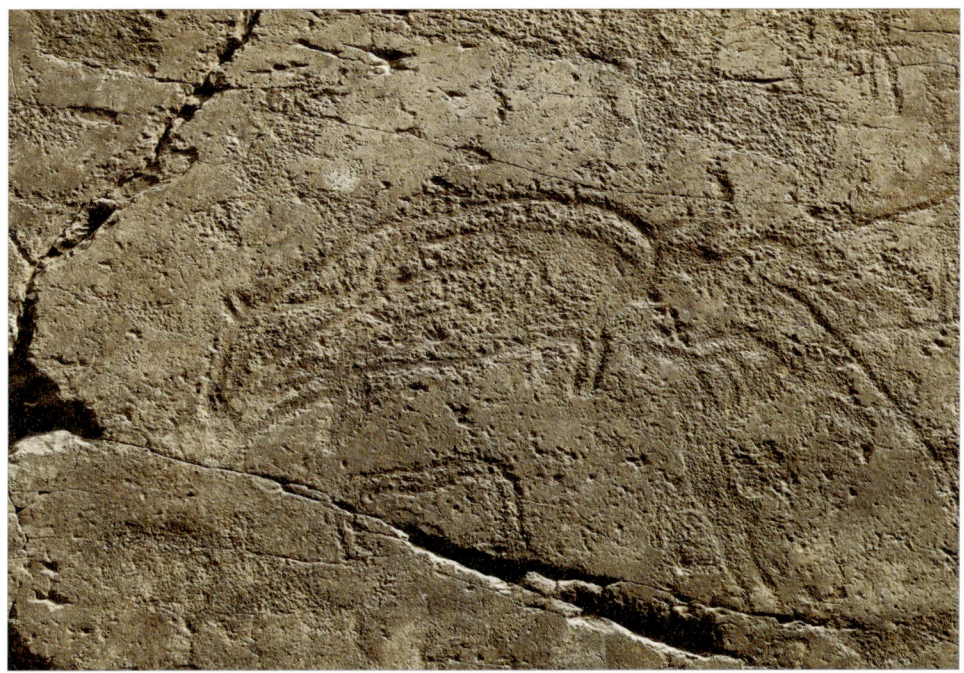

Photo 42. Surface I–D, humans (anthromorphes) and wild boars (sus scrofa)

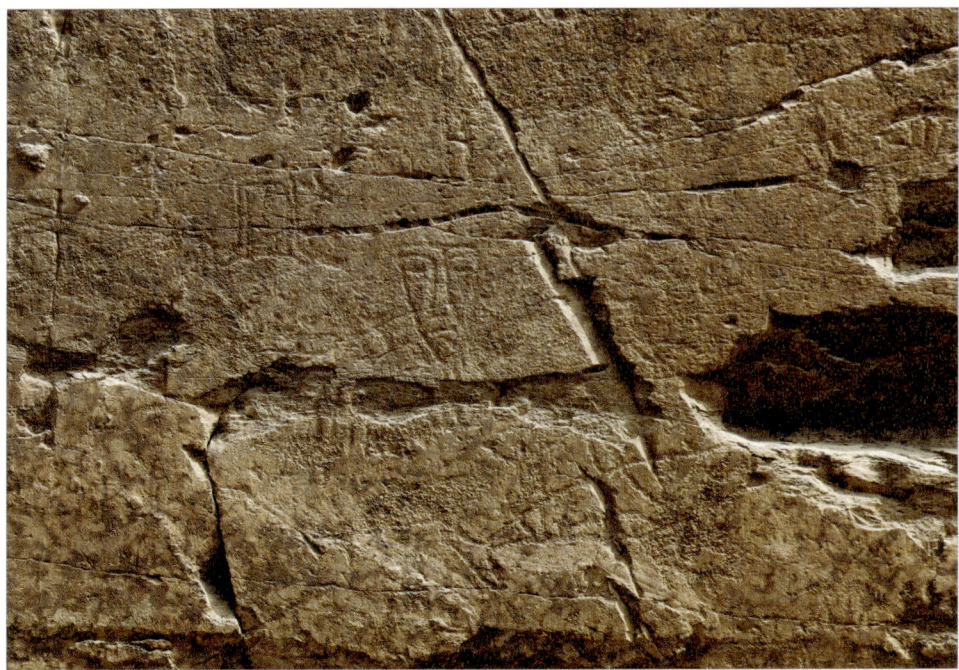

Photo 43. Area of surface I–D (bottom)

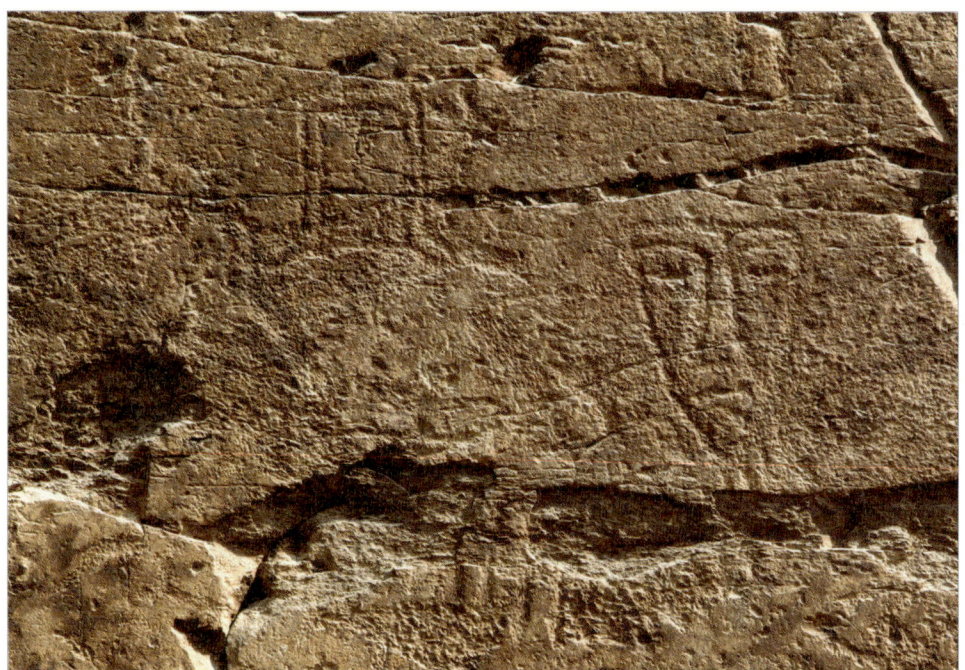

Photo 44. Surface I–D, human faces and tool figures

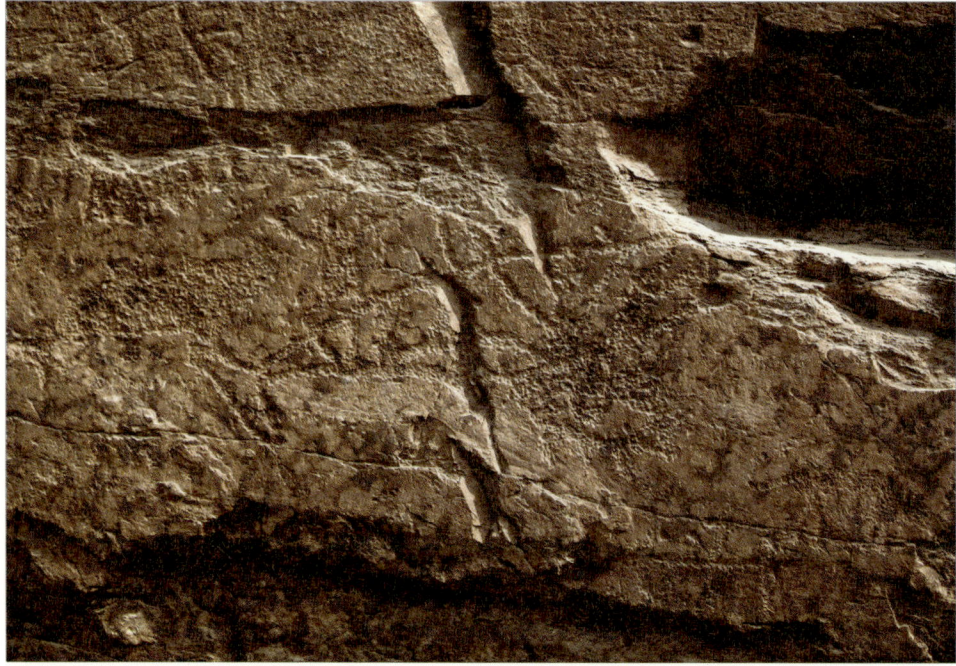

Photo 45. Surface I–D, cetacean (cetacea) and floats (float)

The Bangudae Petroglyphs in Ulsan

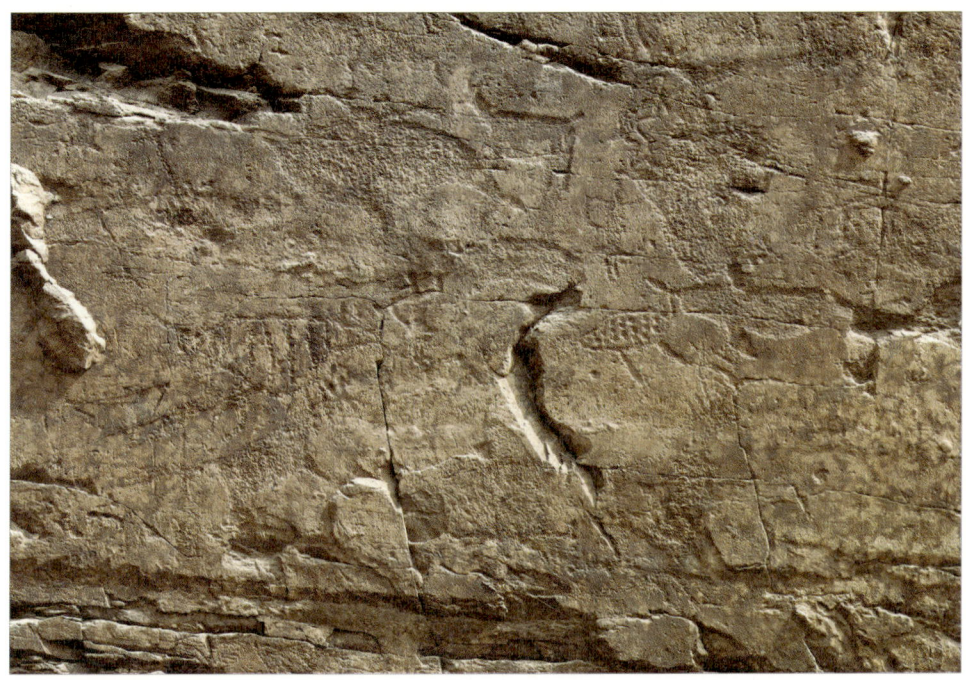

Photo 46. Bottom part of surface I–D (east)

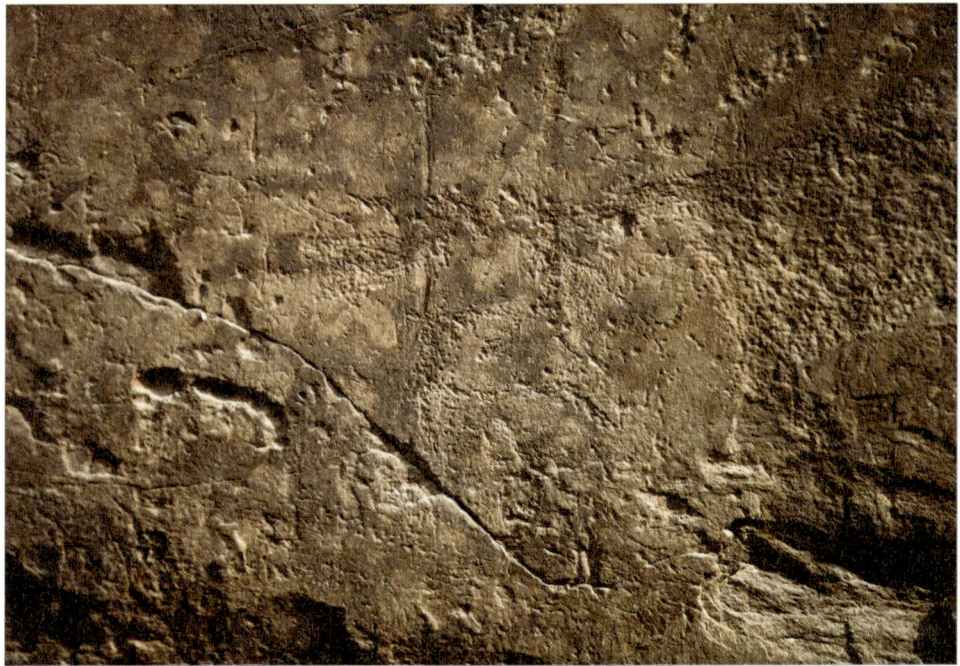

Photo 47. Surface I–D, deer (cervus nippon)

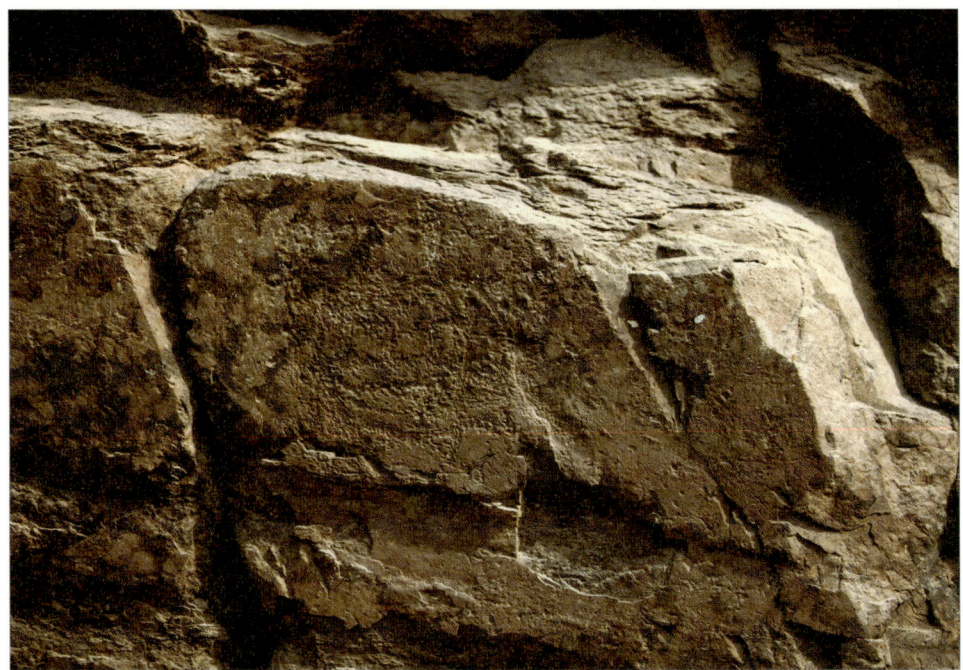

Photo 48. Surface I–D, deer (cervus nippon) and tools (tool figures)

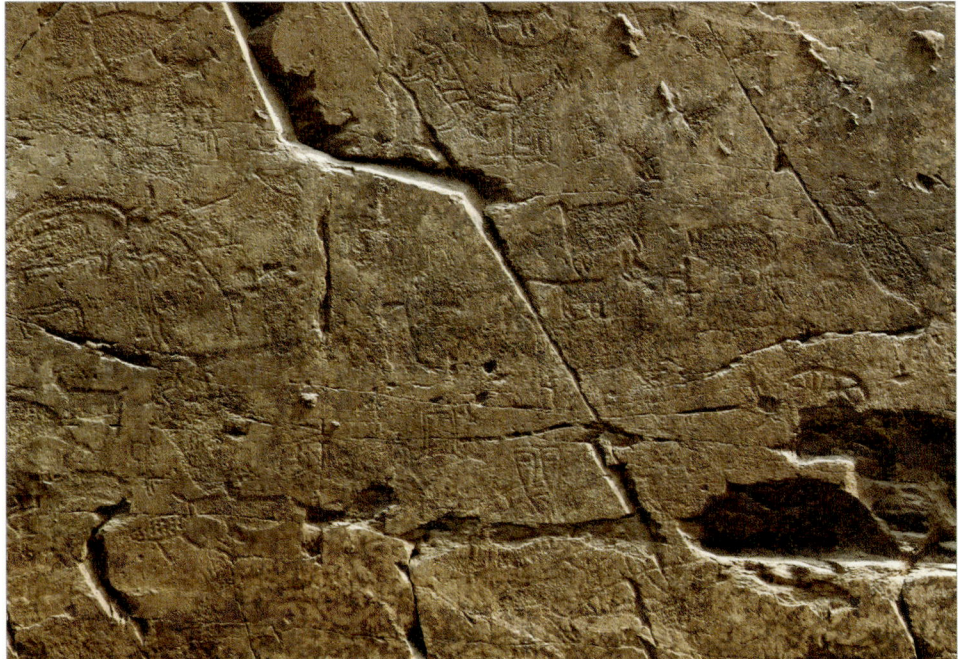

Photo 49. Area of surface I–D, E (middle)

The Bangudae Petroglyphs in Ulsan

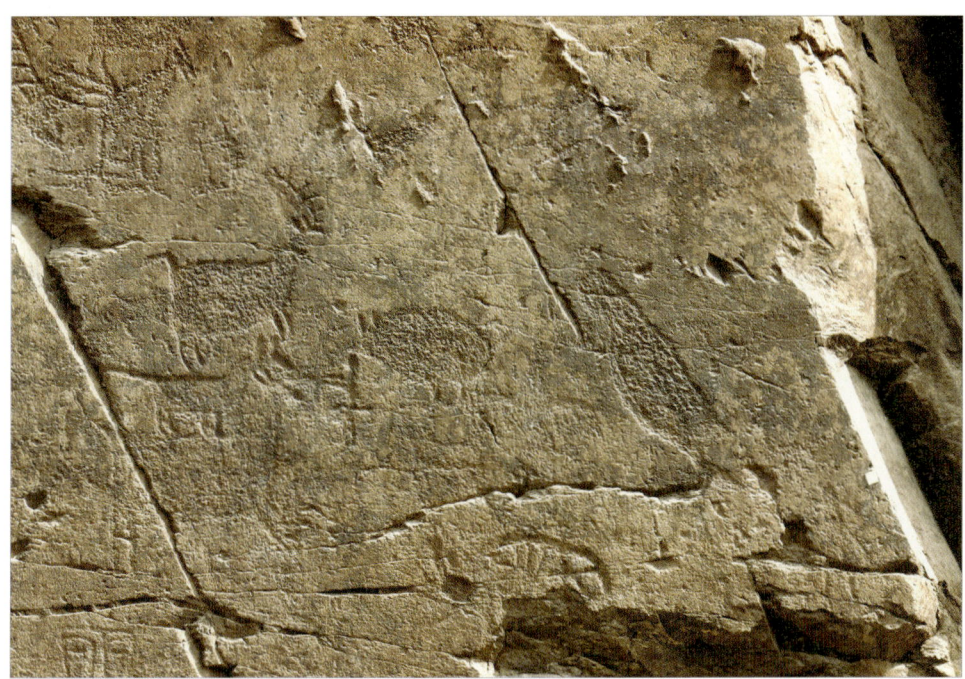

Photo 50. Area of surface I–E (west side)

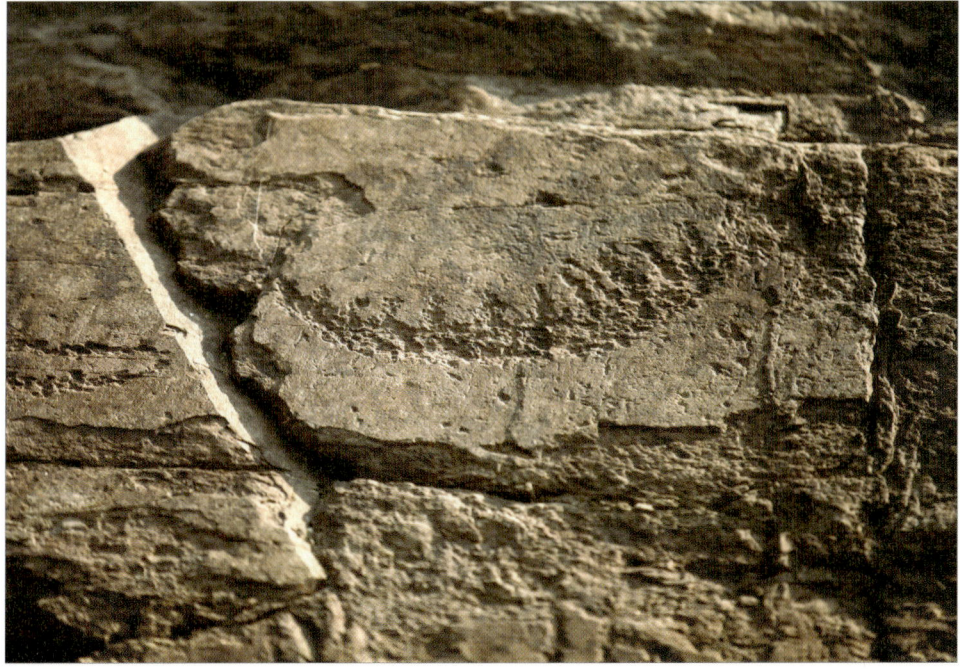

Photo 51. Surface I–E, boat

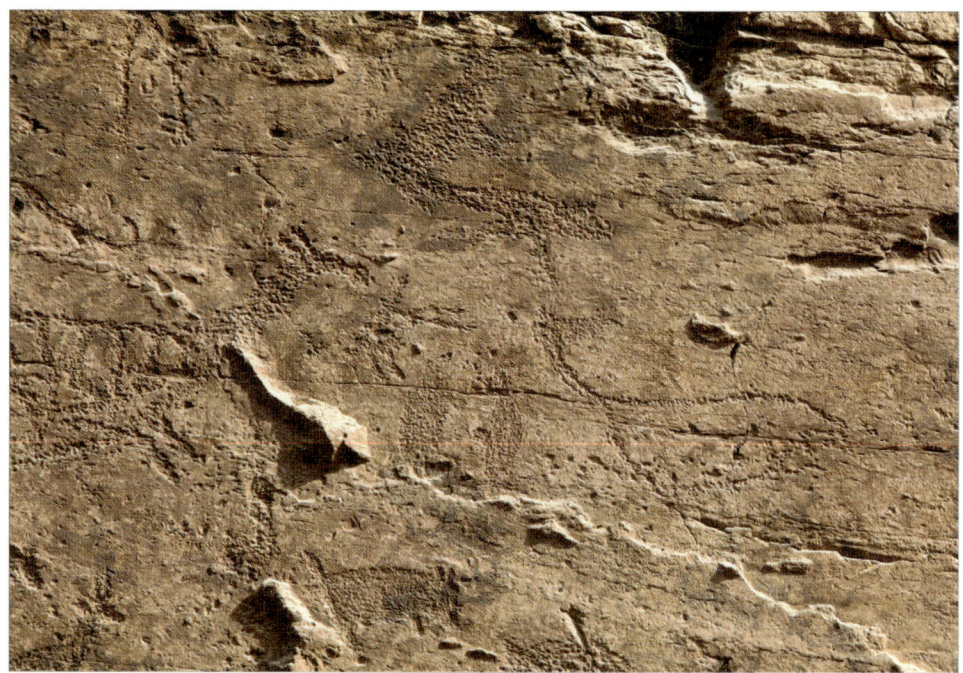

Photo 52. Area of surface I–E (top)

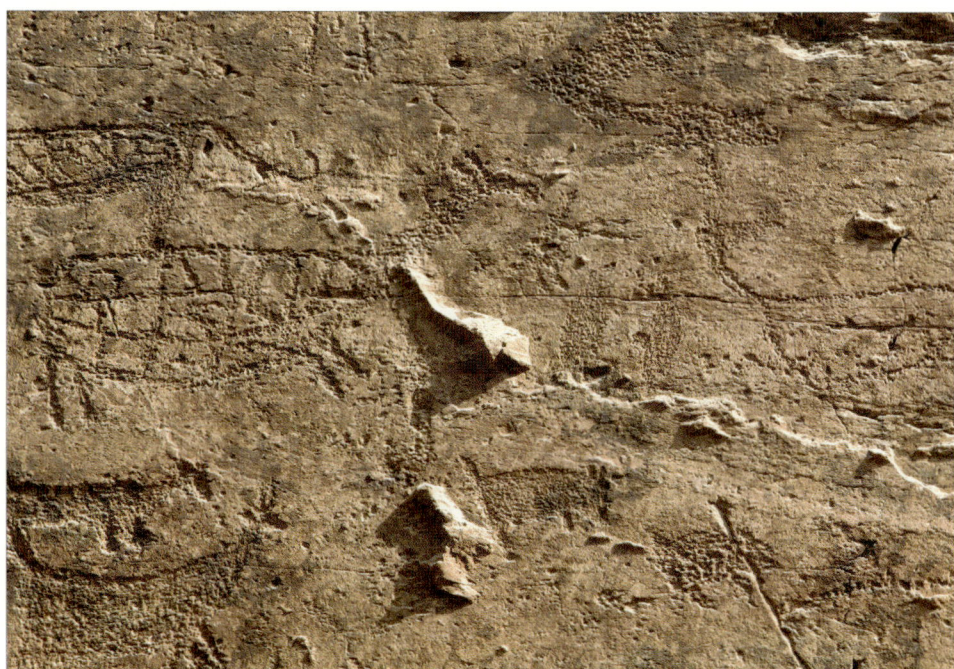

Photo 53. Surface I–E, deer (cervus nippon)

The Bangudae Petroglyphs in Ulsan

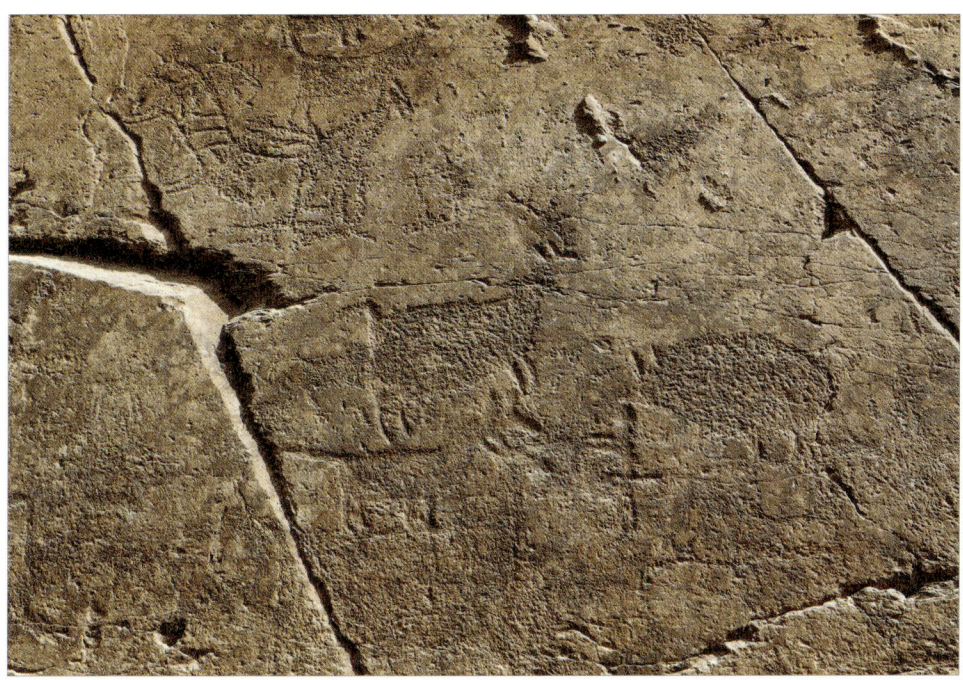

Photo 54. Surface I−E, animals that chases deer

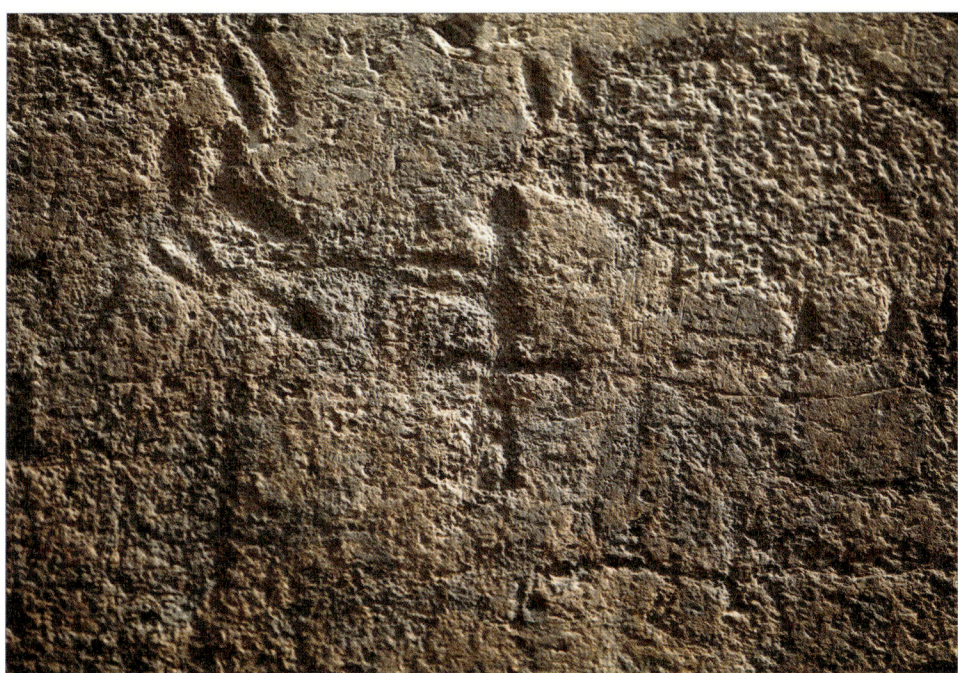

Photo 55. Surface I−E, hunters and animals (zoomorphes)

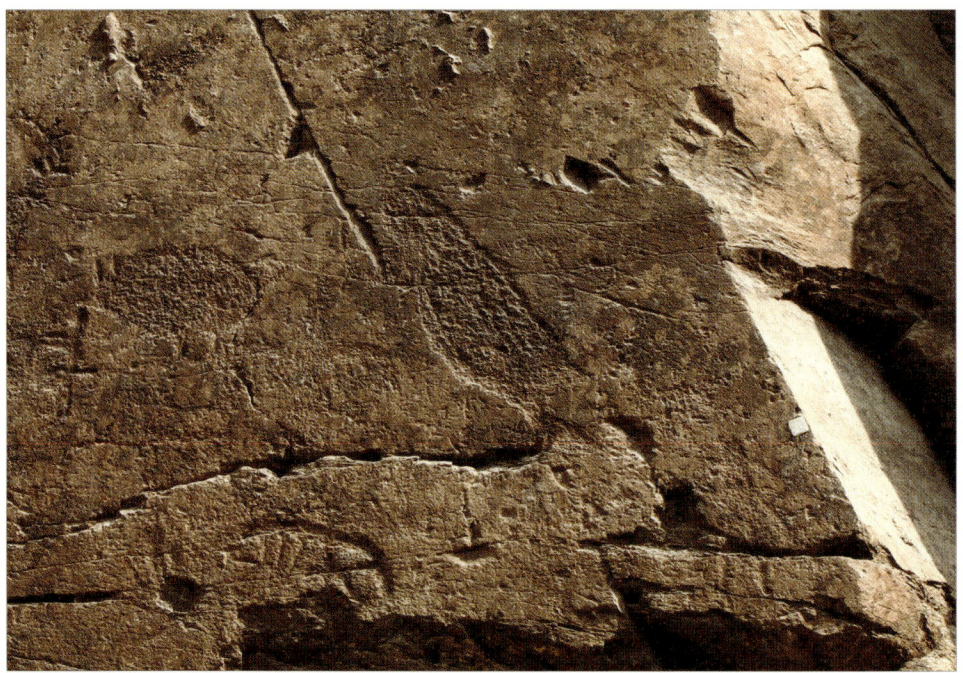

Photo 56. Surface I–E, F

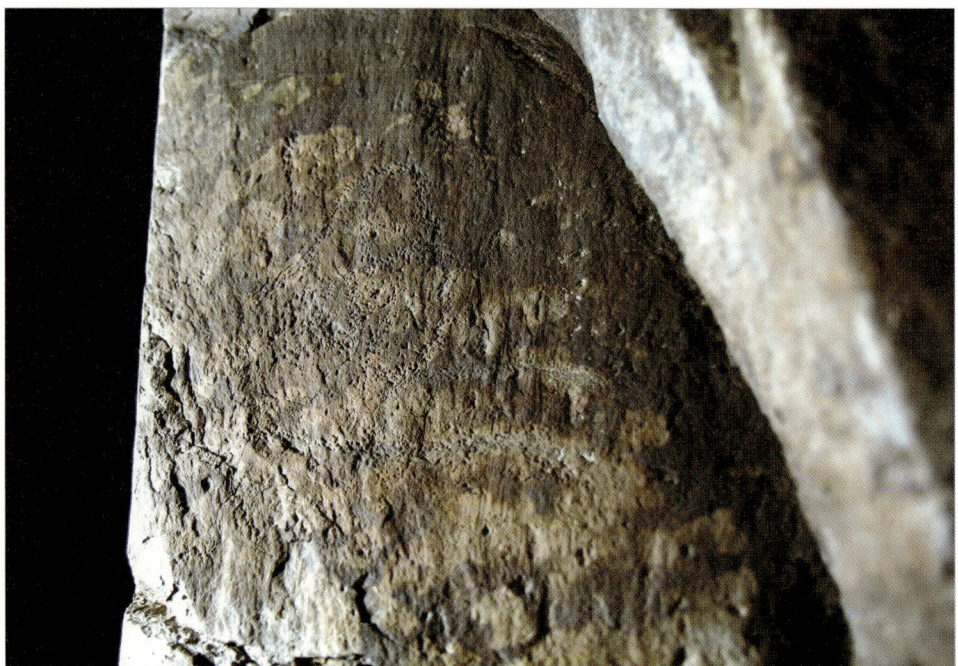

Photo 57. Surface I–F, animals (zoomorphes)

The Bangudae Petroglyphs in Ulsan

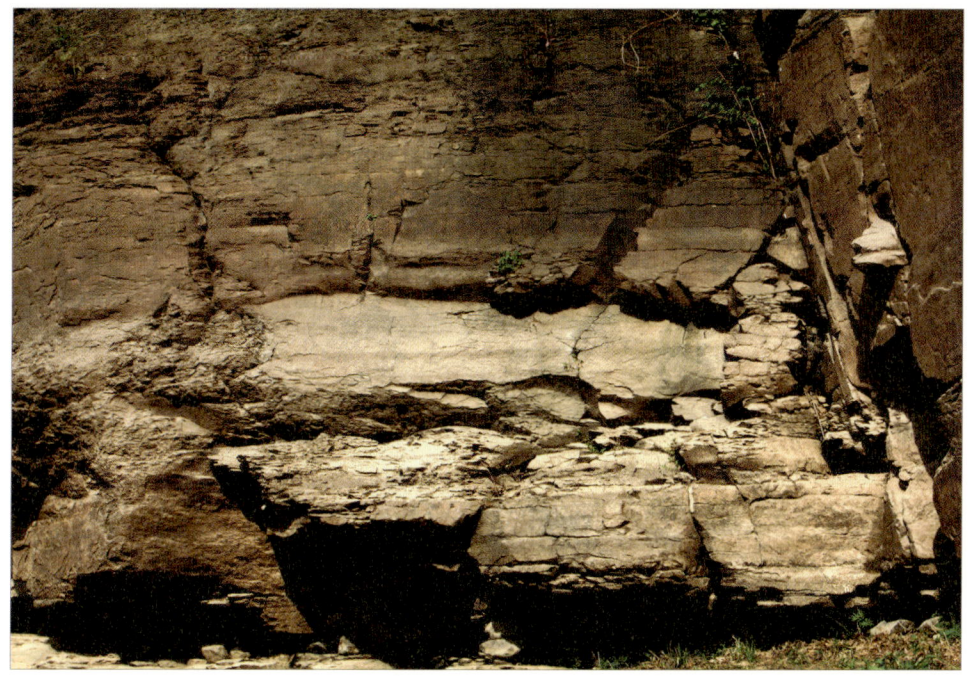

Photo 58. A complete view of surface II

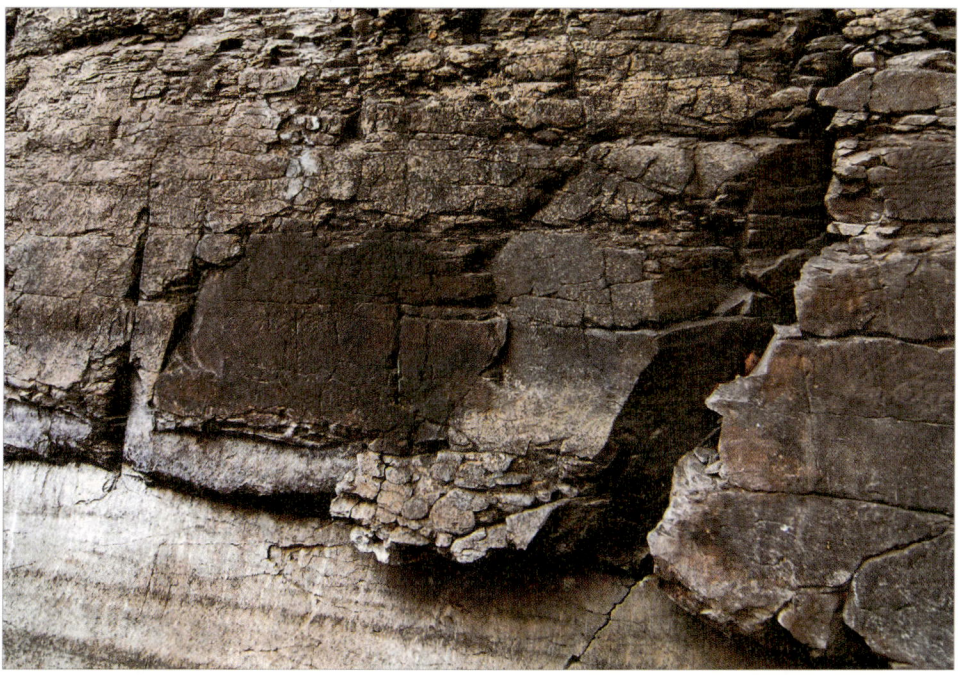

Photo 59. Surface II–A, B

Appendix

147

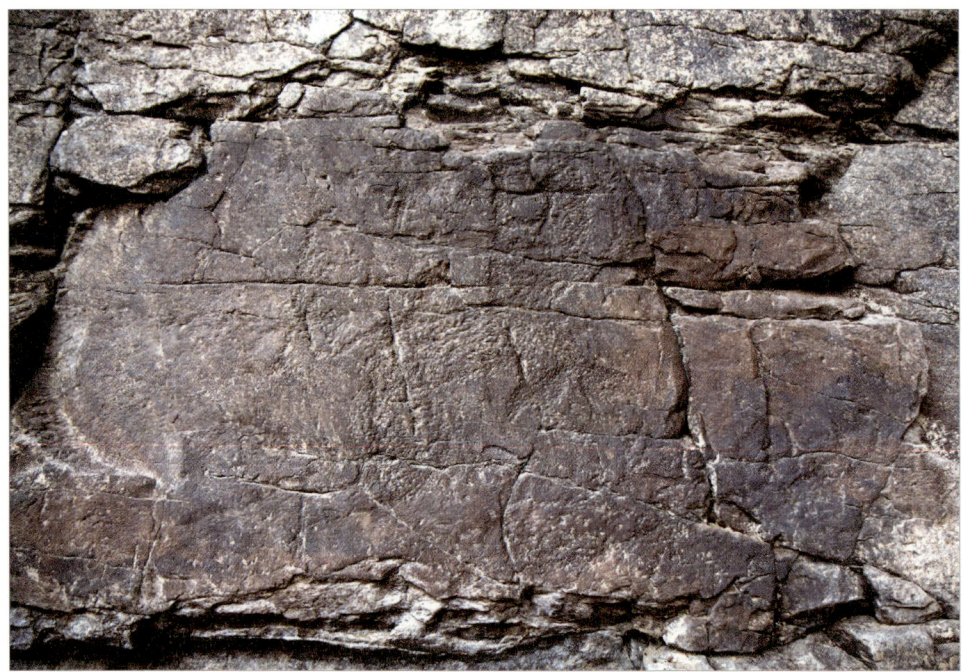

Photo 60. Surface II–A, cetaceans (cetacea) and animals (zoomorphes)

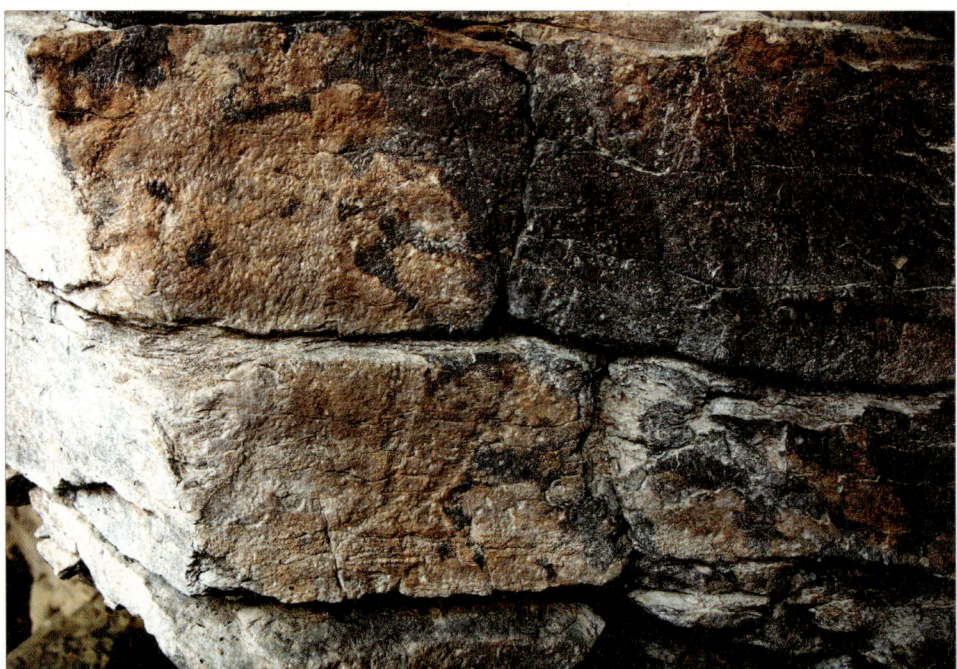

Photo 61. Surface II–D, cetaceans (cetacea)

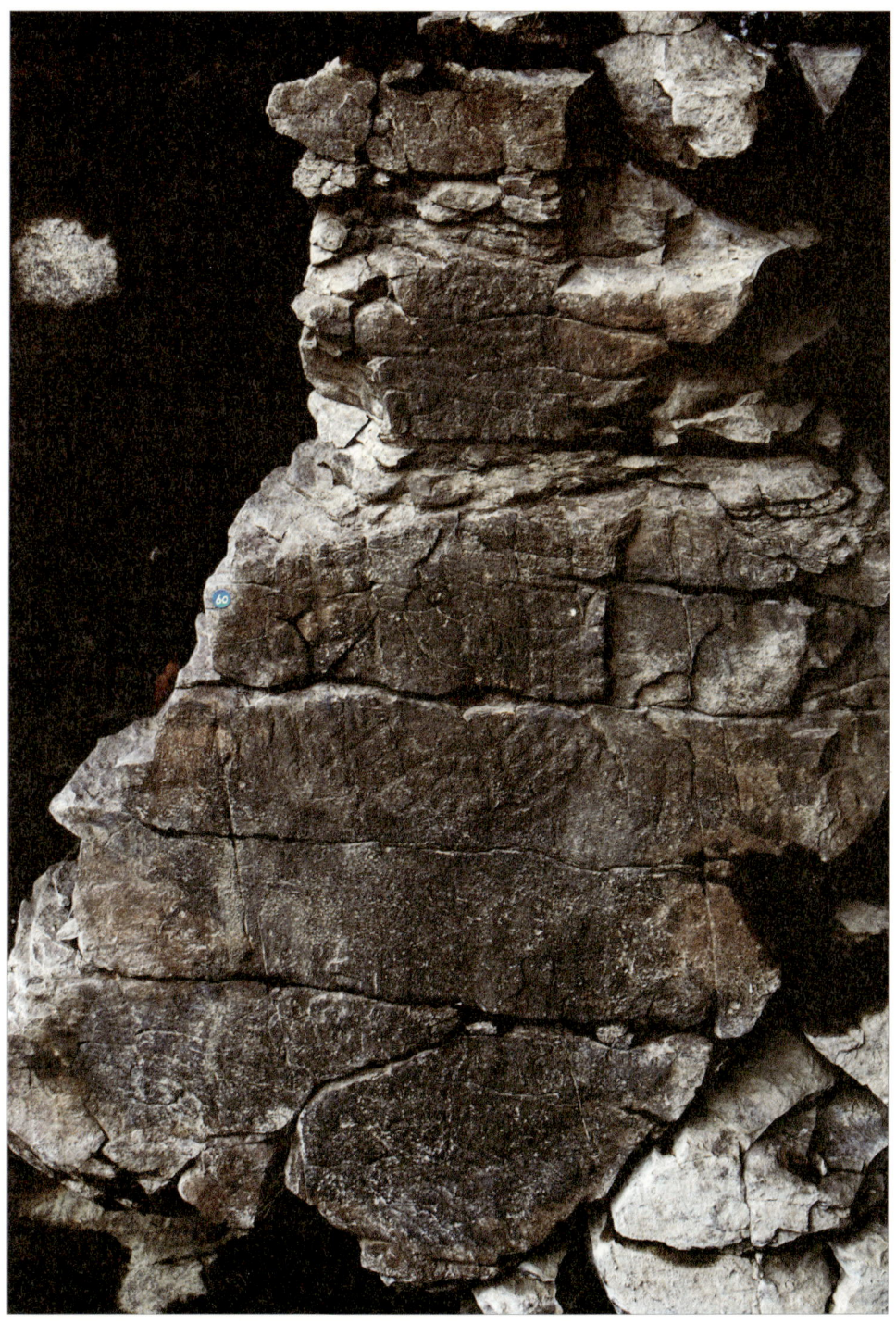

Photo 62. Surface II, cetaceans (cetacea) and nets (net)

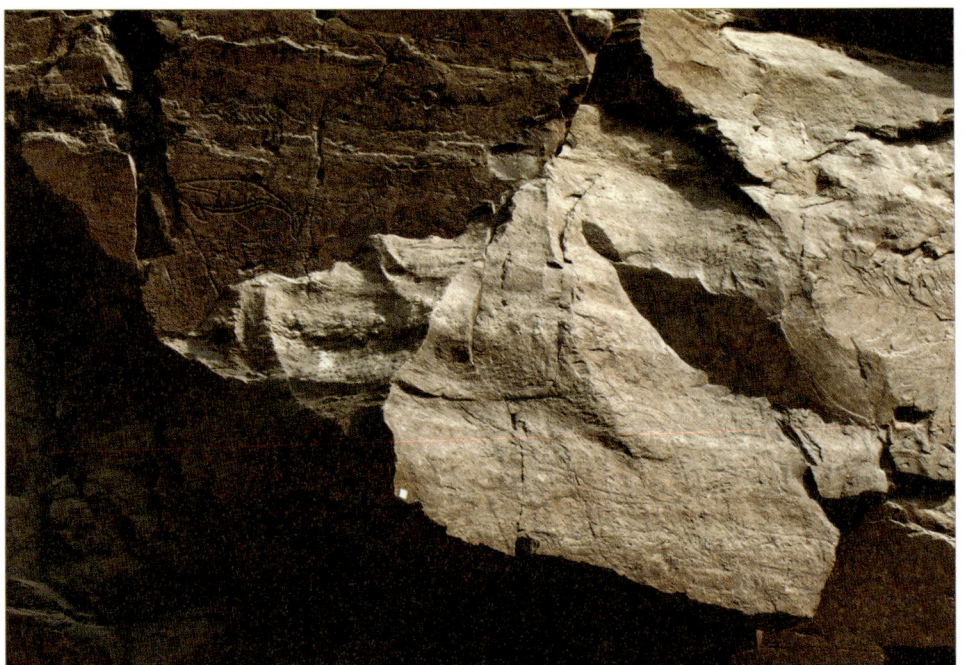

Photo 63. Surface Ⅲ–A, B

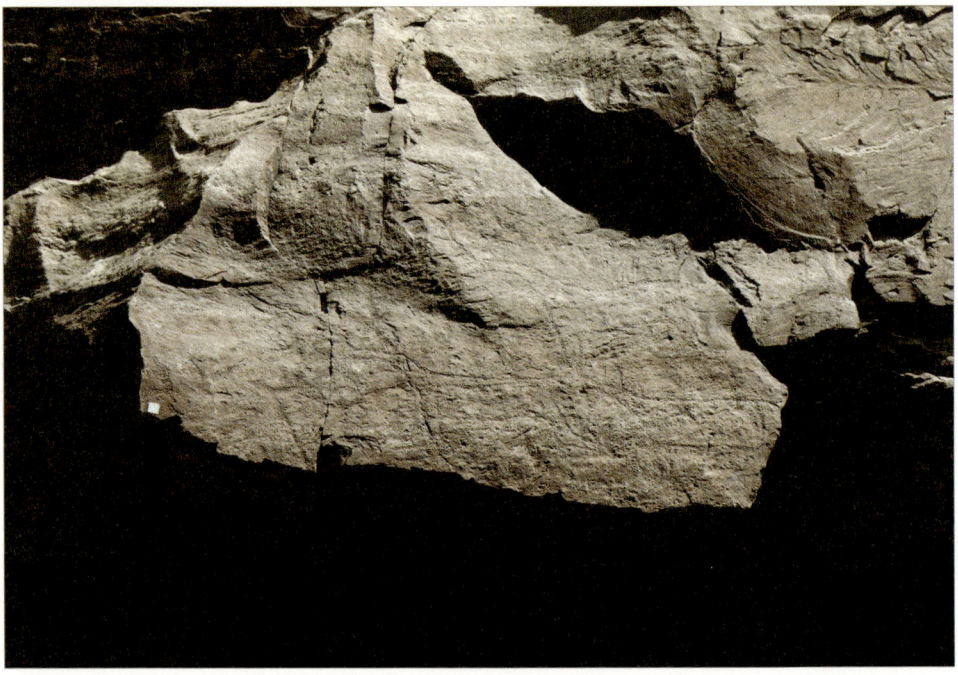

Photo 64. Surface Ⅲ–B, cetaceans (cetacea) and deer (cervus nippon)

The Bangudae Petroglyphs in Ulsan

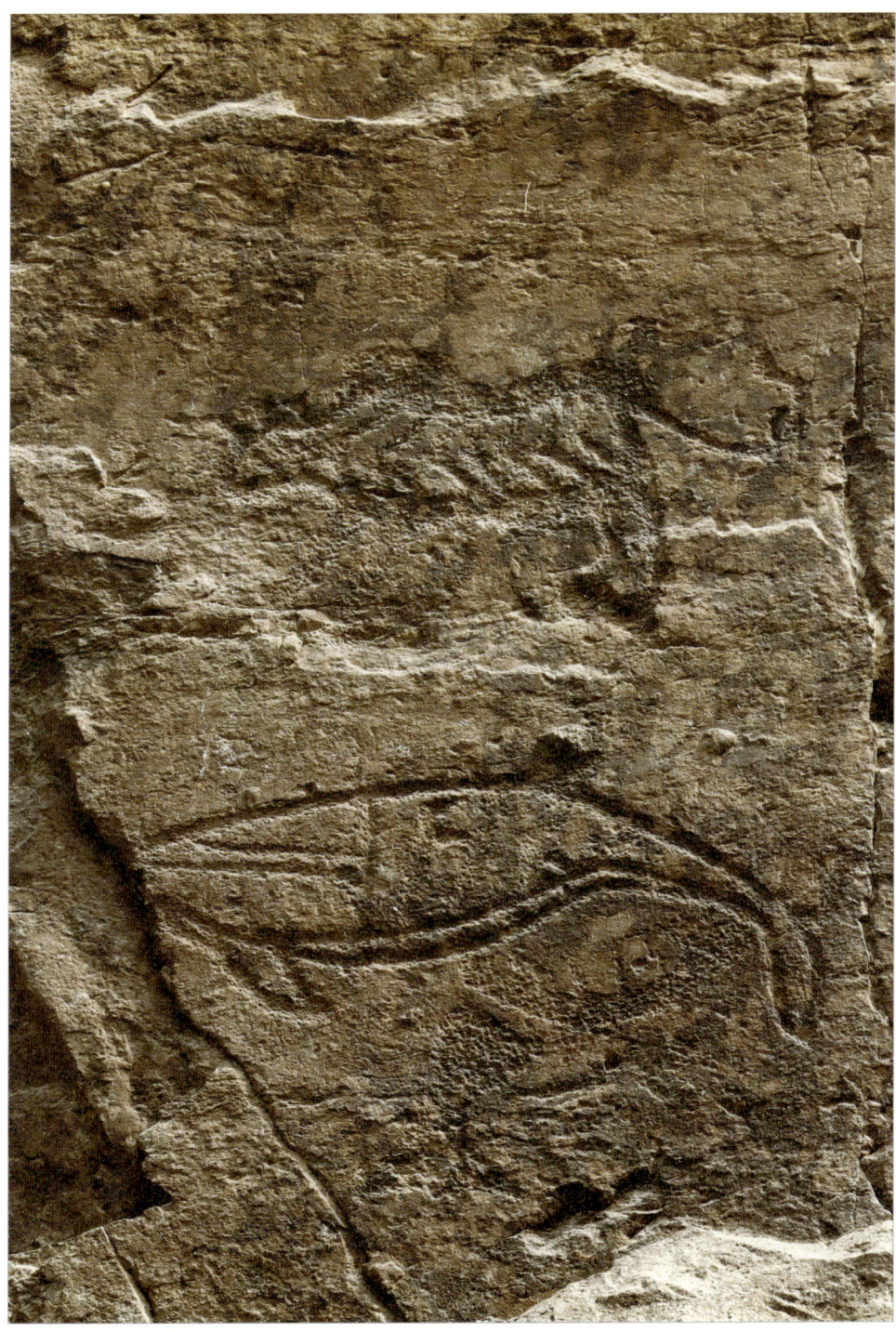

Photo 65. Surface Ⅲ–A, cetaceans (cetacea) and nets (net)

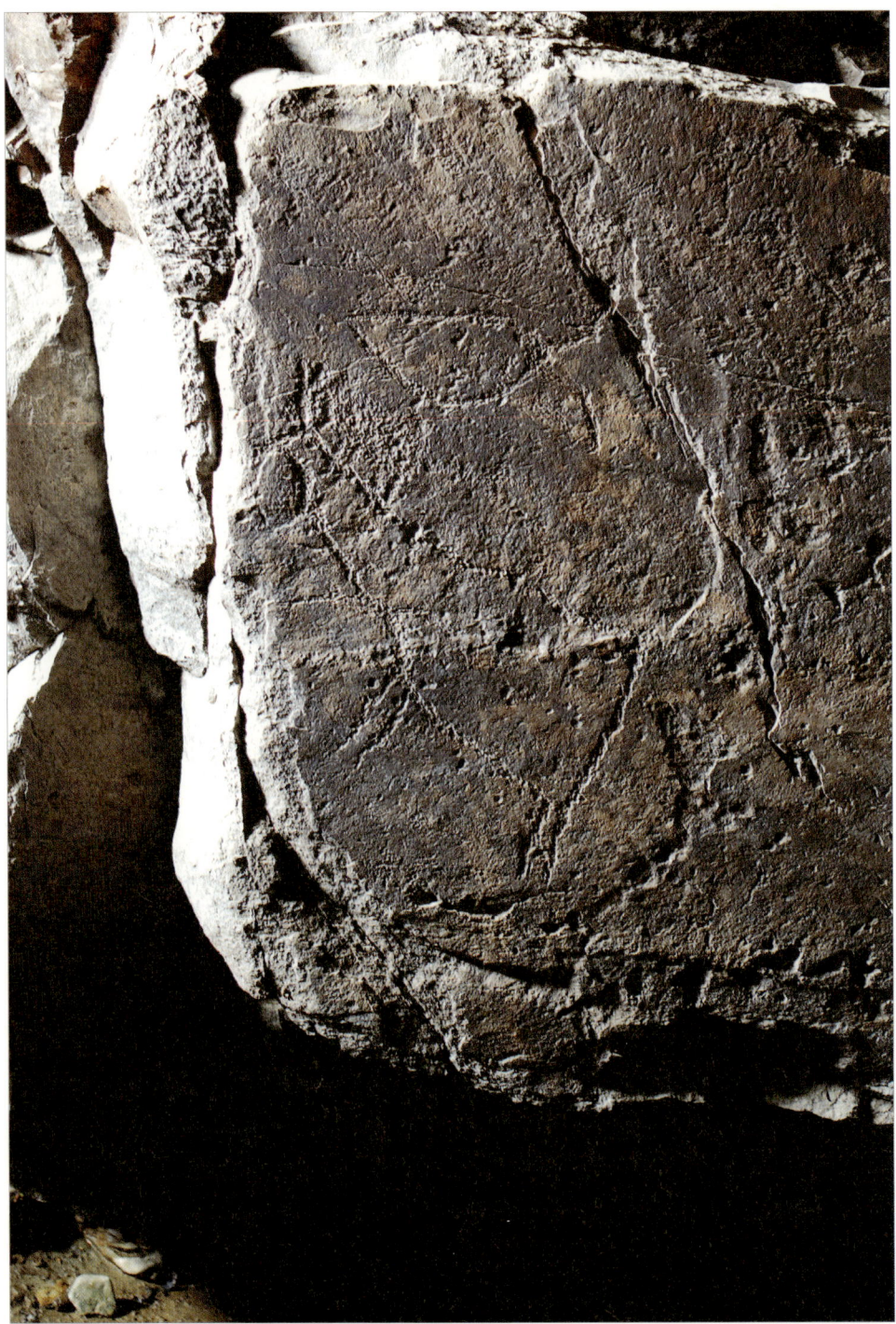

Photo 66. Surface III–C, deer (cervus nippon) and unidentified

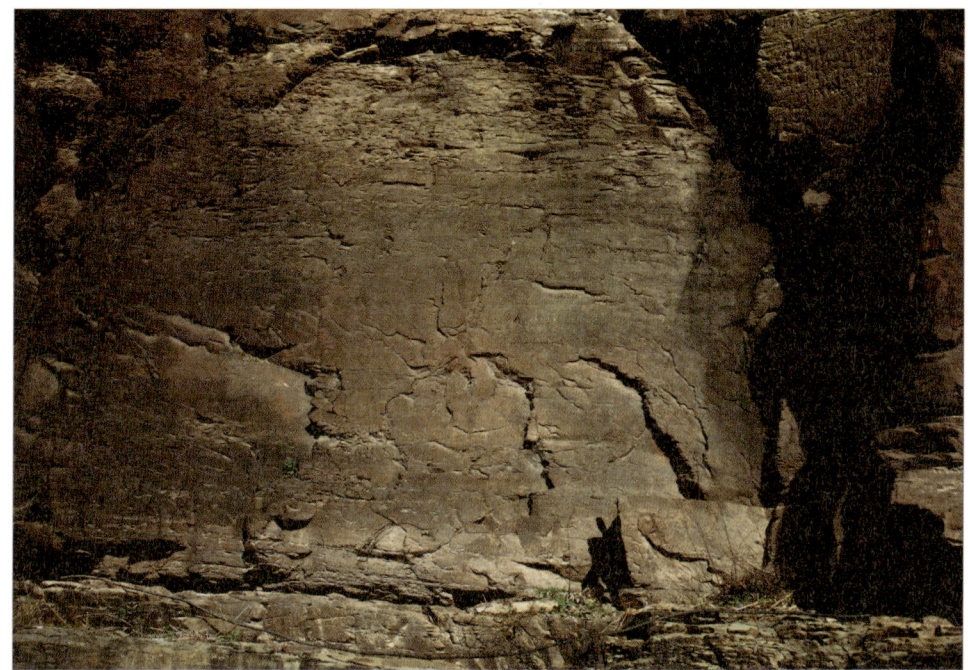

Photo 67. Surface Ⅳ (east side)

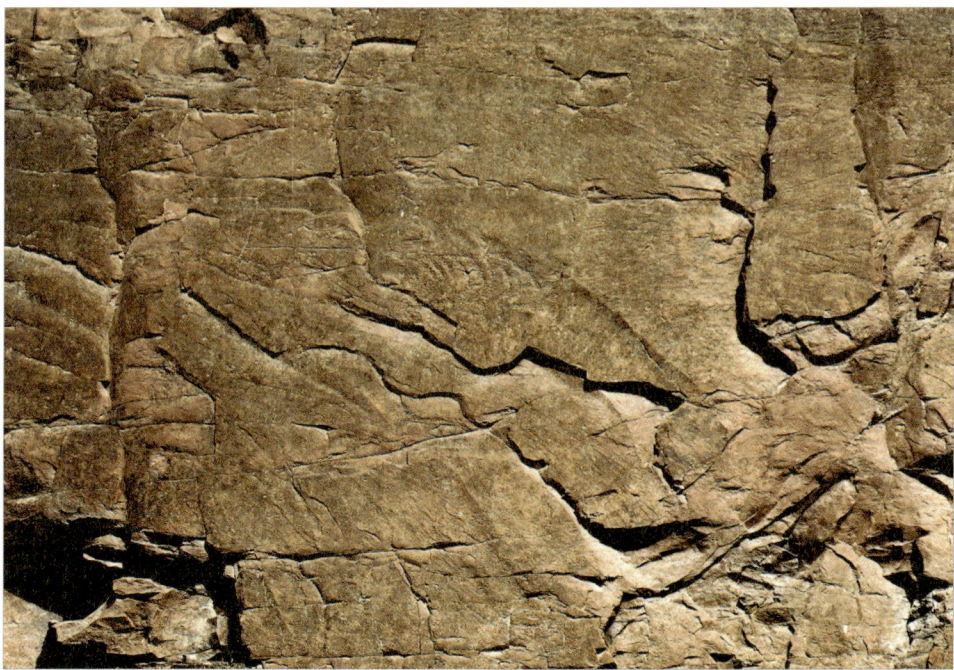

Photo 68. Surface Ⅳ–A, tigers (panthera tigris) and half finished animals

Appendix

153

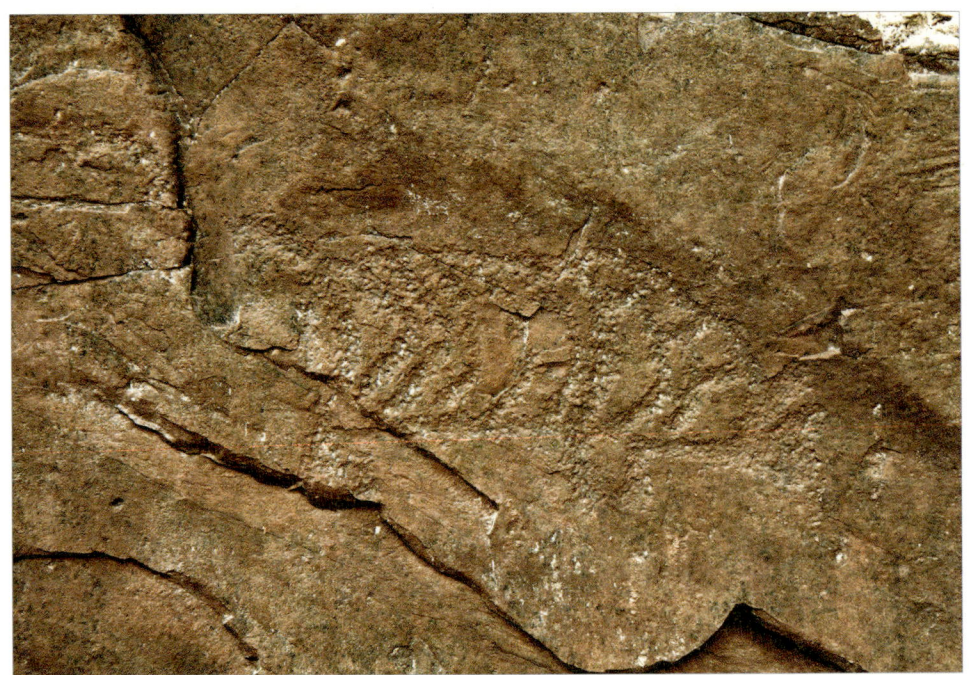

Photo 69. Surface Ⅳ–A, tiger (panthera tigris)

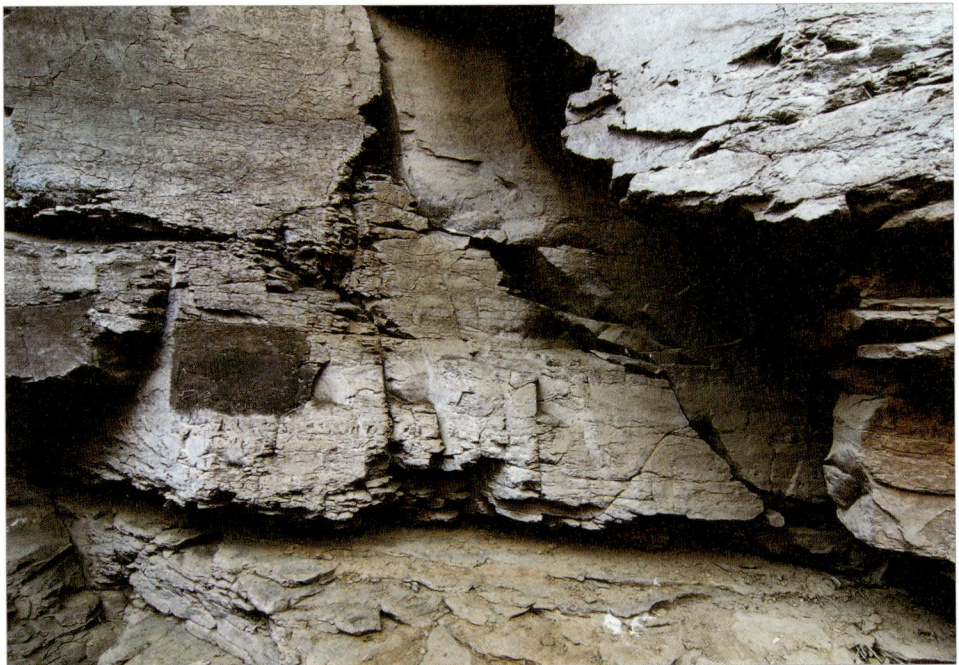

Photo 70. Surface Ⅳ–B, C

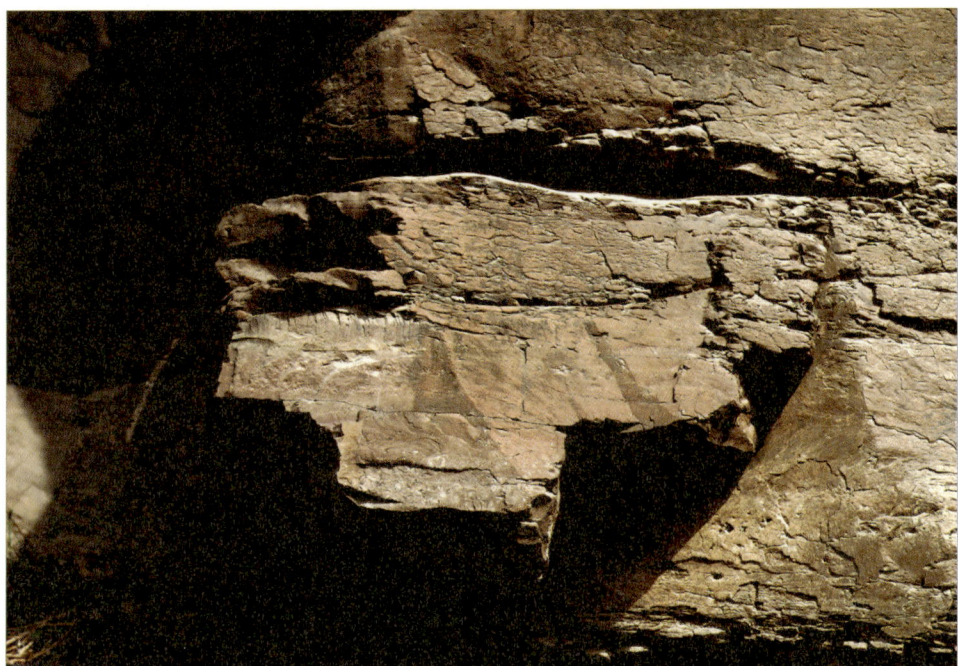

Photo 71. Area of surface IV–B

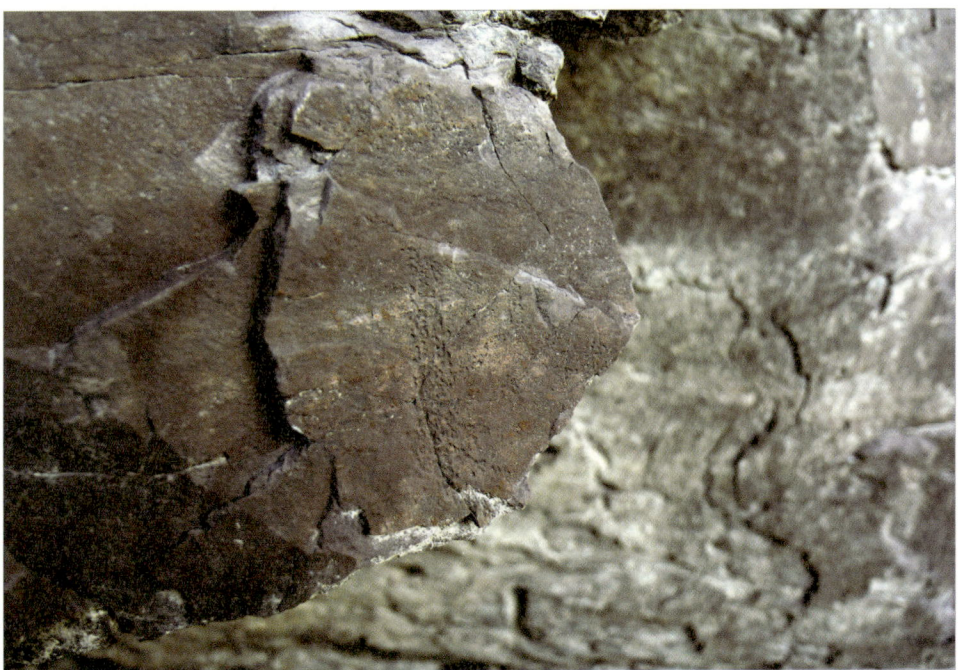

Photo 72. Surface IV–B, unidentified figures

Appendix

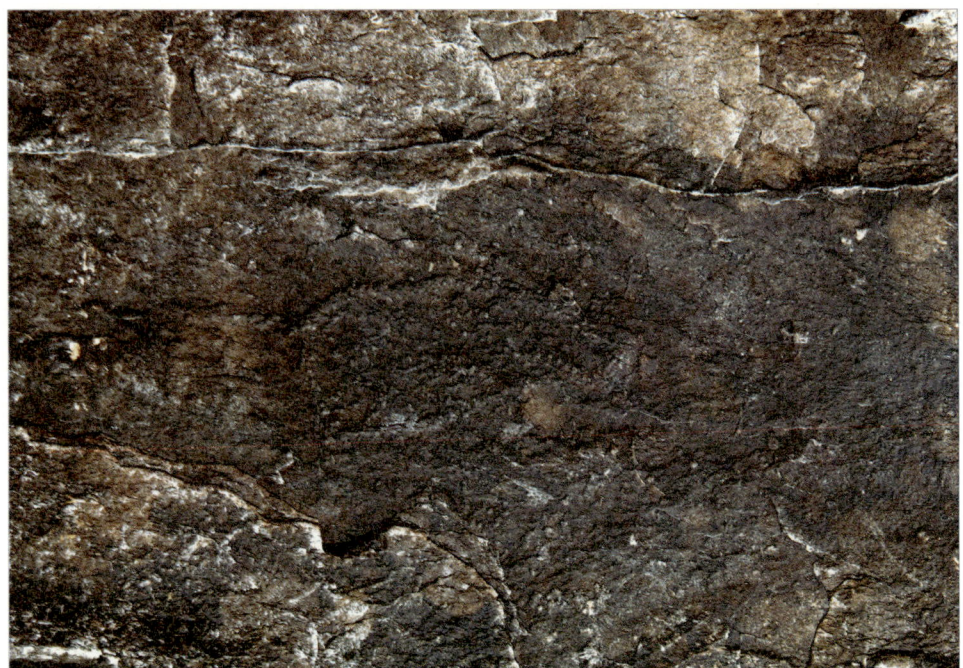

Photo 73. Surface IV–B, animals (zoomorphes)

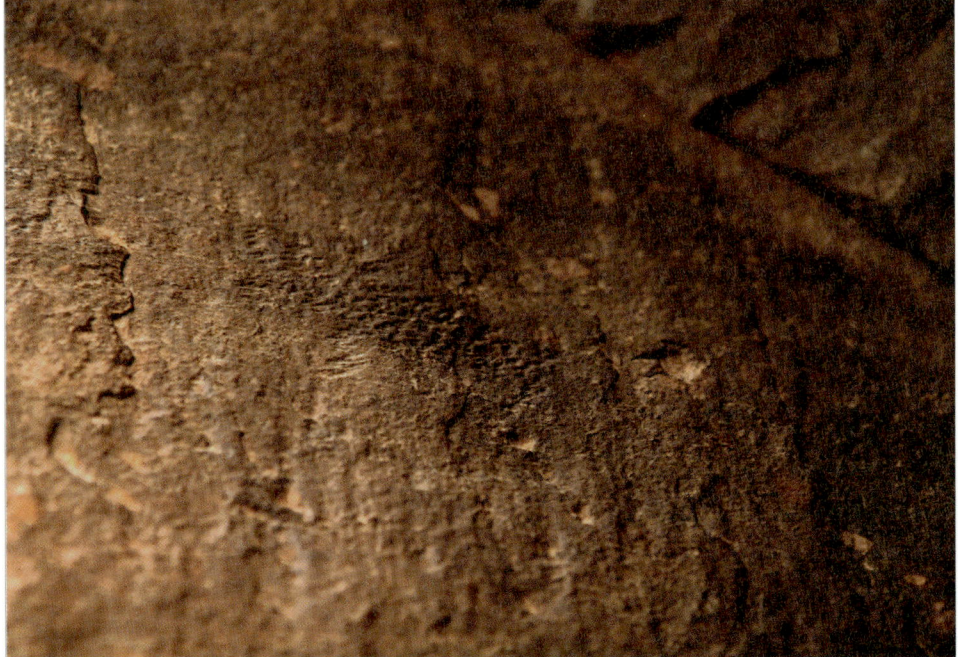

Photo 74. Surface IV–C, animals (zoomorphes)

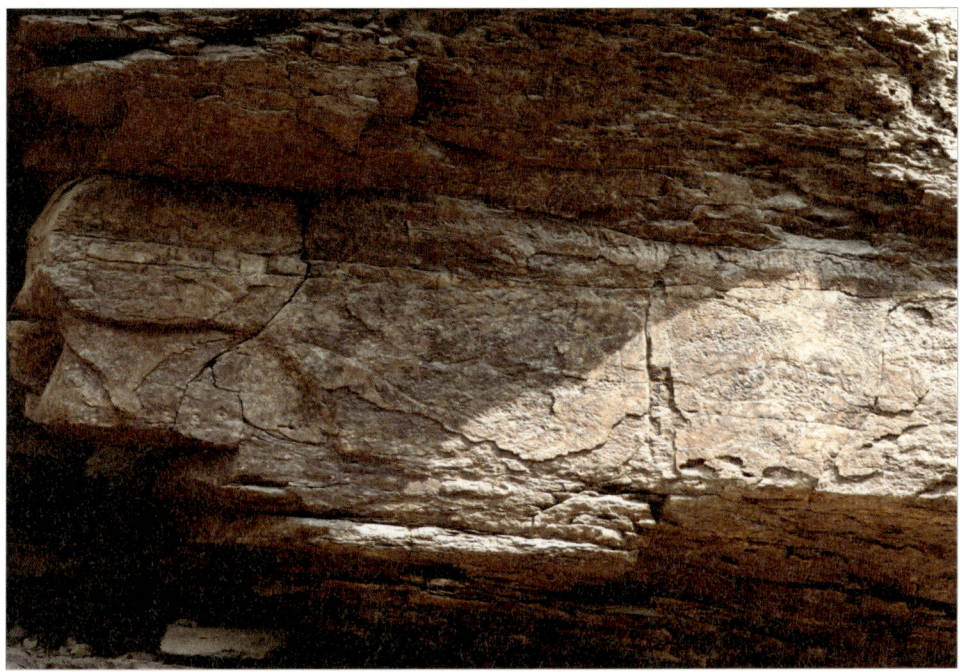

Photo 75. A complete view of surface IV–D

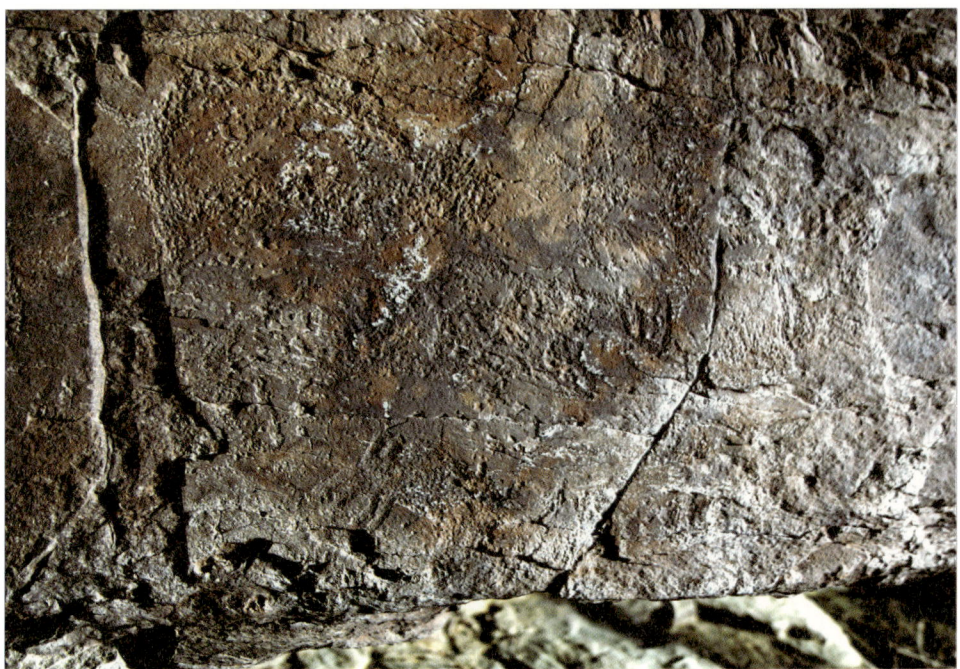

Photo 76. Surface IV–D, canine

Appendix

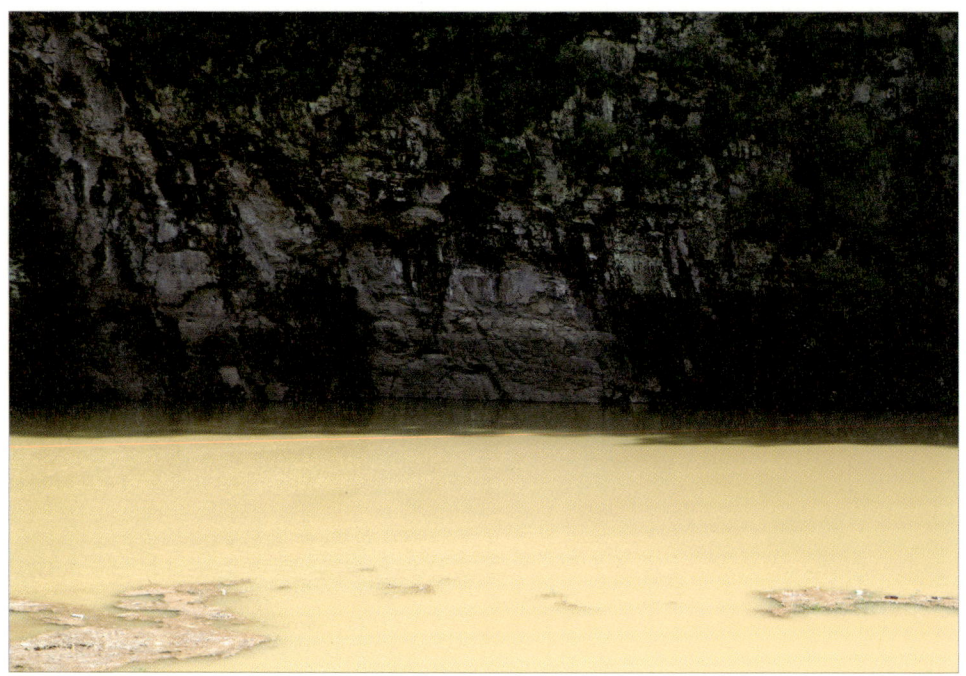

Photo 77. The petroglyphs were submerged underwater (October 06, 2016).

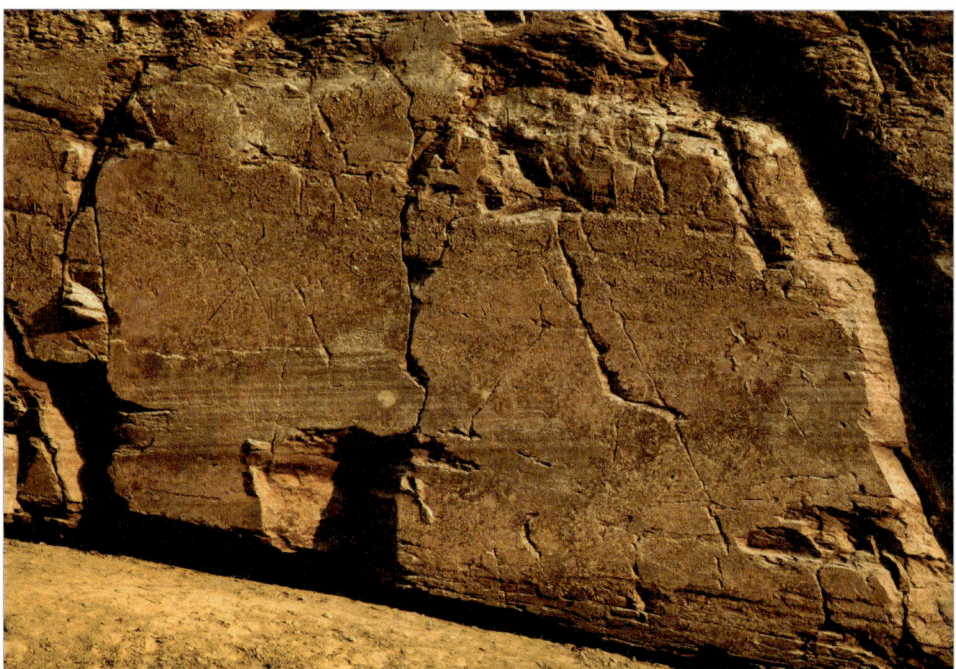

Photo 78. The condition of contaminated the Bangudae Petroglyphs (April 18, 2009)

The Bangudae Petroglyphs in Ulsan

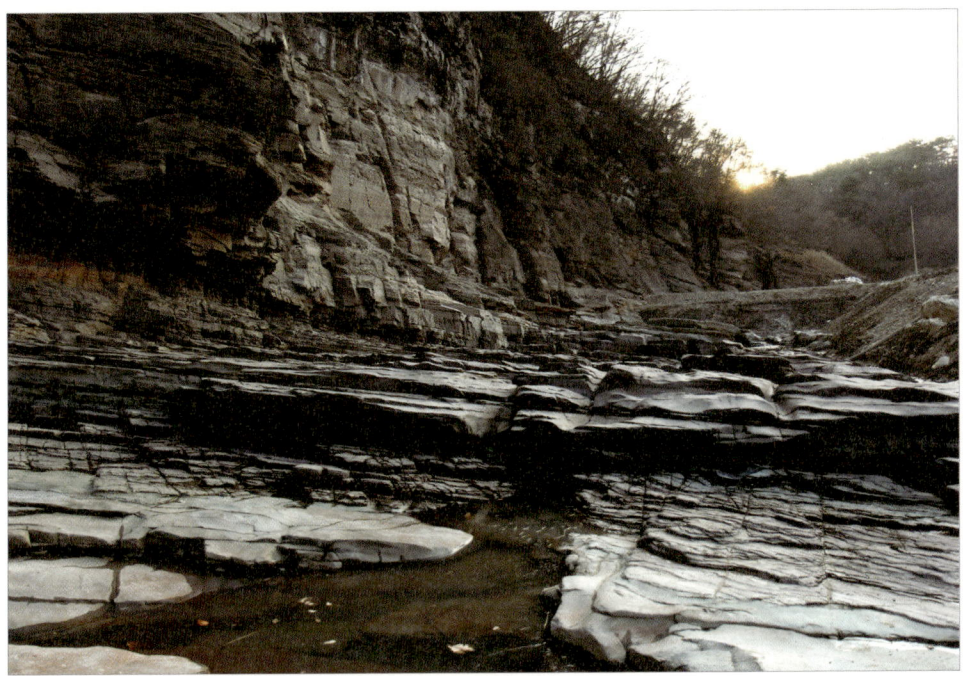

Photo 79. The lower part of the Bangudae Petroglyphs (east→west)

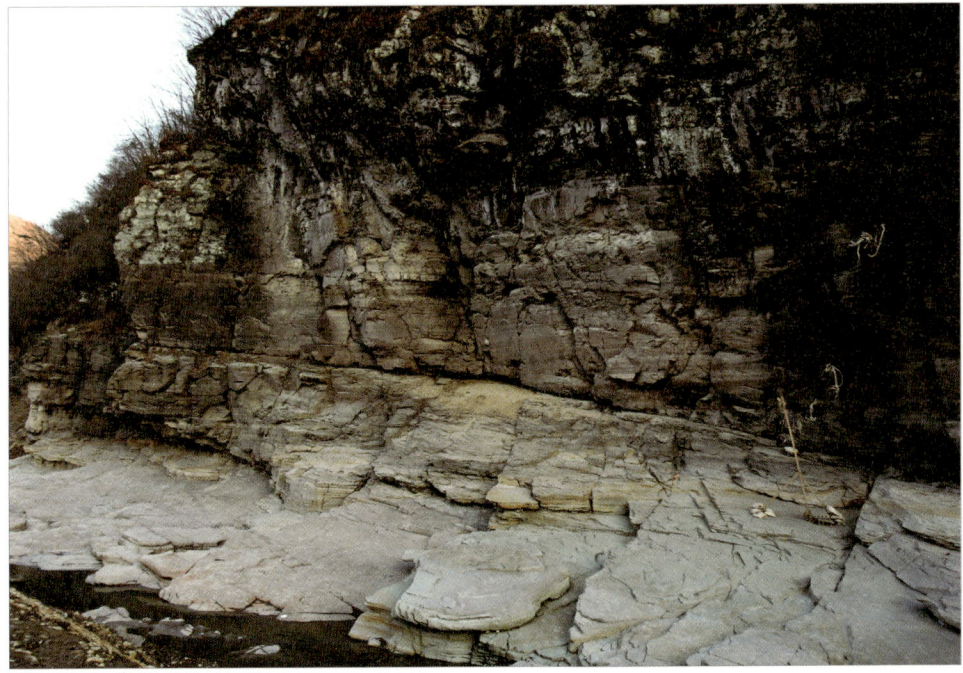

Photo 80. The lower part of the Bangudae Petroglyphs (west→east)

About the Authors

Jeon Hotae

Dr. Jeon Hotae is a historian specialized in ancient history of Korea. He received his Ph.D. from Seoul National University and is currently a professor at its Department of History and Culture. He is also a director of the Bangudae Petroglyphs Institute, University of Ulsan. He has published numerous books and articles on Koguryeo mural paintings as well as ancient Chinese art and culture. He has organized many exhibitions on Koguryeo tomb paintings both inside and outside of Korea.

Rhee Hawoo

Dr. Rhee Hawoo is a research professor at the Bangudae Institute, University of Ulsan. He received his Ph.D. from Gyeongju University. His research focuses on the ritual meaning of Korean petroglyphs. He also has contributed to the field by discovering a number of petroglyphs sites. Dr. Rhee actively publishes books and articles on Korean and East Asian petroglyphs.

Park Younghee

Dr. Park Younghee is a prehistorian and formerly professor at Dongseo University. She graduated Ewha University (B.A. and M.A. in history) and received a Ph.D. from Museum National d'Histoire Naturelle, in France. She served as a curator at Dankook University Museum and also had taught at Ewha University and Yeonsei University.

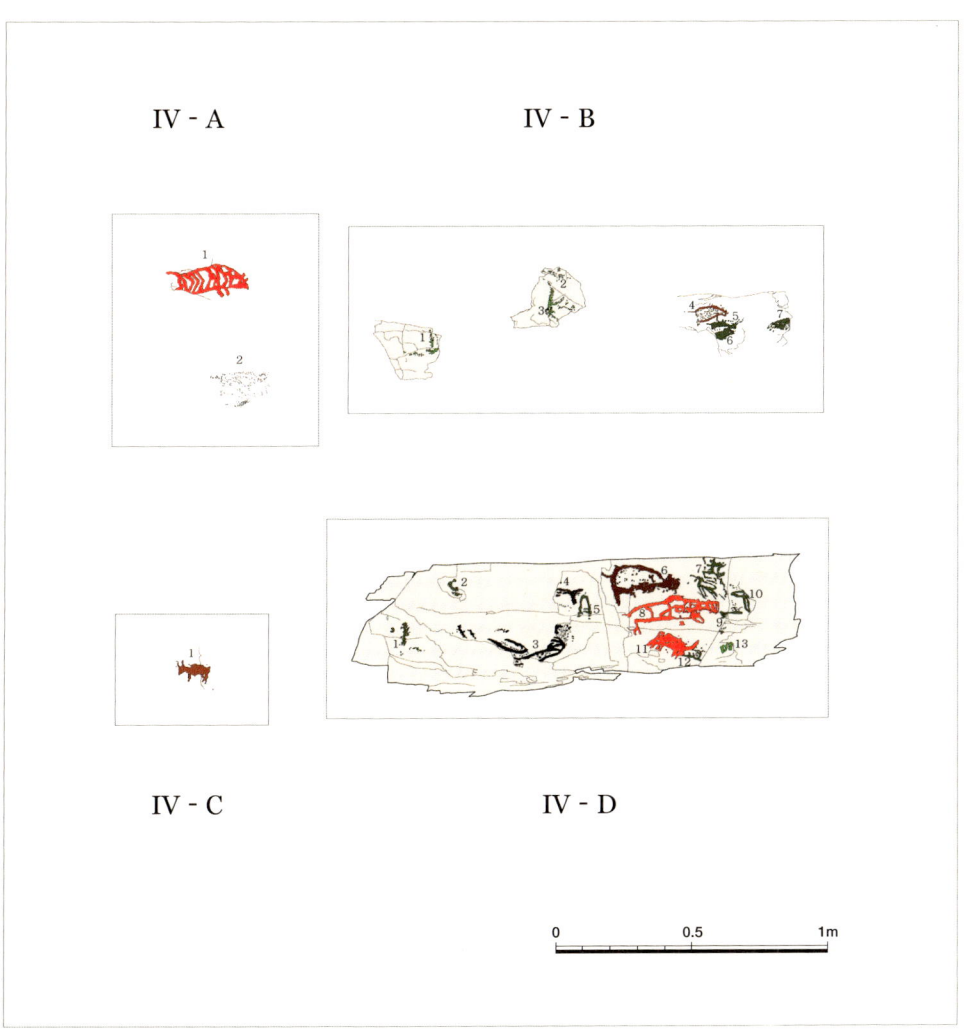

IV - A   IV - B

IV - C   IV - D

0   0.5   1m

Fig. 61. The Bangudae Petroglyphs surface Ⅳ (actual measurement)